TOWARD A COMPREHENSIVE TEST BAN

TOWARD A
COMPREHENSIVE
TEST BAN

Steve Fetter

Ballinger Publishing Company
Cambridge, Massachusetts
A Subsidiary of Harper & Row, Publishers, Inc.

International Standard Book Number: 0-88730-281-5

Library of Congress Catalog Card Number: 88-19238

Printed in the United States of America

Library of Congress Cataloging-in-Publication Data

Fetter, Steve.
    Toward a comprehensive test ban.

    Includes bibliographies and index.
    1. Nuclear weapons — Testing.   2. Nuclear arms control.
I. Title.
JX5133.A7F48   1988   327'.174   88-19238
ISBN 0-88730-281-5

To Emily

CONTENTS

LIST OF FIGURES

LIST OF TABLES

LIST OF ABBREVIATIONS AND ACRONYMS

ABM	antiballistic missile
ACDA	Arms Control and Disarmament Agency
ACM	advanced cruise missile
ADM	atomic demolition munition
AEC	Atomic Energy Commission
AFAP	artillery-fired atomic projectile
ALCM	air-launched cruise missile
ANFO	ammonium nitrate and fuel oil
ASAT	antisatellite
ASROC	antisubmarine rocket
ASW	antisubmarine warfare
ATB	advanced tactical bomber (stealth bomber)
B	bomb or bomber
BMD	ballistic missile defense
C^3	command, control, and communications
CCD	Conference of the Committee on Disarmament
CD	Committee on Disarmament
CDS	command disable system
CEP	circle of equal probability
CIA	Central Intelligence Agency

cm	centimeter
CTB	comprehensive test ban
CTBT	comprehensive test ban treaty
DOB	depth of burst
DoD	Department of Defense
DoE	Department of Energy
DT	deuterium-tritium
EMP	electro-magnetic pulse
ENDC	Eighteen Nation Disarmament Conference
EPW	earth-penetrating warhead
ESD	environmental sensing device
ft	foot
GLCM	ground-launched cruise missile
HIE	hide-in-earthquake
Hz	hertz (cycles per second)
ICBM	intercontinental ballistic missile
ICF	inertial-confinement fusion
IHE	insensitive high explosive
INC	insertable nuclear component
INF	intermediate nuclear forces
JCS	Joint Chiefs of Staff
keV	kiloelectron-volt
kg	kilogram
kJ	kilojoule
km	kilometer
kt	kiloton
ktap	kilotap (kilodyne/cm^2/s)
LANL	Los Alamos National Laboratory
lb	pound

LiD	lithium-deuteride
LLNL	Lawrence Livermore National Laboratory
LTBT	Limited Test Ban Treaty
LYTTB	low-yield threshold test ban
LYTTBT	low-yield threshold test ban treaty
m	meter
MAD	mutually assured destruction
MADM	medium atomic demolition munition
MaRV	maneuvering reentry vehicle
m_b	seismic compressional wave (P-wave) magnitude
MCs	military characteristics
MeV	megaelectron-volt
MILSTAR	military strategic and tactical relay
MIRV	multiple independently targeted reentry vehicle
MRV	multiple reentry vehicle
M_s	seismic Rayleigh-wave magnitude
Mt	megaton
MX	missile experimental (Peacekeeper)
NBD	nuclear depth bomb
NCA	National Command Authority
NDEW	nuclear directed-energy weapon
nmi	nautical mile
NPT	Non-Proliferation Treaty
NRDC	Natural Resources Defense Council
NTM	national technical means
NTS	Nevada Test Site
OSI	on-site inspection
PAL	permissive action link
PBV	post-boost vehicle

p_d	probability of detection
PNE	peaceful nuclear explosion
PNET	Peaceful Nuclear Explosions Treaty
$p(q\|x)$	probability of misclassifying an explosion
psi	pounds per square inch
$p(x\|q)$	probability of misclassifying an earthquake
RV	reentry vehicle
SADM	special atomic demolition munition
SALT	Strategic Arms Limitation Treaty
SAM	surface-to-air missile
SDI	Strategic Defense Initiative
SDIO	Strategic Defense Initiative Organization
SLBM	submarine-launched ballistic missile
SLCM	submarine-launched cruise missile
SNM	special nuclear material
SNR	signal-to-noise ratio
SRAM	short-range attack missile
SSBN	nuclear-powered ballistic missile submarine
START	Strategic Arms Reductions Talks
STS	stockpile-to-target sequence
SUBROC	submarine rocket
TBM	tactical ballistic missile
TNT	Trinitrotoluene
TTBT	Threshold Test Ban Treaty
W	warhead

ACKNOWLEDGMENTS

Books are rarely, if ever, the product of a single mind, and this book is no exception. I am indebted to many people who have contributed to my ideas and to the accuracy of their exposition. In particular, I would like to thank Carol Alonso, Tom Bache, Bill Bookless, Paul Brown, Ash Carter, Dennis Fakely, Richard Garwin, Charles Glaser, Jim Hannon, John Holdren, John Immele, Kent Johnson, J. Carson Mark, Joe Nye, Paul Richards, and Lynn Sykes, each of whom took time to comment at length on early drafts of the chapters. I am especially grateful to Warren Heckrotte for lending his critical eye to the entire manuscript. I must also thank my colleagues and the staff at CSIA for their encouragement and good humor. Finally, this book could not have been completed without the love and support of my wife, Marie.

1 INTRODUCTION

A ban on all nuclear testing is one of the oldest and most elusive proposals to control nuclear armaments. For over thirty years, a succession of U.S. presidents have stated that a comprehensive test ban (CTB) is a goal of U.S. policy. Perhaps because the idea of a CTB has been around so long, there is a tendency not to think very hard about it. Concerned citizens, defense intellectuals, policymakers, military leaders, and weapon designers continue to reiterate many of the same arguments made decades ago, even though the strategic and political environment has changed considerably.

After three decades of analysis and discussion, the test ban question is still far from being resolved. Although the late 1980s have witnessed renewed public and congressional support for a test ban, the Reagan administration and the U.S. nuclear weapons establishment as a whole remain opposed to further restrictions on testing, despite repeated Soviet statements that they are now willing to accept any verification measures the United States deems necessary. All of the Democratic candidates in the 1988 presidential campaign support a CTB or a one-kiloton threshold test ban treaty. I believe that the time is ripe for a thorough reexamination of the issues surrounding a test ban. This book challenges the conventional wisdom of CTB proponents, who claim that a CTB would end the arms race and curb proliferation and that the problems of verifying a ban have long since been solved; and of CTB opponents, who claim that the United States must test as long

1

as it depends upon nuclear deterrence for its security and that the Soviets could obtain important advantages by cheating. This book is intended primarily for policymakers and citizens in the United States who are trying to determine the relevance of a CTB in today's world, but I hope that it will also be useful to arms control experts and to citizens of other countries.

We begin by reviewing the long history of test ban negotiations and by isolating the key issues. The following chapters discuss in detail the subjects that are central to the current test ban debate: weapon modernization, stockpile confidence, verification, nuclear strategy, proliferation, and the politics of détente. Although the first three of these subjects are technical, it should be emphasized that the crucial judgments in these areas cannot be apolitical. Although agreement is possible on technical facts in principle (and even this is often impossible in practice), one must still judge the relative political and strategic importance of these facts. I have tried to be evenhanded in my assessments, but my bias in favor of a test ban inevitably shows through. There is always a tension between objectivity and advocacy whenever science and politics mingle, as they certainly do in the test ban case.

PAST TEST BAN NEGOTIATIONS

The long and often fascinating history of test ban negotiations could fill several volumes, but only a brief overview can be presented here.[1] Proposals for a nuclear test ban did not surface until almost a decade into the nuclear age. The rate of testing was fairly low in the late 1940s (only nine nuclear explosions took place during the years 1945 through 1950),[2] and the hazards to public health from fallout were not widely recognized. Nuclear arms control efforts immediately after World War II focused on general and complete disarmament, or schemes designed to remove nuclear weapons and the ability to produce them from all nations. The flagship of such proposals was the Baruch Plan, which was submitted by the United States to the United Nations in June 1946. The plan would have turned over all nuclear activities — reactors and research facilities as well as weapon development — to an international agency, which would have performed thorough and unrestricted inspections of all parties and reported violations to the U.N. Security Council. The Security Council would then have voted to mete out punishment, which might have included war and the use of nuclear weapons, to those found cheating. Unlike other U.N. decisions, the Baruch Plan would not have permitted the permanent members of the Security Council to veto these actions.

In retrospect, there was little possibility that the Soviet Union could have accepted a proposal that required such a substantial surrender of its sovereignty, especially since the plan did not satisfy Soviet security goals. The United Nations was overwhelmingly pro-American at the time, and the Soviets must have feared that the plan's inspection and enforcement provisions would have been used to interfere in their internal affairs. The United States would have secured a permanent monopoly on nuclear know-how and the Soviet Union would have been frozen into a position of inferiority. The Soviets obviously believed that building their own nuclear arsenal provided a safer route than the Baruch Plan for eliminating the American nuclear advantage. The United States and the Soviet Union exchanged proposals for general and complete disarmament over the next decade in an attempt to sway world opinion. With the detonation of the first Soviet weapon in 1949 and the outbreak of the Korean War a year later, a compromise on nuclear matters was nowhere in sight.

Eisenhower and the Moratorium

The idea of banning nuclear tests appeared suddenly in 1954, after the United States detonated a large thermonuclear device, code-named BRAVO, on an island in the South Pacific on 1 March. The explosion's 15-megaton yield was twice that expected, and shifting winds deposited fallout on a Japanese fishing boat and on the nearby Marshall Islands. Dozens suffered from radiation sickness and one of the fishermen died. Fear about the health effects of fallout touched off a series of protests against nuclear testing, lead by some of the world's most respected statesmen and scientists.

The Soviet Union, which had included a test ban as part of an arms control proposal as early as May 1955, was quick to capitalize on the worldwide outrage against atmospheric testing. American officials, on the other hand, sought to minimize the hazards of fallout. The United States consistently maintained that testing was necessary to develop advanced weapons to deter Soviet aggression. This was a period of tremendous growth and innovation in the U.S. nuclear stockpile: high yield-to-weight thermonuclear bombs, various battlefield nuclear weapons, and ballistic missile warheads were just being developed. Roughly one third of all nuclear weapon types ever to enter the U.S. stockpile were tested during the late 1950s.[3]

Meanwhile, public pressure for a test ban continued to mount. It had become increasingly apparent that negotiations for general and complete disarmament would never bear fruit. Indeed, the Eisenhower administration, while reassessing its position in 1955, had decided that advocating complete nuclear disarmament would no longer serve U.S. interests. When Adlai Stevenson made the test ban a central issue in the 1956 presidential race, the Soviets informally offered a test ban as a separate proposal. When the British exploded their first thermonuclear weapon in May 1957, the Soviets proposed a ban on thermonuclear weapon tests. During the later half of 1957, the Soviets made two offers for a three-year moratorium on testing. All were rejected. The United States offered a two-year moratorium, but this was rejected because it was linked to a cutoff in the production of fissile material. (In the absence of additional arms control measures, a cutoff would have left the United States with a much larger number of nuclear weapons than the Soviet Union.)

After 1957, public pressure to end the radioactive contamination of the environment could no longer be ignored by Eisenhower. The United States suffered propaganda drubbings each time it refused to consider a test ban as a separate issue. While the debate within a badly divided U.S. government gathered momentum, the Soviet Union announced on 31 March 1958 (just four days after Khrushchev became premier) that it would refrain from testing if other nations did not test. In a major policy shift, Eisenhower responded one week later by proposing that scientists from the two countries meet to discuss how compliance with a test ban could be verified. Although the Soviets maintained that verification posed no problems, Khrushchev, perhaps feeling that the meeting was politically necessary for Eisenhower, agreed.

The Conference of Experts.   The Conference of Experts to Study the Possibility of Detecting Violations of a Possible Agreement on Suspension of Nuclear Tests was convened in Geneva on 1 July 1958. Less than two months later, the conferees concluded that a control system composed of 160 to 170 control posts scattered around the world would be capable of detecting and identifying atmospheric explosions yielding more than 1 kiloton and underground explosions with yields greater than 5 kilotons. The conference was widely reported as a great success, and test ban proponents expected a treaty to follow quickly.

The Moratorium. Just two days after the Conference of Experts ended, Eisenhower called for formal test ban negotiations to begin. He also announced that the United States would suspend all nuclear testing for one year while the negotiations took place, provided that the Soviet Union did the same. Both countries rushed to do what they thought might be their final nuclear tests; together, the United States and the Soviet Union did as many tests in the twelve months before the moratorium began as they had done in the previous twelve *years.*[4] Following this flurry of tests, none were done for almost three years.

The United States, the Soviet Union, and the United Kingdom opened the Conference on the Discontinuance of Nuclear Tests in Geneva on 31 October 1958. The conferees made rapid progress in identifying their differences, which were mostly related to the nature and activities of the control organization. In short, the Americans and the British wanted an international organization operated by majority rule, with mandatory on-site inspections (OSIs) whenever ambiguous events were detected to guard against the possibility of Soviet cheating. The Soviets, who feared that OSIs would only amount to legalized espionage, insisted that they be able to control all activities within their own borders. The U.S. fear of Soviet cheating and the Soviet fear of U.S. spying have proved to be a shaky foundation for arms control negotiations ever since.

To make matters worse, the United States introduced new technical data that made the detection of underground explosions seem more difficult than before. A great increase in the complexity of the control system was necessary to compensate for this apparent loss in detection capability. Moreover, U.S. studies suggested that there were a number of techniques by which relatively high-yield explosions might escape detection. It was claimed, for example, that a 300-kt weapon that was exploded inside a large underground cavity would result in the same seismic signal as a 1-kt tamped explosion.[5] These studies also identified problems with detecting explosions in space and at very high altitudes, although a special working group of the Geneva conference, convened in June 1959, concluded that this could be solved by placing satellites in orbit around the earth.

To overcome these difficulties, the Eisenhower administration proposed to ban only those tests that could be verified with the control system defined by the Conference of Experts. In February 1960, the United States introduced a draft treaty that would have banned all atmospheric and underwater tests, tests in space to an unspecified distance from the earth, and underground tests producing a seismic magnitude greater than 4.75 on the Richter scale. The draft treaty included criteria, based on technical considerations, that would have resulted in an average of twenty OSIs in the Soviet Union each year. The Soviet Union agreed to this general framework but called for a ban on all space tests and a moratorium on underground tests below magnitude 4.75. The Soviet Union also stated that the number of OSIs must be decided by political, not technical, criteria; some Soviet negotiators hinted in private that three inspections per year might be acceptable. In response, the United States and the United Kingdom agreed to a moratorium of limited duration on space and underground tests, but they did not agree with the Soviet Union on the duration of the moratorium.

The two sides now appeared close to agreement. The only major issues awaiting resolution were the annual number of OSIs, the length of the moratorium on small underground tests, and the composition of control system personnel. Many analysts expected that these issues would be resolved in the forthcoming Big Four summit meeting in Paris, planned to start on 16 May 1960. When an American U-2 reconnaissance plane was shot down over the Soviet Union on 2 May, however, the summit and the test ban went down with it. Formal negotiations continued, but the Soviets withdrew their compromise position. Later, Eisenhower said that the greatest regret of his presidency was his failure to convert the moratorium into a comprehensive test ban treaty (CTBT).[6]

Kennedy and the LTBT

From the beginning, President Kennedy and his administration were eager to negotiate an end to nuclear testing. They wasted little time in reviving the threshold proposal that seemed close to agreement the previous year, but it became clear that Khrushchev was no longer anxious for a treaty. Perhaps, as in the Berlin crisis, he wanted to test the mettle of the new president. In April 1961, the United States and the United Kingdom introduced the first complete treaty text tabled by either side. Predictably, the intrusiveness of the control system was the main sticking point. The West proposed twelve to twenty OSIs per year, while the Soviets offered only three. There were also differences about the nature of the control system administrator, the number of detection stations on Soviet soil, and the composition of the detection station staff.

Resumption of Testing. Many observers in the West viewed the unwillingness of the Soviets to compromise in the Geneva negotiations as unreasonable and deliberate. These feelings were vindicated when, on 30 August 1961, the Soviet Union announced its intention to resume nuclear testing the next day. The test series that followed was the largest ever conducted, with one test every other day for two months, including a huge 58-megaton explosion. This unprecedented and extravagant series must have been planned at least six months in advance. It is reasonable to assume that Khrushchev, perhaps under pressure from the military, ordered test preparations to begin soon after the U-2 incident.

The abrupt resumption of testing cast a pall not only over the test ban negotiations but over decades of U.S.-Soviet arms control talks as well. Those analysts who suggest that the Soviet Union is interested in arms control only as a method to increase its relative military advantage use the moratorium as the quintessential example of such behavior. The test ban talks, they say, lulled the United States while the Soviet Union prepared a vast test series. Although there is truth to this argument, it is overstated.

First, the moratorium was not a formal agreement. In August 1958, Eisenhower announced that the United States would suspend tests for a period of one year if the Soviet Union did not test. In addition, he stated that the moratorium would be extended on a year-to-year basis if a control system was installed and if progress was being made on reaching arms control agreements. The Soviet Union rejected the proposed moratorium and specifically criticized the conditions the United States had laid down as the requirement for its continuation. When the Soviet Union tested after 31 October 1958, Eisenhower stated that the United States was relieved of its obligation to suspend tests. Nevertheless, both sides stopped testing. About one year later, the United States announced that it would extend the moratorium to the end of the year, and the Soviet Union announced that it would not test as long as the "Western Powers" did not test. At the end of 1959, Eisenhower stated that the United States would no longer be bound by the moratorium, although it would announce any resumption of testing in advance. Khrushchev noted in an interview that the United States might resume testing at any moment. The Soviet Union cited French testing, which began in February 1960, as an excuse for its resumption of testing. Thus, the moratorium was created by a series of unilateral declarations (none of which were broken), not by a formal agreement.

Second, the United States was also secretly preparing to resume testing. After a tough meeting with Khrushchev in Vienna in June, and with the negotiations in Geneva stalemated, Kennedy ordered the Atomic Energy Commission to take the steps necessary to resume testing in about six months.[7] After the Soviet Union began testing, Kennedy tried to delay U.S. resumption — especially resumption of atmospheric testing — as long as possible in order to maximize the U.S. propaganda advantage. It is not unreasonable to assume that the United States might have been the first to test early the next year if the Soviet Union had not started testing in September (although Kennedy would certainly have given more than one day's notice). Indeed, Soviet intransigence during the 1961 negotiations may have been an attempt to goad the United States into breaking the moratorium first.

Third, there is no evidence that the Soviet Union obtained a military advantage by its actions. Although many observers claimed that the Soviets had learned valuable information about high-altitude explosions and high-yield weapons, this never resulted in a meaningful advantage.

With the test ban negotiations stalemated, the superpowers sponsored the creation of the Eighteen Nation Disarmament Conference (ENDC), later known as the Conference of the Committee on Disarmament (CCD), and today as simply the Committee on Disarmament (CD). Perhaps because realistic arms control negotiations were making little progress, the United States fell back to drafting yet another treaty for general and complete disarmament. The U.S. government fully recognized that the primary purpose of such activities was simply to influence world opinion in favor of the West. But the massive Soviet and American atmospheric testing programs that followed the moratorium served to renew public concern about fallout and the dangers of an uncontrolled arms race. The United States and the United Kingdom reduced their demand for on-site inspections, but by then the Soviet position had retrogressed to no inspections at all. In August 1962, the West proposed two alternate treaties at the ENDC: one banning all tests, and the other banning all but underground tests. Both approaches were rejected by the Soviet Union, the first because it required inspections, and the second because it allowed testing to continue.

The Limited Test Ban Treaty.   The Cuban missile crisis in October 1962 is often credited for bringing the United States and the Soviet Union back to the negotiating table in earnest. There is little doubt that the crisis temporarily removed the abstract quality from the balance of terror and in so doing motivated Kennedy and Khrushchev to take whatever steps they could to back away from the brink. The most obvious step at the time was to negotiate a test ban treaty.

In December 1962, the Soviet Union proposed that unmanned, tamperproof seismic stations (black boxes) be used to supplement national means of verification. Later that month, Khrushchev wrote to Kennedy offering two to three inspections per year. Khrushchev had apparently been lead to believe, as a result of a misunderstanding between U.S. and Soviet ambassadors, that this compromise would result in a treaty and on this basis had gone to great lengths to convince the Politburo to agree to offer three inspections. When the Kennedy administration responded by reducing its demand from twelve to eight inspections, Khrushchev felt betrayed. Kennedy had in fact authorized as few as six inspections (Harold Brown, then director of defense research and engineering, mentioned publicly that five would be acceptable), but Khrushchev was immovable. He would not (and probably could not) offer more than three. Kennedy was already in danger of losing his frail support in Congress by having offered only eight. Khrushchev withdrew his inspection offer entirely in April. Thus, the negotiations stalled once again early in 1963.

Determined not to let the test ban die, however, the two leaders continued their efforts. In response to a personal letter from Kennedy, Khrushchev agreed to receive a high-level delegation directly, in order to circumvent the formal negotiations that were deadlocked in Geneva. On 10 June, Kennedy gave a landmark commencement address at American University, in which he called for a relaxation in tensions between the superpowers. He announced that although he still preferred a CTBT, he was willing to consider a limited treaty, for which there was considerable support in the U.S. Senate. In a speech delivered in East Berlin on 2 July, Khrushchev indicated that he would accept a limited treaty.

Kennedy sent Averell Harriman, a former ambassador to the Soviet Union who was well respected in both countries, as head of the U.S. team. His instructions were to achieve a CTBT if possible, but when he arrived in Moscow the Soviets were only willing to discuss a limited agreement. With underground testing set aside, verification could be accomplished with national technical means (NTM), thus eliminating the problem of on-site inspection. The negotiations, which began on 15 July, ended just ten days later with the signing of the Treaty Banning Nuclear Weapons Tests in the Atmosphere, in Outer Space and Under Water, or, as it is known in the United States, the Limited Test Ban Treaty (LTBT).

Despite the popularity of the LTBT, Kennedy still faced a major battle for its ratification in the U.S. Senate. Although some analysts maintained that the Soviets could cheat on even a limited agreement, most opponents of the LTBT objected to it because they felt that continued atmospheric testing would be a net benefit to U.S. security. They argued, for example, that atmospheric tests were essential to develop an antiballistic missile system to protect against Soviet attack and that allowing only underground tests would slow the development of new nuclear weapons, such as pure-fusion weapons, that could revolutionize warfare. In support of the treaty, members of the Kennedy administration claimed that the LTBT would eliminate fallout, limit proliferation, slow the arms race, and catalyze the negotiation of more beneficial agreements in the future. After an intense, two-week-long debate in August, the Senate advised ratification by a vote of eighty to nineteen. The treaty was ratified by President Kennedy on 7 October 1963 and entered into force three days later.

Kennedy had to pay a high price for Senate support of the treaty. The Joint Chiefs of Staff (JCS), whose backing seems to have been essential for Senate approval, made their endorsement of the LTBT contingent on the implementation of four "safeguards." These safeguards were: (1) the conduct of a comprehensive and aggressive underground nuclear testing program, (2) the maintenance of modern nuclear weapon laboratories, (3) the maintenance of the ability to resume atmospheric testing on short notice, and (4) the improvement of the capability to verify compliance with the treaty. Skeptics and opponents of the treaty later ensured that these safeguards were implemented to the fullest extent—thereby decreasing the value of the treaty in relaxing East-West tensions and slowing the arms race. There was considerable concern expressed in the Senate hearings that a general euphoria would break out and the security of the United States would be impaired by the resulting lack of vigilance and preparedness.

In retrospect, the concerns of conservative senators and the Joint Chiefs of Staff were unfounded. Euphoria did not break out. Underground testing turned out to be relatively easy, and the rate of U.S.

testing increased substantially after the LTBT was signed. Weapon development has proceeded almost unimpeded, and lack of knowledge about atmospheric weapon effects has had no obvious effect on U.S. security. For precisely these reasons, however, the LTBT failed to slow the arms race.

Although the preamble of the LTBT states that the parties seek "to achieve the discontinuance of all test explosions of nuclear weapons for all time" and that they are "determined to continue negotiations to this end,"[8] the ratification of the LTBT marked the end of serious negotiations for a long time. With the cessation of atmospheric testing (except for occasional French and Chinese tests), public concern over fallout and public support of a CTB diminished greatly. Kennedy's other reasons for seeking a comprehensive test ban — to limit proliferation and slow the arms race — still remained, however, as did his strong personal conviction to end testing. Some analysts argue that if he and Khrushchev had remained in power another four years, a CTB would have been achieved, although Kennedy would have had to overcome vigorous opposition from the weapon laboratories, the JCS, and conservative senators.

Johnson and the NPT

Johnson inherited many of Kennedy's policies, but he did not share Kennedy's enthusiasm for a CTB. A CTB remained part of Johnson's official arms control agenda largely for propaganda purposes. Other issues, such as arresting nuclear proliferation (China exploded its first weapon in October 1964), slowing the production of fissile materials, and placing limitations on nuclear weapon systems, were given higher priority. Soon after coming to office, Johnson limited U.S. production of fissile materials (actually, he ended their overproduction) and extracted similar concessions from the Soviet Union. Toward the end of his term, he began the process that lead to the first Strategic Arms Limitation Treaty (SALT). His most significant arms control achievement, however, was the Non-Proliferation Treaty (NPT) of 1968. The link between nonproliferation and a CTB then became a central issue.

The heart of the matter was the inherently discriminatory nature of the NPT. The NPT codified the division of the world into two groups: the nations that had already developed nuclear weapons and those that had not. The nuclear weapon states, particularly the United States, the

Soviet Union, and the United Kingdom, did not want any more members in the nuclear club. (France was against further proliferation but felt powerless to prevent it, while China was then in favor of nations developing a "defensive" nuclear posture to prevent superpower blackmail.) The basic argument of the weapon states was that as nuclear weapons spread to more nations (some of which might be less stable and responsible than the superpowers), the risk of a global war involving all nations would increase. Therefore, the security of nonnuclear states would be enhanced if they agreed to forgo nuclear weapons altogether.

Although many of the nonweapon states, particularly neutral states such as Sweden and India, were sympathetic with this reasoning, they wanted to know what the weapon states were willing to do in exchange for their forbearance. The weapon states had already promised to assist the nonweapon states in harnessing the peaceful uses of nuclear energy, but this was not enough. Why, the nonweapon states argued, should the burden of decreasing the risk of war fall only on them? Should not the weapon states also be required to take steps to reduce the probability of a devastating nuclear war? If nuclear weapons were "bad," why should some states be allowed to continue to test and deploy new types? These nonweapon states took the word "proliferation" to encompass vertical, as well as horizontal, proliferation. Some states regarded the whole affair as a transparently cynical attempt by the superpowers to lock lesser states into positions of inferiority. After all, the superpowers readily admitted that nuclear weapons were vital for their own security; why shouldn't these weapons be useful to other states as well? A handful of nuclear weapons could be a great equalizer in a conflict, and many states were loath to surrender this possibility, especially if they were uncertain about the intentions of a regional adversary or about the quality of the security guarantees of a nuclear ally.

The superpowers soon found that a treaty would be impossible without responding to these concerns in some way. Sweden insisted that the weapon states commit themselves to a CTBT, but, referring to the impasse over on-site inspection, the superpowers refused. (In fact, Sweden claimed that a CTBT would be as effective as the NPT in slowing proliferation.) The neutrals contented themselves with a restatement in the NPT's preamble of the pledge made in the Limited Test Ban Treaty to end all nuclear tests for all time and with Article VI of the NPT, which called upon the nuclear weapon states "to pursue negotiations in good faith on effective measures relating to cessation of the nuclear arms race at an early date and to nuclear disarmament. . . ."[9] Most nonweapon states implicitly understood this language to refer to a CTBT, which is clearly demonstrated by the fact that, despite a steady stream of SALT negotiations, the nonnuclear states have complained consistently that the nuclear states are not living up to their obligations under Article VI. In the NPT Review Conferences in 1975, 1980, and 1985, for example, the superpowers were called upon to negotiate a CTBT. Moreover, many of the states that are not parties to the NPT cite the lack of a CTBT as an excuse for their continued refusal to sign. Whether a CTBT would actually deter proliferation is arguable, but it is interesting to note that India almost certainly would not have conducted its first and only explosion (which, in turn, spurred Pakistan's nuclear efforts) if the LTBT or the NPT had included a complete ban on testing.

Nixon, Ford, and the TTBT/PNET

Like Johnson, President Nixon half-heartedly reaffirmed each year, for the sake of world opinion, the willingness of the United States to negotiate a CTB. Nixon may have felt, in view of his decision to exclude the possibility of banning multiple independently targeted reentry vehicles in the SALT talks, that testing was needed to develop the next generation of ballistic missile reentry vehicles. In any case, restrictions on antiballistic missile systems and SALT were the main thrusts of Nixon's arms control policy, and these were decoupled from the issue of underground testing. Congressional interest in a CTB was aroused in 1972, but election-year politics, the Vietnam War, and SALT intervened.

The Threshold Test Ban Treaty. At the end of May 1974, President Nixon sent a delegation to Moscow to discuss limitations on nuclear testing. The reasons for the sudden interest of the Nixon administration in a test ban treaty are not entirely clear; some analysts have suggested that the treaty was arranged simply to maintain the momentum of the détente process. Earlier in the year, Nixon and Brezhnev had agreed to a June summit, at which they hoped to sign a follow-on agreement to SALT, but it became increasingly apparent that a treaty would not be ready. To fill the gap, the two sides agreed to consider a threshold test ban. Both leaders felt a need to sign a treaty — especially Nixon, who may have been hoping this would help restore confidence in his flagging presidency. The Threshold Test Ban Treaty (TTBT) was negotiated in time to be signed at the summit meeting on 3 July 1974. One month later, Nixon resigned.

The main effect of the TTBT was to restrict underground weapon tests to specified test sites and to yields of less than 150 kilotons. This differed from previous U.S. threshold proposals, which had incorporated a seismic, rather than a yield, threshold. The Soviets had apparently decided that a seismic threshold would have put them at a significant disadvantage, since explosions of a given yield at their test site would have produced larger seismic magnitudes than similar explosions at the Nevada test site. In any case, an equitable agreement based on a seismic threshold certainly would have been more difficult to work out than one based on yield. The treaty was to be verified by NTM, supplemented by an exchange of pertinent data, such as the location of each test and the geology underlying the test sites.

The Peaceful Nuclear Explosions Treaty.   Part of the reason that the TTBT was negotiated quickly was that the most difficult problem — accommodating peaceful nuclear explosions — was deferred to another treaty. It was agreed that the TTBT would not take effect until its companion, the Peaceful Nuclear Explosions Treaty (PNET), had been negotiated. The United States, once enthusiastic about the potential of PNEs, had since lost interest, but the Soviet Union by now had a major PNE program that it wished to save. It would not have been difficult to accommodate PNEs if their yields were less than the threshold, but the Soviet Union wanted the option of using explosives much larger than 150 kilotons. The problem was that the development of high-yield weapons might continue under the cover of a PNE program. In 1959, the Soviet Union demanded internal inspections of PNE devices to ensure that they were not being used for weapon development. The United States agreed (pending congressional approval), but later changed its position because such inspections would have revealed sensitive information.

This problem was eventually solved in the PNE talks by permitting multiple explosions with an aggregate yield of up to 1,500 kilotons, but with the yield of individual explosions limited to 150 kilotons. Because the Soviet Union allowed detailed OSIs as part of this agreement, many saw the PNET as a watershed in superpower arms control. It should be noted, however, that this concession did not necessarily guarantee that OSIs would be offered in future agreements; OSIs were only allowed in this case because it was the price the Soviet Union was willing to pay to continue PNEs. After eighteen months of intense negotiations, the PNET was signed by Presidents Ford and Brezhnev on 28 May 1976.

The TTBT and PNET were controversial in the arms control community. Although supporters claimed that the treaties represented a small but significant step toward a CTB, skeptics maintained that the treaties were seriously flawed. First, argued opponents of the treaties, the 150-kt threshold was far above any reasonable threshold based on seismic detection criteria. The most common threshold discussed before the TTBT was a seismic magnitude of 4.75, which corresponds to a yield of roughly 10 kilotons in hard or water-saturated rock. Moveover, seismic detection and identification capabilities had improved considerably since a threshold of 4.75 was first proposed in 1960. The 150-kt threshold was undoubtedly chosen so that it would have had little effect on warhead development programs already under way in both countries. Second, the TTBT was set to enter into force nearly two years after it was signed. Although arguably justified by the absence of the companion PNET, the delay allowed the design and testing of the latest generation of high-yield weapons to be finished. Third, the PNET legitimized the idea of making exceptions for PNEs, which, it was thought, would complicate the negotiation of a CTBT.

In the final analysis, the treaties did little to keep the spirit of détente alive. Not wanting to risk a Senate debate in an election year, President Ford did not push for ratification. The treaties remain unratified to this day, although both parties have promised not to test above 150 kilotons.

Carter and the CTB

Carter was the first U.S. president since Kennedy to make the CTB a serious arms control initiative. Just days after his inauguration in January 1977, and again in a speech to the United Nations in March, Carter announced his intention to seek an end to all nuclear testing. His main reason: to strengthen efforts to prevent nuclear proliferation. Although the administration's "deep-cuts" proposal was rejected when Secretary of State Cyrus Vance and Soviet Foreign Minister Andrei Gromyko met in Moscow later in March, they did agree to resume trilateral negotiations on a CTB. Formal negotiations began in Geneva on 3 October 1977.

According to most reports, the negotiations made rapid progress. The issue of peaceful nuclear explosions, which many expected to be a major stumbling block, was resolved when Brezhnev announced in November that the Soviet Union was willing to accept a moratorium on PNEs for the duration of a CTB. The second major obstacle was the issue of on-site inspections. In a draft treaty presented to the United Nations the previous year, the Soviet Union indicated that it would be willing to accept voluntary OSIs as proposed by Sweden more than a decade earlier. In a reversal of long-standing U.S. policy, the Carter administration also adopted the concept of voluntary OSIs, since it had decided that their deterrent effect would be about the same as that of a fixed number of mandatory OSIs. In addition, the Soviet Union accepted the idea of a fixed number of automatic, tamperproof seismic stations being installed on their territory to supplement national means of verification, although provisions for this installation were not worked out in detail. The Soviet Union agreed to accept ten stations, but only if each of the other parties accepted an equal number. The United Kingdom refused, claiming that only one station should be sufficient to monitor its much smaller land area. Both nations saw this as a matter of principle, and both refused to compromise.

It had become apparent that there was considerable opposition to a CTB from within the Western governments. This time, the main arguments against a CTB, in the United Kingdom as well as in the United States, revolved around the need to ensure the continued reliability of the stockpile of proven weapon systems. In hearings before Congress in August 1978, representatives from the nuclear weapon laboratories, the Department of Defense, and the Joint Chiefs of Staff asserted that problems would eventually occur with an important warhead and that it would be difficult to reestablish confidence without nuclear tests. Later, the directors of the two nuclear weapons laboratories visited the White House to emphasize this point. CTB opponents also raised the need to modernize the stockpile and doubts about the verifiability of an accord, but these issues were secondary to that of stockpile confidence. The obvious reasons for this priority were that the "need" to build new types of weapons was not nearly as popular as the need to maintain deterrent forces and that the CTB negotiations were making great strides in securing effective verification procedures.

To placate CTB opponents, Carter sought a treaty of limited duration. Although this pleased the Soviets, whose position was that a treaty of unlimited duration was possible only with the participation of the French and the Chinese, they were upset by the inability of the Carter administration to decide on a specific duration for the treaty. Carter decided to seek a five-year treaty in May 1978, but then changed, amid growing congressional unrest, to a three-year treaty in September; later, the administration decided that the treaty should be renegotiated and reratified instead of merely reviewed and renewed after the expiration date. Even so, the critics were not satisfied — they wanted an explicit commitment to resume testing after the end of the treaty.

The negotiations were never completed. Brezhnev and Carter had decided that SALT II should come before a CTB. Not wanting to upset the JCS, who did not favor a CTB but whose support was crucial to the success of SALT II, Carter pushed the CTB no further. Negotiations slowed considerably after the Soviet invasion of Afghanistan in December 1979 and were recessed on 20 November 1980.

The Reagan Years

President Reagan had a very different view of arms control than most of his predecessors. During his campaign, Reagan decried what he saw as a growing U.S. strategic inferiority vis-à-vis the Soviet Union. SALT, in his view, was part of the problem, not part of the solution. The desirability of a test ban was not questioned explicitly until a year into his presidency, when Eugene Rostow, then director of the Arms Control and Disarmament Agency (ACDA), told the Committee on Disarmament that a CTB would not reduce the threat of nuclear weapons or help maintain the stability of the nuclear balance. Several months later, in June 1982, the United States formally announced that the trilateral CTB talks would not be resumed. Difficulties with verification were cited as the reason for the decision. Moreover, the administration said that it could not submit the TTBT and PNET to the Senate for ratification until more effective verification procedures were agreed upon by the Soviet Union. The administration later accused the Soviet Union of violating the TTBT by consistently testing at yields above 150 kilotons, a charge that has been disputed almost unanimously by scientists outside the government.

When the United Kingdom fell in line with the U.S. position, all the nuclear powers except the Soviet Union were against a CTB. Other nations were not willing let the issue die, however. Later that year, the Soviet Union introduced a draft CTBT to the U.N. General Assembly, and in December the United States was the only nation to vote against a resolution to resume trilateral negotiations toward a CTB. In May 1984, the leaders of six nonaligned nations — Argentina, Greece, India, Mexico, Sweden, and Tanzania — called for an end to the production and testing of nuclear weapons. This appeal, which became known as the "Five Continent Peace Initiative," has been repeated on several occasions since. In August 1985, Mexico suggested that a conference of the parties to the LTBT be organized with the purpose of amending the treaty to include underground tests. The ability of the Soviet Union to conduct coherent arms control negotiations during this time was impaired by the deaths of three Soviet leaders — Brezhnev, Andropov, and Chernenko — in four years.

Two events occurred in 1985 that forced the Reagan administration to alter its position on nuclear testing, if only cosmetically. First, a new and youthful Soviet leader, Mikhail Gorbachev, had just assumed office. In a move reminiscent of Khrushchev, Gorbachev announced just a few months after coming into office that the Soviet Union would unilaterally suspend all nuclear testing beginning 6 August 1985 (the fortieth anniversary of the destruction of Hiroshima) and invited the other nuclear powers to join the moratorium. The Reagan administration dismissed the offer as mere propaganda, claiming that "a flurry" of Soviet tests had just been done. The available evidence, however, indicates that the Soviet Union had conducted *fewer* tests than normal.[10] More sincerely, the administration claimed that continued U.S. testing was necessary to redress the nuclear imbalance. As if to indicate its disdain, the United States invited the Soviet Union to witness a U.S. test on 8 August. Gorbachev extended the moratorium three times, but to no avail. After a nineteen-month, self-imposed moratorium, the Soviet Union resumed nuclear testing in February 1987.

When it became apparent that the Reagan administration would not join in the Soviet moratorium, private discussions between U.S. and Soviet scientists began about how to break up the logjam. A private agreement emerged in May 1986 between the Natural Resources Defense Council (NRDC) and the Soviet Academy of Sciences to establish seismic monitoring equipment near the Kazakhstan nuclear test site in the Soviet Union. The NRDC agreement was widely hailed as a breakthrough for arms control negotiations. But critics disparage the value of the seismic data collected and point out that after the moratorium ended, the Soviet military first required the equipment to be shut down during nuclear tests and then ordered the station to be relocated far from the test site.

The other event in 1985 was the NPT Review Conference. Predictably, the nuclear nations were scored for not living up to their obligations under Article VI. The United States and the United Kingdom were criticized especially for their refusal to resume CTB negotiations, but the Soviet Union escaped censure. Unlike past administrations, Reagan's would not even give lip service to the CTB. ACDA Director Kenneth Adelman told the conference that "a CTB will not reduce the number of nuclear weapons in the world by one, nor will it, in the near term, make the world any safer." Another Reagan spokesman said "we believe a ban must be seen in the context of a time when we do not need to depend on nuclear deterrence to ensure security and stability. . . ." In other words, by the time a CTB would be acceptable to the administration, it would be irrelevant.

Congress was upset at this reversal of long-standing U.S. policy. Resolutions were adopted in both houses of Congress calling on the president to resume CTB negotiations. To divert attention, Reagan began formal negotiations with the Soviets on test restrictions in July 1986. It quickly became apparent, however, that the two sides had quite different agendas: the Soviet Union wanted a CTB, whereas the United States merely wanted to improve TTBT verification. Despite a strong lobbying effort by the administration, in October 1986 the House passed, by a margin of 234 to 155, legislation to ban U.S. tests above 1 kiloton for one year. With the Reykjavik summit drawing near, Reagan urged Congress "not to tie his hands," and the low-yield threshold legislation was derailed. In another attempt to sidetrack the CTB debate, the administration forwarded the TTBT and the PNET to the Senate for their advice and consent in 1987 (but this was made contingent on the Soviet Union accepting more effective verification procedures). A Senate version of the House low-yield threshold legislation subsequently failed to pass.

Summary

Several important lessons can be learned from the history of test ban negotiations. The most important lesson is that the test ban issue will not go away. Despite repeated attempts by leaders in all nuclear weapons states to downplay its importance, the CTB has remained one of the most important items — if not *the* most important item — on the world's arms control agenda. Given the robustness of the support for a CTB in the past, it is only logical that leaders should have a well-informed position on the test ban in the future.

Second, the most critical variables in determining the prospects for a test ban are the attitude of the U.S. president and the degree of support he enjoys from Congress. Given the large institutional barriers against a CTB, the president must be enthusiastic about a test ban and have a broad base of support to have a chance for a treaty. President Kennedy, who satisfied both of these criteria, faced a heated Senate debate over a limited treaty and was forced to accept conditions (the JCS safeguards) that greatly limited the political value of the agreement. A weaker or less enthusiastic president would not have had a chance. It appears that a broader American-Soviet rapprochement is an essential precondition for the achievement of a CTBT. We may now be witnessing the beginning of such a rapprochement in Gorbachev's policy of "glasnost."

Finally, it is interesting to note the moderating influence of Congress in the test ban debate and in treaty discussions in general. For example, Congress could be highly critical of Carter's CTB negotiations in 1978, yet demand that Reagan resume these negotiations only a few years later. This apparently paradoxical behavior can be explained by remembering that a two-thirds majority is required for the Senate to advise ratification of a treaty, while only a simple majority is required to pass laws and resolutions. The House, moreover, has been consistently more pro-CTB than the Senate. Thus, a large majority of congressmen can favor a test ban, but a minority of senators can block a treaty.

TEST BAN ISSUES

One of the most striking features of the test ban debate is the large number of issues that have been raised and the rapid shifts that have taken place in the relative importance of these issues. The topics that have been central at some point in the debate are reviewed below; those that are still relevant form the basis for subsequent chapters.

Fallout

If nuclear explosions did not produce fallout, it is unlikely that a test ban would have emerged as a separate arms control initiative. The fear of adverse health effects from fallout, made frightening by the BRAVO test and by the appearance of radioactivity in mother's milk and children's teeth, triggered the public outcry against testing, and these public protests caused formal negotiations to take place. Eisenhower, as leader of a loose alliance of democracies, could ill afford to ignore public opinion. Khrushchev, as head of an unpopular and militarily inferior nation, could not resist the opportunity to score propaganda victories by advocating a test ban, thereby possibly weakening the Western alliance. Thus, the two leaders, both probably convinced that continued nuclear testing was important to the security of their country, were thrust together by public opinion in search of a test ban. Given the insincerity of prior proposals, it is reasonable to assume that progress in nuclear arms control would have been delayed much longer if fallout had not made the test ban an urgent issue.

Fallout is no longer an important consideration in the test ban debate; therefore it is not discussed further in this book. The LTBT was a great success in limiting the health effects of nuclear testing. The average dose from atmospheric fallout is now less than the extra dose one would receive from a chest X-ray or a cross-country airline flight. France, though not a party to the LTBT, has refrained from testing in the atmosphere since 1974, in response to protests from Australia and New Zealand. Even China has not tested in the atmosphere since 1980. Small amounts of radioactivity occasionally are released during underground explosions, but the resulting health effects are negligible.

Weapon Modernization

The fundamental reason for weapon testing, today as in Eisenhower's time, is to develop new nuclear weapons. The fundamental objection to a test ban has always been that the development of new nuclear weapons is necessary to support the national security policies of the nation. Weapon modernization can be evolutionary (e.g., developing a warhead whose size, shape, and weight are optimized for use on a certain missile) or revolutionary (e.g., developing weapons based on new physical principles, such as thermonuclear weapons or X-ray lasers). Nuclear testing is also necessary to equip warheads with the latest safety and security features and to test the effects of nuclear explosions on various types of military hardware.

The popularity of this rationale for testing has risen and fallen with the overall mood of the nation with regard to nuclear weapons. When the public has perceived the Soviet Union as an impending threat to peace, weapon modernization and nuclear testing have generally gained support; when the public has perceived the nuclear arms race itself as the greater threat, however, test bans have enjoyed more support. The swing in public opinion during the late 1970s illustrates this point vividly: in the 1977–1978 CTB debate, when public support for military spending was low, the defense community scarcely raised the modernization argument; instead, it was content with objections based on maintaining the reliability of existing weapons. In the early 1980s, however, when public support for military programs was much greater, it could be stated quite candidly that continued testing was necessary for new weapon systems designed to respond to the perceived Soviet threat. The support for modernization in the 1980s has resulted in a number of new weapon designs for cruise missiles, enhanced-radiation artillery shells, improved bombs, and MX and Pershing II warheads, as well as a plethora of novel ideas, including earth-penetrating warheads, insertable nuclear components, and nuclear directed-energy weapons such as the X-ray laser. The effect of forgoing nuclear testing on weapon system modernization is discussed in Chapter 2.

Strategy

Requirements for weapon modernization should be dictated by military strategy, but often this relationship has not been explicit in policy discussions. The stated policy of the United States regarding nuclear weapons is one of deterrence; that is, nuclear weapons are stockpiled in order to deter war. There is a broad base of support for the concept of nuclear deterrence, probably because there does not seem to be any rational or viable alternative. But deterrence comes in dozens of flavors, and there is little agreement within the defense community or the American public about what *kind* of deterrent posture the United States should adopt.

The official U.S. deterrent posture is one of "flexible response" or "countervailing strategy." This strategy requires that the United States have the ability to carry out limited nuclear attacks and to deny victory to the adversary at any level of nuclear violence. Accordingly, the United States has made plans and acquired weapons to carry out a wide variety of limited nuclear attacks, including attacks on missile silos, command and control centers, and other military targets. In this view, the credibility of nuclear deterrence rests on the willingness to use nuclear weapons to achieve a rational goal of national policy. Supporters of this view argue that relying on the ability to destroy cities, which does not require sophisticated weapons or careful planning, is not a credible deterrent and may therefore actually increase the probability of war.

Many arms control advocates, on the other hand, believe that a policy of "minimum deterrence" would be more effective in preventing war. They argue that the very act of planning for limited nuclear war increases the risk of war and reinforces dehumanizing images of the opposing national leadership. In this view, the weapons acquired to support the countervailing strategy (e.g., the accurate warheads on the MX, Pershing, and Trident II missiles) may increase Soviet fears of a preemptive U.S. attack during a crisis. Moreover, advocates of minimum deterrence claim that the use of nuclear weapons during war would be extremely difficult — if not impossible — to control. An illusory belief that limited nuclear war is possible could draw both countries into a mutually devastating general nuclear war. Advocates of minimum deterrence believe it would be safer to admit that a nuclear war cannot be won and should not be fought and to maintain a minimum of nuclear forces on both sides to decrease residual anxiety about the possibility of an attack.

It is not my purpose here to argue which of these types of deterrence is more correct but simply to indicate the very different implications these views have for support of a test ban treaty. If one believes that minimum deterrence is safer than a countervailing strategy, for example, then much of the weapon modernization prevented by a test ban is a stabilizing influence that contributes to peace; if one believes the opposite, however, then a test ban prevents the development of new weapons that are necessary to strengthen the psychology of deterrence. The role of strategy in the test ban debate is discussed in Chapter 5.

Stockpile Confidence

Nuclear weapons, like any piece of sophisticated hardware, are not perfect. They deteriorate with age at an unspecified rate, and they may have unrecognized design flaws. At some point in the future or under some deployment conditions, deterioration or design flaws may reduce the yield of a weapon type or even cause it to fail completely. This has happened several times in the past, and nuclear testing was used to correct these problems and to restore confidence in the reliability of the stockpile. Opponents of a CTB claim that unexpected aging or design flaws will almost certainly be discovered in the future and that nuclear testing will be required to restore confidence in these systems. In this view, the president would be presented with an unavoidable choice when such problems occurred under a CTBT: abrogate the treaty or accept decreased confidence in the stockpile. CTB opponents argue that decreased stockpile confidence undermines deterrence and makes war more likely.

Proponents of a CTB recognize the importance of stockpile confidence but claim that there are many ways to restore confidence short of nuclear testing. First, nonnuclear testing may indicate, as it has in some cases in the past, if a problem will affect the yield. Second, aged warheads can be replaced by warheads manufactured to the original specifications. Third, a similar warhead can be substituted for the problem warhead. Fourth, one could take special precautions before a CTBT is negotiated, such as developing substitutes for the components most likely to deteriorate. In addition, CTB proponents maintain that the reliability of nuclear weapons far exceeds that of other military equipment, such as missiles and command and control systems, and that reliability requirements for nuclear weapons can be relaxed substantially without significantly decreasing the reliability of the system as a whole. Those CTB proponents who prefer minimum deterrence point out that high reliability is only necessary for dangerous nuclear war-fighting strategies; they suggest that we simply accept a lower degree of confidence in our nuclear forces.

CTB opponents maintain that many of these suggestions are impractical or unworkable. Since it is often difficult to duplicate certain materials or manufacturing processes, CTB opponents argue that remanufactured weapons would have to be tested in order to have confidence that they would work. Remanufacturing also rebuilds old problems into new warheads; the temptation to fix the problem may be irresistible, which would introduce untested designs into the stockpile. Substitution is not acceptable in all cases, and the substitute might also fail. Finally, CTB opponents argue that experienced weapon designers are vital to the success of nonnuclear solutions to reliability problems and that it would be impossible to have experienced designers without an active nuclear testing program. The stockpile confidence issue is examined in Chapter 3.

Peaceful Nuclear Explosions

Perhaps in reaction to the tremendous destructive capacity of nuclear weapons, scientists were generally optimistic in the 1950s and 1960s about the potential of the peaceful uses of nuclear energy to contribute to the well-being of humanity. In June 1957, the AEC started Project Plowshare to investigate the nonmilitary uses of nuclear explosives, which later became known as "peaceful nuclear explosions" (PNEs). A total of forty-eight PNE experiments were done under Project Plowshare to explore isotope generation for medical and nuclear physics experiments, earth-moving, oil and gas stimulation, and the creation of cavities for underground storage.[11] Congress was enthusiastic about PNEs, and many senators based their support of the LTBT on the Kennedy administration's assurance that Project Plowshare could go forward under the treaty. Public concern about the release of radio-nuclides to the environment increased in the 1970s, however, and industrial interest waned. Policymakers, including many early Plowshare advocates, concluded that the social, political, and economic costs of PNEs far outweighed their potential benefits. The last U.S. PNE experiment was done in 1973, and in 1977, one year after the PNET had been signed, Project Plowshare ended.

Soviet interest in PNEs lagged somewhat behind that of the United States. In the test ban negotiations of the late 1950s, for example, the Soviet Union argued that PNEs should be banned along with weapon tests. Stimulated perhaps by the claims being made for PNEs in the United States, the Soviet Union began PNE experiments in 1965. By 1973, the year of the last Plowshare explosion, it had done about thirty-nine PNEs to explore their feasibility for a wide variety of tasks, including earth-moving, mineral development, storage cavity creation, deep seismic sounding, oil and gas stimulation, and extinguishing gas-well fires.[12] The use of PNEs seemed attractive in the last four of these tasks, and the Soviet Union pressed to keep the PNE option open in the TTBT negotiations in 1974. As noted above, this resulted in the PNET in 1976. Although the Soviet Union offered in 1977 to suspend PNEs for the duration of a CTBT, they continue to have an active program. Over one hundred large explosions have been detected outside of the normal Soviet nuclear testing sites; these are presumed to have been PNEs.

Peaceful nuclear explosions create obvious problems for a test ban because they can have military value. First, it has proved impossible to find a mutually satisfactory arrangement whereby PNEs can be less restricted than military tests. The early proposal of PNE-device inspection was rejected because it would have revealed sensitive information about weapon design. (The main goal of PNE-device design is to minimize the fraction of fission energy released, thereby minimizing the generation of radioactivity; thus, PNE devices are quite sophisticated.) One might also determine that a PNE device was not being used to gather militarily significant information by sampling the debris left behind after the explosion, but apparently even this approach is not foolproof. Unless this problem can be solved, PNEs must be subject to the same restrictions as weapon tests. Second, even if PNEs are not being used as a cover for military tests, the production, fielding, and firing of PNEs would help to maintain the infrastructure necessary for weapon testing. Since the United States has no PNE program, this would lead to asymmetries in the ability to test clandestinely or to resume testing quickly if the treaty is abrogated. Since the Soviet Union has been willing in the past to give up PNEs in exchange for a CTBT, the PNE issue is not examined further in this book.

Verification

It should be obvious from the brief history presented above that problems with verification have always been at the center of the test ban debate. The United States has consistently emphasized adequate verification procedures because it is apprehensive about Soviet cheating; the Soviet Union has consistently avoided intrusive inspections because it fears that these would be used as opportunities for spying or interference in its internal affairs. Key issues have been the military significance of a given level of cheating, and whether verification must be accurate enough to ensure high confidence that significant cheating is not taking place or merely sufficient to deny other parties high confidence that they could cheat with impunity. Generally, CTB proponents have argued that verification procedures are adequate to deter parties from significant cheating, while opponents have insisted that significant cheating would be possible by a determined adversary.

Although seismic methods have improved tremendously since test ban negotiations first began, there is still disagreement about whether seismic systems could identify clandestine nuclear explosions with high probability, without generating huge numbers of false alarms caused by earthquakes and chemical explosions. Nonseismic methods of verification exist but are subject to even greater uncertainties than seismic means. And while the Soviets have finally agreed to allow OSIs, Americans are now divided on whether the contribution of OSIs would be sufficient to warrant the detailed negotiations that would be required to include them in a treaty. Evasion scenarios have been identified that might allow significant testing to escape detection, but there are disagreements about the practical difficulties involved. These issues are discussed in detail in Chapter 4.

Proliferation

One of the strongest rationales for a test ban during the Kennedy and Carter administrations was the belief that it would strengthen efforts at preventing nuclear proliferation. Three reasons are often given for this belief. First, parties to a CTBT relinquish their right to test nuclear weapons, which makes the development of such weapons more difficult. Nations would naturally be less confident in an untested weapon than in a tested weapon and therefore may be less likely to develop weapons in the first place. Second, a CTBT would strengthen the NPT regime by partially fulfilling the obligations of the nuclear nations in Article VI of the NPT to take actions to end the arms race. Most nations feel that a CTB is the largest single step that the superpowers could take toward satisfying this obligation. A CTBT would also remove the discriminatory aspect of the NPT to a certain extent, thus eliminating a key excuse that some nations, such as India, Brazil, and Argentina, have used for not signing the NPT. It would be politically difficult for these nations to refuse to sign a CTBT since a CTB is not discriminatory. Third, by agreeing to a CTBT the nuclear nations would diminish the prestige value of nuclear status somewhat, and the nonnuclear nations would give up nuclear testing as a route for acquiring prestige, thus weakening the rationale for proliferation in some nations.

Test ban opponents, however, are quick to point out that a nation's decision to develop nuclear weapons is based almost entirely on regional rivalries and has very little to do with agreements made between the superpowers. Furthermore, they point out that it is not difficult for a nation with a large industrial base to develop primitive nuclear weapons without testing and to have high confidence that they will work. Finally, test ban opponents maintain that for many non-signatories of the NPT, the lack of a CTB is merely a convenient excuse for not signing. If these nations are interested in developing nuclear weapons, and if they believe that nuclear testing would be important to achieve this goal, a CTBT will not change their minds. The effect of a CTBT on nuclear proliferation is discussed in Chapter 5.

Détente and Politics

Closely related to the issue of proliferation is the significance of political moves and propaganda gains made by advocating a CTB. The propaganda defeats that the United States suffered in the late 1950s at the hands of the Soviets convinced Eisenhower's secretary of state, John Foster Dulles, to support a test ban. Even if Americans do not believe that a test ban is in the security interests of the United States, most American allies favor a CTB. There is a widespread belief that the cohesiveness of the Western alliance is vital to U.S. security, and U.S. presidents have been forced on several occasions to voice support for a test ban to appease allies (and congressional critics). If the Soviet Union presses the test ban issue and appears to concede to U.S. demands for better verification procedures, the United States may find it very difficult politically not to sign a CTBT.

In view of the thirty-year-long impasse on test ban issues, a CTBT would be a vivid symbol of superpower détente. For those observers who feel that the superpowers are caught in the vicious cycle of an action-reaction arms race, détente would be a large contribution to a stable peace. For those who feel that the basic and unchanging Soviet goal is world hegemony, on the other hand, détente would only lull the West into a dangerous false sense of security. The relationship between détente and a CTB is discussed in Chapter 5.

TYPES OF TESTING RESTRICTIONS

This book focuses on a comprehensive test ban. Taken literally, the word "comprehensive" implies a ban on all nuclear explosions, regardless of purpose, size, or method of creation. There are many nuclear explosions, however, that we may not want to ban. So-called hydronuclear experiments, for example, can result in a nuclear yield equivalent to only a few grams of high explosive. These tests could be valuable in assessing the safety and reliability of nuclear weapons without full-scale nuclear tests. In addition, there is great interest in inertial-confinement fusion (ICF). In the ICF process, large lasers or particle beams are focused on a small sphere of fusion fuel, compressing and heating it. With large enough lasers or particle beams, ICF may eventually be capable of creating miniature nuclear explosions yielding the equivalent of a ton of high explosive. A source of this size would be useful for weapon effects testing and perhaps even for electricity generation. If such experiments were to continue, a CTBT should actually be an extremely-low-yield threshold test ban treaty, with the threshold set at perhaps 10 tons.

Although a comprehensive test ban has been the central goal of most test ban proponents, other ideas, such as a low-yield threshold test ban (LYTTB) and a test quota, have recently received attention in the United States. These proposals are attractive for those observers who fear that undetectable Soviet cheating under a CTBT may be more of a risk to national security than unrestricted testing by both countries below some threshold; for those who feel that some nominal amount of testing is required to maintain stockpile confidence or to appease domestic critics of a CTBT; or for those who simply are philosophically opposed to banning unverifiable activities. The two most widely mentioned thresholds for an LYTTBT are 1 kiloton and 10 kilotons, although thresholds of 3, 5, and 15 kilotons have also been proposed. A test quota is designed to allow stockpile confidence problems to be fixed. Based on current practices, the value usually proposed for the quota is one or two tests per year, with each test yielding less than 10 or 20 kilotons. The Senate's proposed Nuclear Explosions Control Act of 1987 combined these two ideas by establishing a 1-kt threshold for routine testing and by allowing two reliability tests of less than 15 kilotons each year.

At the present time (late 1987), there appears to be much more support in the United States for an LYTTBT or test quota than for a

CTBT. Given the almost certain opposition of the Department of Defense, the Department of Energy, and the Joint Chiefs of Staff, Senate support for a CTBT does not seem possible in the near future, no matter how enthusiastic a future president might be. Nevertheless, the CTBT is still the central idea in the debate — all other proposals are the result of compromise. Few CTBT opponents favor other restrictions on testing (except as a way of avoiding a CTB), and few CTBT proponents favor an LYTTBT (except as a step toward a CTB). For this reason, this book will focus specifically on a CTB. Low-yield thresholds and test quotas are mentioned as well, but only as modifications of the central idea of a CTBT.

NOTES

1. This review of the history of test ban negotiations has been gleaned from many sources, including G. Allen Greb, "Comprehensive Test Ban Negotiations, 1958–1986: An Overview," in Jozef Goldblat and David Cox, eds., *Nuclear Weapon Tests: Cessation or Limitation?* (Oxford: Oxford University Press, 1988); Glenn T. Seaborg, *Kennedy, Khrushchev, and the Test Ban* (Berkeley: University of California Press, 1981); Glenn T. Seaborg, *Stemming the Tide: Arms Control in the Johnson Years* (Lexington, Mass: Lexington Books, 1987); Herbert F. York, *Making Weapons, Talking Peace: A Physicist's Odyssey from Hiroshima to Geneva* (New York: Basic Books, 1987); National Academy of Sciences, "Nuclear Test Bans," in *Nuclear Arms Control: Background and Issues* (Washington, D.C.: National Academy of Sciences Press, 1985); Robert A. Divine, "Early Record on Test Moratoriums," *Bulletin of the Atomic Scientists* 42, no. 5 (May 1986): 24–26; and "Agreements and Treaties Other than SALT and the NPT," in Coit D. Blacker and Gloria Duffy, eds., *International Arms Control: Issues and Agreements* (Stanford: Stanford University Press, 1984). In addition, annual reports of the Arms Control and Disarmament Agency to Congress, congressional hearings on the LTBT and the CTB, and participants in those negotiations were consulted.
2. Neil Joeck and Herbert F. York, "Countdown on the Comprehensive Test Ban," University of California Institute on Global Conflict and Cooperation (1986), p. 21.
3. Thomas B. Cochran, William M. Arkin, Robert S. Norris, and Milton M. Hoenig, *Nuclear Weapons Databook*, vol. II: *U.S. Nuclear Warhead Production* (Cambridge, Mass.: Ballinger Publishing Company, 1987), pp. 10–11.
4. Cochran, et al., *U.S. Nuclear Warhead Production*, pp. 151–159, list as many U.S. explosions from 7/24/57 to 10/30/58 as during the previous twelve years. Jeffrey I. Sands, Robert S. Norris, and Thomas B. Cochran, "Known Soviet Nuclear Explosions, 1949–1985," Nuclear Weapons Databook Project Working Paper NWD 86–3, Natural Resources Defense Council, June 1986, pp. 13–16, list as many Soviet explosions from 9/24/57 to 11/03/58 as during the previous eight years.
5. A.L. Latter, R.E. LeLevier, E.A. Martinelli, and W.G. McMillan, "A Method of Concealing Underground Nuclear Explosions," *Journal of Geophysical Research* 66, no. 3 (March 1961): 943–46. This work was originally published as a RAND report dated 30 March 1959.

6. Herbert York and G. Allen Greb, "The Comprehensive Nuclear Test Ban," Discussion Paper No. 84 (Santa Monica, Calif: California Seminar on Arms Control and Foreign Policy, June 1979), p. 8.

7. See Seaborg, *Kennedy, Khrushchev, and the Test Ban*, pp. 68–78.

8. Preamble, "Treaty Banning Nuclear Weapon Tests in the Atmosphere, in Outer Space and Under Water," reprinted in Blacker and Duffy, *International Arms Control*, p. 366.

9. Article VI, "Treaty on the Non-Proliferation of Nuclear Weapons," reprinted in Blacker and Duffy, *International Arms Control*, p. 395.

10. Jeffrey S. Duncan, "How Many Soviet Tests Make a Flurry?" *Bulletin of the Atomic Scientists* 41, no. 9 (October 1985): 9–10.

11. I.Y. Borg, "Nuclear Explosions for Peaceful Purposes," in Jozef Goldblat and David Cox, eds., *Nuclear Weapon Tests: Cessation or Limitation?* (Oxford: Oxford University Press, 1988).

12. Ibid.

2 MODERNIZATION

The most immediate effect of a comprehensive nuclear test ban would be to slow or halt the development of nuclear weapons. Most Americans agree that a CTB would prevent the development of new nuclear warheads, but there is no consensus in the United States on whether this would be good or bad for the security of the nation. First, there is no consensus about which nuclear strategy is best. Although most Americans support deterrence, this only masks great differences of opinion about what type of deterrence minimizes the risk of war. Advocates of a war-fighting deterrent posture, for example, require more innovation in weapon systems than advocates of minimum deterrence. Second, Americans disagree about the military capabilities necessary to support a given strategy. Supporters of minimum deterrence, for example, may dispute how this deterrent force should be distributed among the different classes of weapon systems (bombers, land-based missiles, and sea-based missiles). Finally, even if Americans agree about the military capabilities necessary to support a given strategy, we may still disagree about the degree to which nuclear testing is required to achieve these capabilities.

This chapter focuses mainly on this last source of disagreement. It examines, in a general way, the types of modernization that may be possible in the future and the degree to which nuclear testing would be required to support these developments. Although references to deterrent strategy are often made to elucidate the key issues, an explicit discussion of the relationship between strategy and modernization is reserved for Chapter 5. It is often said that nuclear testing is valuable — and sometimes essential — in modernizing military forces in several ways: (1) to increase the safety and security of nuclear warheads, (2) to develop custom-designed nuclear warheads for new delivery systems, (3) to develop special nuclear weapons for new military missions, and (4) to test the effects of nuclear weapons on military equipment. Each of these rationales for testing will be examined below.

SAFETY AND SECURITY

Most people agree that if nuclear weapons must exist, they should be as safe and secure as possible. To be safe, nuclear weapons should be immune from accidents such as a nuclear explosion or a dispersal of plutonium if a bomb is dropped accidentally. To be secure, nuclear weapons should be protected from unauthorized use by both terrorists and armed forces personnel.

Nuclear Safety

No known accident with nuclear weapons has resulted in an appreciable nuclear yield, because a large number of nuclear reactions will take place only if the chemical explosive is detonated symmetrically. Weapons are designed so that this is not possible with a detonation at one point in the high explosive, as might happen in an accident. This attribute is called "one-point safety." The official definition of one-point safety in the United States requires that "in the event of a detonation initiated at any one point in the high explosive system, the probability of achieving a nuclear yield greater than 4 pounds of TNT equivalent shall not exceed one in one million."[1] Although it is difficult to find assurances in the unclassified literature that particular weapon designs are one-point safe, it is generally assumed that all U.S. nuclear weapons currently deployed meet this criterion. Future designs might further minimize the probability of a nuclear accident, but the current risks are perceived to be so low that improving nuclear safety is not a persuasive reason to continue nuclear testing: a change in viewpoint from the time of the moratorium, when nuclear safety was a key issue.

It is also remotely possible that during an accident the arming system might supply the proper signal to detonate the weapon. To guard against this, many weapons have environmental sensing devices (ESDs), which allow the weapon to detonate properly only after it has gone through the normal stockpile-to-target sequence (STS). ESDs in missile warheads and bombs can sense acceleration and altitude and will permit the weapon to detonate only if the missile has been launched or the bomb dropped from a given altitude. Most weapons also incorporate electrical safety systems that isolate the warhead electrical system to prevent accidental power surges and to disconnect the power until the weapon receives the proper arming code. The further refinement of such devices would not be prevented by a CTB.

Plutonium-dispersal Safety

Even in the absence of a nuclear yield, accidents involving nuclear weapons can have serious environmental and political effects. About thirty accidents have occurred with U.S. nuclear weapons in aircraft, and in about one quarter of these accidents the high explosive detonated. The majority of these incidents occurred in the 1950s, when long-range bombers and the procedures for handling nuclear weapons were relatively young. Two accidents resulted in widespread plutonium contamination: in 1966, a B52 bomber crashed in Palomares, Spain, and in 1968, another crashed in Thule, Greenland.[2] In no case since the incident at Thule has the high explosive detonated or burned, but accidents still happen. The latest incidents occurred in 1980, when the chemical fuel of a Titan II missile exploded, and a B52 carrying nuclear weapons caught fire.

One of the most effective ways to reduce the possibility of plutonium dispersal is to minimize the probability that the high explosive will detonate in an accident. For this reason, most U.S. weapons designed after 1976, such as the B61-3, B61-4, and B83 bombs; the W80 and W84 cruise missile warheads; and the W81 Standard-2, W85 Pershing II, and W87 MX missile warheads use an insensitive high explosive (IHE). Stray bullets and crashes will not detonate IHE. Since IHE is significantly less energetic than normal high explosives, nuclear weapons must be redesigned to use it. A CTBT would therefore prevent old warheads from being replaced by new warheads-that use IHE (unless, of course, the delivery system could use one of the IHE warheads that was already developed for another system). It should be noted that use of IHE reduces but does not eliminate the plutonium-dispersal problem, since a fire or an explosion of missile propellant could cause even IHE to burn or explode.

Fortunately, as Table 2–1 shows, the strategic systems thought to be most vulnerable to accidents are being deployed with IHE. With the planned replacement of the short-range attack missile (SRAM) warhead and the replacement of old bombs by the B61 and B83 bombs, the entire strategic bomber force—which is more accident-prone than the intercontinental ballistic missile (ICBM) and submarine-launched ballistic missile (SLBM) forces—will only use weapons with IHE. The new MX missile uses IHE in its W87 warhead, and the planned Midgetman mobile missile could use this warhead also. If the comprehensive use of IHE is desired in the ICBM force, the Minuteman missiles could be retired, or they could be modified to use the W87 warhead, although the range of the Minuteman III would be shorter (or only two warheads could be deployed per missile) due to the greater weight of the W87 compared to that of the current Minuteman warheads. No SLBM warheads use IHE, perhaps because they do not pose a threat to the civilian population while they are deployed at sea. But U.S. submarines are in ports near heavily populated areas about half the time, so SLBMs may pose a greater risk of plutonium dispersal than ICBMs. Nevertheless, the Navy deliberately chose not to use IHE in the new W88 warhead for the Trident II missile because its greater weight would decrease the missile range somewhat. One can hardly fault a CTB for preventing the use of IHE on SLBMs when new SLBM warheads are being designed without IHE. If it became necessary to use IHE on SLBMs after a comprehensive test ban took effect, the Trident II probably could be modified to use the MX warhead.

The situation with tactical weapons is similar. Of the 10,000 warheads designated for tactical use, over half will incorporate IHE by the end of the decade, including all bombs and cruise missiles. About 25 percent of the remaining warheads are slated for replacement in the early 1990s. Another 20 percent are nuclear artillery shells, which, because of their small size, make the use of IHE difficult.[3] Some tactical weapons, such as atomic demolition munitions and artillery shells, are relatively invulnerable to accidents since they are kept in storage depots and are not regularly deployed in the field.

Table 2–1.   The Use of IHE and PALs in the Projected Nuclear Arsenal of the Late 1990s, Assuming a CTBT Is Negotiated in the Early 1990s.

Warhead	Approx. Number[a]	IHE?[b]	PAL?[b]	Delivery System
		Strategic Systems		
W56	500	no	yes	Minuteman II ICBM
B61	1,000	yes	yes	B52, B1, ATB bombers
W62	650	no	yes	Minuteman III ICBM
W76	2,400	no	no	Trident I/II SLBMs
W78	950	no	yes	Minuteman III ICBM
W80	3,150	yes	yes	ALCM, ACM
B83	1,500	yes	yes	B52, B1, ATB bombers
W87	1,550	yes	yes	MX, Midgetman ICBMs
W88	2,400	no	no	Trident II SLBM
W??	1,700	yes	yes	SRAM II
Total	15,800			
		Tactical Systems		
W44	575	no	no	ASROC ASW
W55	285	no	no	SUBROC ASW
B57	900	no	yes	NDB ASW
B61	2,500	yes	yes	tactical aircraft
W70	1,285	no	yes	Lance TBM
W79	1,000	no	yes	8″ artillery
W80	800	yes	yes	SLCM
W81	300	yes	yes	Standard-2 SAM
W82	1,000	no	yes	155 mm artillery
B83	1,000	yes	yes	tactical aircraft
W84[c]	500	yes	yes	GLCM
W85[c]	120	yes	yes	Pershing II TBM
Total	10,300			

a. Number of warheads projected from current estimates given in Robert S. Norris and William M. Arkin, "Nuclear Notebook," *Bulletin of the Atomic Scientists* 43, no. 5 (June 1987): 56. Assumes 100 MX and 500 Midgetmen are equipped with the W87, that the B83 replaces old strategic bombs, that the W82 and W79 replace the W48 and W33 on a one-for-one basis, and that the Trident II warheads are half W76s and half W88s. (The deployment of W79s and W82s has been temporarily limited by Congress to a total of 925 warheads.) Approximately 300 special atomic demolition munitions (SADMs) that have been removed from Europe are not included. No replacement for the SADM is planned. The Pershing Ia is assumed to be replaced by the Pershing II (but see note c below). The W69 warhead for the SRAM is assumed to be replaced by a new warhead for the SRAM II; initial deployment is planned for 1992. Replacement warheads for the W55 and B57 are expected to enter full development engineering in the next year or so, with the replacement for the W70 lagging somewhat further behind. These replacements would presumably make use of IHE and PALs.

b. Use of PALs and IHE taken from Thomas B. Cochran, William M. Arkin, and Milton M. Hoenig, *Nuclear Weapons Databook*, vol. I: *U.S. Nuclear Forces* (Cambridge, Mass.: Ballinger Publishing Company, 1984). ICBMs have PALs controlling the missile launch, not warhead arming, and ESDs that prevent arming except after missile launch.

c. The GLCMs and Pershing II missiles will be removed from Europe (and destroyed) under the Intermediate-range Nuclear Forces (INF) Treaty signed in December 1987, although the warheads will still be available for use elsewhere. The GLCM warhead, for example, can probably be used on ALCM or SLCM, and the Pershing II warhead may be usable on ICBMs or SLBMs.

Thus, the common statement that only one third of all currently stockpiled U.S. warheads use modern safety features[4] does not tell the whole story, since modernization programs that are already well under way will greatly increase IHE usage in the remaining systems, regardless of future restrictions on nuclear testing. If the use of IHE is considered to be of utmost importance, then programs to design and test a version of the Trident II warhead using IHE should begin, along with development engineering on replacements for the remaining tactical warheads. The desire to increase warhead safety is not a permanently operating argument against restrictions on nuclear testing.

Security

Environmental sensing devices provide a measure of security, since unauthorized personnel cannot detonate weapons equipped with ESDs without simulating the stockpile-to-target sequence. A guard or terrorist who stole a ground-launched cruise missile (GLCM), for example, could not use the missile against a target of his choice because the missile would only be armed just before it reached the target preprogrammed into its memory.

To provide an extra measure of assurance that nuclear weapons cannot be used by unauthorized persons, most weapons are fitted with permissive action links (PALs), which act as a sophisticated electromechanical lock on the weapon's arming system. The weapon becomes operational only after the proper authorization code — which is held by the National Command Authority — is entered into the PAL. The latest PALs require a six-digit (category D PALs) or twelve-digit (category F PALs) code, and the number of attempts is limited so that one cannot try all possible codes. Most weapons also incorporate a mechanism that will render a weapon unusable by destroying key components if an attempt is made to bypass the PAL.

Table 2–1 indicates the use of PALs on the strategic and tactical warheads that will compose the nuclear arsenal in the 1990s. Except for naval weapons, which are presumed to be less vulnerable to theft by terrorists, all nuclear weapons are protected by PALs. A test ban would not prevent extending PAL technology to existing naval weapons, because category D PALs operate on components that do not require nuclear tests to certify their reliability. A CTB would prevent using the newer category F PALs, however, which automatically disable the warhead upon intrusion.

Insertable Nuclear Components. For safety reasons, in the earliest nuclear bombs, such as the Nagasaki-type weapons, the fissile material was inserted into the weapon en route to the target. The concept of insertable nuclear components (INCs) has been revived recently as a way to provide the ultimate in safety and security. Since INC warheads normally would be deployed without fissile material, there would be absolutely no possibility of a nuclear accident, plutonium dispersal, or unauthorized use. It is also claimed that INCs would make certain weapon systems more survivable because there would be fewer inhibitions about deploying the system throughout the countryside. The use of INCs could also save money, since nuclear weapons would no longer require the protection of guard forces. The development of INCs would entail extensive nuclear testing.

The significance of the additional safety, security, and survivability provided by INCs is unclear, however. First, warhead safety is already very high in one-point safe warheads using IHE, as is the security of warheads protected by PALs. It is sometimes said that INCs would prevent the fissile material in U.S. tactical nuclear weapons from being captured by the Soviets should deployment positions be overrun by a Soviet attack, but it is difficult to believe that there is any credible scenario in which this would be an important factor in the outcome of a war. Even so, there are other ways of denying the capture of fissile material that do not require nuclear testing, such as by detonating a small, shaped charge to destroy the weapon. With regard to survivability, INCs could actually make weapon systems *less* survivable because the delivery of INCs to widely dispersed weapons during war might be difficult or impossible. Finally, it is not clear that INCs would save money, because INC warheads would be more expensive than normal warheads and because guards would still be needed to protect the weapon system itself.

The United States has had the technical capability to build INCs for some time, yet it has not done so. In all likelihood, the military has decided that, on balance, the extra safety and security provided by INCs is not worth the trouble. With the withdrawal of short- and medium-range missiles from Europe, the rationale for INCs will dim considerably. Although it is conceivable that INCs might be appropriate for a particular application in the future, the inability to develop

INCs during a test ban would hardly appear to be a crucial flaw, according to any reasonable deterrent strategy.

NEW DELIVERY SYSTEMS

Contrary to popular belief, the nuclear competition between the United States and the Soviet Union has not been characterized by a growing number of weapons of increasing yield, at least not on the U.S. side. The total number of nuclear weapons in the U.S. stockpile has not varied by more than about 15 percent in the last twenty-five years, and the total yield of the arsenal has declined by 75 percent since 1960.[5] The competition can be much better described as a continual increase in counterforce, or the ability to destroy the opponent's forces. The nature of the driving force behind this increase has been the subject of a lively debate for decades, with one side claiming that the ever-growing Soviet threat is responsible, and the other maintaining that technological opportunity has fueled the growth in military effectiveness. Opponents of the CTB tend to favor the former explanation; proponents, the latter.

Increased military effectiveness has been primarily achieved not through changes in doctrine or operations but by refining the methods of delivering nuclear weapons to their targets to make them more accurate and less susceptible to enemy counterattack. For example, improvements in missile and guidance technologies have increased the accuracy of ICBMs by an order of magnitude, and advances in stealth and cruise missile technology have greatly increased the survivability of bombers, despite sophisticated air defenses. The evolution of delivery vehicles has been the principal reason for nuclear weapon development and testing over the past twenty-five years. Although new delivery vehicles can almost always be designed to accommodate an existing warhead, the military effectiveness of the weapon system can often be improved by using a new, custom-designed warhead. Using custom-designed rather than existing warheads is usually said to be cost-effective because warheads are much cheaper than the systems that deliver them (typically accounting for only 10 to 15 percent of the complete system cost)[6] and because system performance can be sensitive to warhead design.

In the past, the main reasons for using custom-designed warheads were that they could sufficiently increase the yield-to-weight ratio, accuracy, survivability, and safety of the system to justify the additional research and development costs. To take a recent example, consider the decision to deploy a custom warhead and reentry vehicle (RV), the W87/Mk-21, on the MX missile. It is well documented that the MX could have used the Minuteman III W78/Mk-12A warhead/RV; indeed, the MX was flight-tested successfully with W78/Mk-12A RVs.[7] The W87/Mk-21 was chosen for several reasons: (1) the Mk-21 RV is more accurate than the Mk-12A, (2) the W87 uses less special nuclear material (SNM) and therefore costs less ($500 million less for 1,000 warheads), (3) the W87 uses IHE for increased plutonium-dispersal safety, (4) the W87/Mk-21 is less vulnerable to antiballistic missile (ABM) attack, (5) the W87 can be built with a higher yield than the W78, and (6) the Department of Defense believes that each leg of the triad should have at least two types of warheads.[8]

Except for the perceived need to use IHE, however, these reasons are less than compelling. The increased accuracy of the MX over Minuteman III, for example, is mainly an argument for a new RV, not a new warhead. First, a new RV, incorporating the latest improvements in fusing and materials technology, could have been designed for the W78 Minuteman III warhead without additional nuclear testing. The resulting accuracy would have been nearly as great as that achieved with the W87/Mk-21. Second, the research, development, and testing costs of the W87, which probably totaled several hundred million dollars, should be subtracted from the savings due to reduced SNM usage. Third, the high-yield option of the W87 adds very little to its effectiveness against military targets. In fact, the additional weight of the W87 may make it less effective than the W78 (for a given RV), since more W78s could be put on a missile or the missile range could be increased. With regard to redundancy, three warhead types were already deployed on the Minuteman missiles (the W56, the W62, and the W78), and it is likely that with minor modifications ICBMs could use SLBM warheads. The point here is not that the W78 could have done as well as the W87 but simply that most of the objectives of the MX could have been achieved without additional nuclear testing.

The list of additional examples is long: the Trident II could have used the W87, W78, or Trident I (W76) warheads instead of the custom-designed W88; the air-launched cruise missile (ALCM) could have been designed to use the SRAM warhead (W69) instead of the W80 (at the expense of IHE); and so forth. All weapon systems deployed after 1972 could have used warheads that were already in the stockpile. Just as astronauts are not redesigned for space travel, nuclear warheads need not be custom-designed for each new missile — careful attention to the packaging would suffice.[9] Of course, using older warheads would have resulted in somewhat less effective military forces (no IHE, lower accuracy, shorter range, higher cost, etc.), but in fact custom-designed warheads are rarely *essential*.

It is often said that repackaged warheads (i.e., warheads that are incorporated into different RVs) would have to be tested, but note that most of the examples given above do not involve repackaging. The Minuteman III warheads, for example, can be used *without modification* on the MX missile. If one desired a new, more accurate RV, however, then the warhead would have to be repackaged. The distribution of components (e.g., guidance and fusing packages) around a warhead can influence its behavior, but these effects can be assessed without nuclear testing. The effect of such components on the implosion of the high explosive or the behavior of neutrons released during nuclear reactions can be evaluated using computer calculations or laboratory-scale experiments. The use of an existing warhead on a delivery vehicle that experiences a more stressing stockpile-to-target sequence could require additional nuclear testing, but none of the examples given above have this problem.

Advocates of the war-fighting variants of deterrence theory would argue that the above analysis begs the question. They would claim that while it is true that new warheads were not required to deploy new systems such as the MX, the marginal improvements in system performance made possible by custom-designed warheads were essential to achieve most of the security goals of these deployments. To advocates of minimum deterrence, on the other hand, refinements such as increased accuracy add nothing to deterrence, since nuclear weapons are basically unusable. It is not necessary to try here to decide between these two views, however, because the reasons for warhead modernization in the past — increased efficiency, accuracy, and safety — are not likely to remain persuasive in the future; in each case the point of diminishing returns has been reached. First, the yield-to-weight ratio of strategic weapons has reached a plateau, beyond which substantial progress is unlikely — at least not without further jeopardizing stockpile confidence or safety.[10] Indeed, yield-to-weight ratio has probably decreased recently with the use of IHE. Second, although the shape of the nuclear device can reduce reentry errors by allowing the reentry vehicle to be more streamlined, the ballistic coefficients of modern RVs are already very high, changes in warhead design are unlikely to result in large additional increases, and reentry errors are relatively insensitive to further increases.[11] Furthermore, progress in RV materials and technology can proceed without nuclear testing. Third, as noted above, the use of modern safety features will be (or at least could be) increased in the next few years to include the large majority of weapons. The most important task remaining here is not nuclear design but convincing the U.S. Navy to accept IHE and PALs.

This analysis does not imply that new weapon designs would fail to increase the performance of future delivery systems; it simply indicates that the marginal returns of evolutionary improvements in the yield-to-weight ratio, ballistic coefficient, and safety of weapons are growing smaller. The justification for further weapon design must come from other sources, such as reducing collateral damage or responding to changes in Soviet forces. These possible rationales for future modernization are examined below. The implications of a quantum leap in weapon physics, which could also drive continued modernization, are covered in the next section.

Reducing Collateral Damage

Some analysts have asserted that the natural evolution of weapon technology has made, and will continue to make, nuclear war less destructive by increasing the accuracy of delivery systems. Increasing accuracy allows the use of smaller weapons to do the same degree of military damage while minimizing the effects of nuclear war on civilians. Nuclear testing could continue to be important in this trend, since efficient, low-yield designs may be required to maximize the capabilities of new, more accurate delivery vehicles. Supporters of this position usually cite the tremendous increase in missile accuracy and the marked decrease in the yield of the stockpile that occurred after 1960 as evidence of this trend. With the arrival of homing missiles such as ALCMs, optimists predict that future missiles may be so accurate that they will not even require a nuclear warhead, perhaps eliminating collateral damage altogether.

This view is mistaken in several ways. First, the decrease in stockpile yield that occurred after 1960 had little to do with the desire to limit collateral damage. The decrease was due simply to the small payload capabilities of ballistic missiles, which were determined to be more survivable and cost-effective than bombers. Multiple independently targeted reentry vehicles (MIRVs) permitted increases in damage while decreasing the yield. In the more recent past, increases in accuracy have not resulted in corresponding decreases in yield. In fact, the opposite has been true: every new warhead has been given the highest yield that was consistent with constraints on safety, weight, cost, and stockpile confidence. Improvements in Minuteman III accuracies were paralleled by a doubling of the warhead yield (from 170 to 335 kilotons), and the MX, although nearly doubling the accuracy of the improved Minuteman, maintains almost the same yield (and, indeed, has an option for a yield 60 percent greater). Similarly, the tremendous improvements in SLBM accuracy have paralleled increased warhead yields: 50 kilotons for Poseidon, 100 kilotons for Trident I, and 475 kilotons for Trident II. Even the cruise missile, which is far more accurate than the MX, carries a 150-kt warhead — ten times more explosive power than the bombs that destroyed Hiroshima and Nagasaki. Surely these recent improvements in accuracy have not even begun to decrease the destructiveness of nuclear war.

This fact is no surprise, since the primary goal of U.S. nuclear strategy has been to limit damage to the United States by destroying the capability of the enemy to wage war, not to limit the deaths of enemy civilians. This strategy includes destroying enemy forces (e.g., ICBMs, ballistic missile submarines, and bombers), command, control, and communications (C^3) facilities, political leadership, and war-related industries. Many of these targets, such as bomber bases, are spread over such large areas that higher accuracy is irrelevant to the effectiveness of the attack. (Indeed, high-yield warheads would be essential to destroy bombers soon after takeoff.) Other targets, such as commercial airports, political leadership, and industrial areas, are collocated with civilian population so that attacks with warheads yielding one-tenth that of today's strategic warheads would still cause an unprecedented number of civilian casualties. It is not even clear whether an adversary could determine that he had sustained a "limited" attack with "small" weapons rather than an all-out attack. Clean weapons (i.e., those deriving only a small fraction of their yield from fission reactions), which would greatly decrease collateral effects from fallout, have been available for decades, but they have not been deployed because they do not give the most "bang for the buck." Similarly, since low-yield warheads do not weigh much less than high-yield warheads, they probably will never be developed.

Increased hardening is another factor that reduces the likelihood that warhead yields will decrease markedly. It is estimated that structures fifty times harder than current Minuteman silos could be constructed,[12] which would require missile accuracies nearly four times greater to destroy. At least part of the reason that Minuteman III yields were doubled, in spite of their increasing accuracy, was to offset "the continued Soviet hardening program."[13] Vast numbers of hardened facilities, including silos, bunkers for leadership, C[3] and special industrial facilities, and even tunnels for submarines in port, are mentioned in *Soviet Military Power* as "threats" that the United States must overcome.[14]

Achieving extremely high accuracies is not as easy as some analysts would believe. Inertial guidance systems, which require no additional information after the missile is launched, have nearly reached the limits of their accuracy, since targeting errors are now dominated by reentry errors. Reentry errors, many of which are random, can only be overcome by supplying additional information to the RV about its position relative to the target and by giving the RV maneuvering capability so that it can compensate for the errors. Additional position information can be supplied in three ways: (1) by equipping the RV itself with an inertial guidance system, (2) by sending navigation information to the RV (e.g., from a satellite), or (3) by using sensors in the RV to guide it to the target (as with the Pershing II missile). Each of these methods for improving accuracy would add weight to the RV, with the result that a given missile could carry fewer RVs. Using warhead inertial guidance plus maneuvering capability could result in targeting errors of as little as 30 meters.[15] With this accuracy, a 35-kt warhead would have the same probability of destroying a hardened target as the 300-kt MX warhead.[16] Although the areas contaminated by fallout may be reduced by an order of magnitude, collateral effects from attacks on targets in or near cities would still be enormous. Further increases in missile accuracy require homing sensors, which, unlike inertial guidance, can be defeated by a determined adversary. Navigation satellite transmissions can be jammed or the satellites destroyed. Infrared sensors can be decoyed or jammed, as can terrain-matching radars such as those used on ALCMs. In short, homing technology is not the end of the battle between offense and defense — it is only another beginning. To reduce the warhead yield to the point where collateral effects become small (less than 1 kiloton), an accuracy of several meters would be required to destroy hardened targets, which would open up the possibility of close-in defenses and even passive barriers. The military planner, confronted with the possibility of unexpected countermeasures or poor terminal guidance performance, is unlikely to request large decreases in the yield of weapons.

Earth-penetrating warheads (EPWs), which burrow into the ground before exploding, offer the possibility of a reduction in yield of more than an order of magnitude while maintaining a given probability of destroying a hardened target. A 10-kt EPW could be as effective as the MX warhead against very hard targets without increases in accuracy and yet generate less than a hundredth of the blast damage at large distances from the target.[17] The thermal effects of the smaller EPW weapon would also be reduced by a large factor. It is not clear to what degree fallout would be reduced by using the smaller EPW. Although it would generate fewer fission products, a larger fraction would condense onto dirt particles, more neutron-induced activity would be formed in the dirt, and the cloud would be denser and would stay at lower altitudes, thus perhaps increasing fallout close to the target. But even if EPWs are capable of reducing collateral damage, there is no guarantee that they would be used in this way. Rather than reducing the yield to keep the kill probability the same, it is more likely that EPWs would be used to destroy targets of increasing hardness with increased probability, thus substituting for terminal warhead guidance. As in the past, these new warheads would probably be given the highest yield feasible in a given size and weight. The huge crater formed by large EPWs could allow one-on-one targeting (if techniques were available to replace launch failures), thus halving the number of weapons required and eliminating the possibility of unknown fratricide effects. Moreover, to the extent that these weapons are successful in interfering with an adversary's command and control, they would make war more difficult to control or terminate. While some analysts claim that the ability of EPWs to destroy the shelters of the political leadership would better deter Soviet leaders from going to war, others fear that the resulting anxiety about decapitation could make leaders more hasty to launch an attack during a crisis.

Lastly, assume that weapons of such low yield and high accuracy may be possible that large-scale military attacks could be conducted without large civilian casualties. Smart missiles could recognize and destroy individual bombers, for example, eliminating the need to barrage bomber bases and airfields. Command posts or factories could be destroyed in the middle of a city without indiscriminate massacre.

Insofar as these developments convinced leaders that a war could be fought and won for objectives more valuable than the war might cost, the probability of a devastating war between the superpowers would increase. What would happen when one side started to lose this war — would the losing side stop at levels that involved minimal civilian casualties, or would it escalate in hope of winning at the next level of battle? Why would any country unilaterally divest itself of the small number of high-yield nuclear weapons it would need to hold an enemy's population hostage, especially when it could never verify that the enemy had done likewise? Without some assurance that mutual destruction was impossible, engaging in direct battle would be one of the most likely ways in which disastrous miscalculations could occur.

Although advocating continued modernization to decrease the destructiveness of the arsenal may sound reasonable, this brief analysis shows that this has not happened in the past, it is unlikely to happen in the future, and even if it were to occur, it may be more likely to increase rather than decrease the risk of general war.

Changing Soviet Forces

The most frequently cited rationale for weapon system modernization is the need to respond to changes in Soviet forces. In fact, it is difficult to think of a U.S. modernization program that has *not* been justified largely in terms of a response to specific Soviet actions. Since the development of new nuclear warheads is often seen as a fundamental part of weapon system modernization, this is used as a reason to oppose restrictions on nuclear testing. Of course, this rationale has meaning only if one believes that the Soviet improvements or the U.S. responses in question alter the military balance, which is fundamentally a function of nuclear strategy. Many of the Soviet developments that appear threatening to an advocate of war-fighting deterrence do not appear so to a proponent of minimum deterrence. For example, advocates of war-fighting deterrence require a response to Soviet hardening or mobility programs, since they believe that deterrence would be weakened if certain targets could not be held at risk; but proponents of minimum deterrence see hardening and mobility as mutually stabilizing, since opponents would be less anxious about preemptive attack during a crisis.

Aside from the issue of strategy, there are two generic types of Soviet modernization: one that requires continued nuclear testing (e.g., X-ray lasers) and one that does not (e.g., hardening). A test ban would prevent the former type of modernization, and as long as compliance with a test ban could be verified, this type could be ignored. Similarly, there are two generic types of U.S. responses to changes in Soviet forces: one that requires continued nuclear testing and one that does not. Since the latter would be available under a test ban, the United States would only need to worry about those permitted Soviet improvements that would necessitate a U.S. response that depends on nuclear testing. It is my contention that such conditions are rarely, if ever, achieved—no matter what nuclear strategy one subscribes to.

Many test ban opponents disagree. Typical of their assertions is the recent statement by three weapon scientists at the Lawrence Livermore National Laboratory that "in the Soviet Union, such developments [requiring a response that necessitates nuclear testing] are mainly nonnuclear and include increased air defense coverage, improved antisubmarine defenses, improved target characteristics (such as hardening), and increasing threats to the survivability of U.S. forces (such as more accurate missiles)."[18] Since this point is central to the CTB debate, let us consider these examples in detail.

First consider air defense. Presumably, the authors of the above passage are referring to three U.S. nuclear developments—the ALCM, the SRAM, and the modern strategic bomb—that made it possible for bombers to cope with improved Soviet air defenses. ALCMs, which are much more difficult to shoot down than bombers, allow bombers to release their weapons without penetrating air defenses. But the important developments that made the ALCM possible—terrain-matching guidance systems and small, high-efficiency turbofan engines—are *nonnuclear*. A custom-designed warhead was not necessary.[19] SRAMs improved survivability by giving bombers the capability to attack air-defense sites. While it is arguable whether a custom-designed warhead was required for the SRAM, the nuclear testing that supported this development was completed two decades ago. A replacement for the SRAM is planned, but this new missile could almost certainly be designed, with little loss in performance, to use an existing warhead (e.g., the SRAM, ALCM, or GLCM warhead). The modern strategic bomb allows bombers to evade air defenses by permitting them to release bombs while flying very low at supersonic speeds. Although the development of bombs that could survive the resulting impact required nuclear testing, a similar capability could have been provided by means that did not require testing (e.g., by using small rockets to slow down an existing bomb before impact or by lofting the bomb into the air and using a parachute). Moreover, the most important contributions to bomber survivability — electronic countermeasures and stealth technology — are completely nonnuclear.

Although the Livermore authors do not mention it, a similar argument has also been made with respect to strategic missile defenses. Since it is the United States, and not the Soviet Union, that is primarily interested in deploying these defenses, it would be in the interest of the United States to ban nuclear testing if it could lead to effective countermeasures against strategic defenses. As obvious as this may seem, the three weapon scientists cited above claim that nuclear testing must continue, nevertheless, in order to evaluate possible nuclear countermeasures (e.g., X-ray lasers), even though continued testing would allow these very technologies to be developed and perfected by the Soviet Union. These scientists suggest that the Soviet Union may already have developed such devices, even though the CIA has stated that it "does not believe that the Soviet Union can deploy nuclear directed-energy weapons without conducting additional explosive tests."[20] Given the difficult technological hurdles that must be crossed before such devices are feasible, the CIA's assessment is likely to be valid for some time. The development of maneuvering reentry vehicles (MaRVs) to evade missile defenses is often cited as a response that would require testing, but a MaRV has in fact already been developed and flight-tested by the United States.[21] One should not forget that there is already a treaty that bans strategic missile defenses. It is illogical to oppose a CTB because testing might be needed to respond to a hypothetical future violation or abrogation of this treaty; nuclear testing could always be resumed if the supreme national interests of the country are jeopardized. The relationship of a test ban to strategic defense is discussed in detail later in this chapter.

The rationale for continued nuclear testing is even weaker in the case of responses to improvements in antisubmarine warfare. Test ban opponents often point out that longer-range missiles were necessary to increase the survivability of ballistic missile submarines, but nuclear testing was not required simply to increase the range of missiles. While it is true a new RV might have been required in order to withstand the higher reentry velocity of a longer-range missile, the new RV could have been designed around an old warhead, or an ICBM warhead/RV could have been used. Custom-designed warheads were required to optimize the military effectiveness of systems (though even here the contribution of nuclear design is marginal), but they were *not* required to increase the survivability of submarines.

Although analysts also often argue that nuclear testing is required to increase the survivability of land-based forces, this argument for continued nuclear testing is even less persuasive than those arguments regarding air- and sea-based forces. The proposed Midgetman missile, for example, could use the MX warhead. The assertion by some analysts that nuclear testing would be required to deploy mobile missiles is simple deception. Although one can certainly devise system requirements that would preclude using the MX warhead (e.g., a lightweight missile carrying two or three RVs), these requirements would only be necessary to increase the cost-effectiveness of the system somewhat, not to secure a more survivable basing mode. If the objections to a test ban are based on economics — that is, that one would buy less "bang for the buck" without custom-designed warheads — then opponents of a CTB should argue this point, rather than pretend that new missiles are impossible without new warheads.

The necessity for nuclear testing to respond to increased hardening of targets is also problematic. First, it should be emphasized that the ability to destroy hard targets is necessary only for advocates of a nuclear war-fighting posture. To supporters of minimum deterrence, this capability is seen as destabilizing. Second, symmetry can be maintained without improving weapon system performance, simply by hardening the corresponding U.S. facilities. Third, as pointed out above, increases in the ability of weapon systems to destroy hard targets are due mostly to increases in accuracy that are unrelated to nuclear design. Improvements in nuclear design have made a contribution to hard-target kill, but these have been minor compared to the combined effects of nonnuclear improvements in guidance and fusing technology. The development of higher-yield weapons would make it easier to destroy hard targets, of course, but the United States and the Soviet Union have already foreclosed this route by signing the Threshold Test Ban Treaty. The only foreseeable significant improvement in hard-target-kill capability that would require nuclear testing is the development of earth-penetrating weapons.

Yet another generic argument against a CTB is that the United States has an advantage over the Soviet Union in nuclear weapon technology; why should the United States relinquish this advantage by agreeing to a test ban? For the types of modernization considered in this section — evolutionary improvements in nuclear weapons to support new delivery vehicles — this argument makes little sense. The United States is close to the performance limits of traditional thermonuclear weapons. It is widely speculated that Soviet warheads are not as efficient as U.S. warheads; a recent article in *Scientific American* estimated that the yield-to-weight ratio of U.S. warheads is 30 to 80 percent greater than that of Soviet warheads.[22] If the United States does indeed have an advantage in yield-to-weight ratio, it would be to the relative advantage of the United States to agree to a test ban now, before the Soviets, also, reach the point of diminishing returns.

NEW MISSIONS

Although nuclear weapon design has been limited to evolutionary improvements over the past twenty-five years, there is no guarantee that this will always be so. In fact, the level of funding and effort at the weapon laboratories on revolutionary designs that many people believe (and some hope) will alter the nuclear balance may be higher than ever before.

Strategic Defense

Nearly every recent discussion of increased restrictions on nuclear testing has implied that the Reagan administration resists a test ban because it would interfere with the Strategic Defense Initiative (SDI). This inference is based on the vigorous research program on nuclear directed-energy weapons (NDEWs) being conducted at the nation's nuclear weapon laboratories: roughly half a billion dollars will be spent on NDEW research this year alone. In addition to the well-known X-ray laser, nuclear weapons that generate particle or microwave beams, shoot pellets at extremely high velocities, pump optical lasers, or create an enormous electromagnetic pulse are being considered for use in defensive systems. The administration's interest in NDEWs is somewhat puzzling, however, since President Reagan has stated repeatedly that a strategic defense would be nonnuclear. The stated rationale for this research is to evaluate the potential of these weapons in Soviet hands, but the administration has been careful not to rule out U.S. deployment of nuclear defensive weapons if they appear promising.

There is a strong consensus in the technical community that the defense of cities is not feasible and that such deployments would actually increase the likelihood of war under most circumstances. Others are more optimistic about SDI technologies and see strategic defense as eventually capable of removing the threat of nuclear annihilation. But the sharp disagreements between these two groups need not lead to similar divisions on test ban issues, because nuclear testing benefits the offense as much as — and probably more than — the defense.

To illustrate this point, consider the characteristics of the X-ray laser, which would have both offensive and defensive capabilities. X-ray lasers were originally envisioned as defensive weapons to destroy missiles in their boost phase. X-ray lasers could be rendered powerless for this purpose, however, by missile boosters that burn out at altitudes of less than 80 kilometers (fast-burn boosters), since the most powerful X-ray lasers could not penetrate deeper into the atmosphere. Although intercepting fast-burn boosters with X-ray lasers is probably not feasible, some strategists maintain that X-ray lasers could do essentially the same job by destroying the post-boost vehicle, or "bus." The bus, which dispenses the RVs on their independent trajectories, travels outside the atmosphere and is almost as easy to track and destroy as a booster. The offense could minimize this opportunity, however, by dispensing the warheads more quickly or by using several smaller buses on each missile, or foreclose the option completely by building single-warhead missiles that do not use a bus.

The RVs could be attacked directly, but they are very difficult to destroy with X-rays. Using optimistic assumptions, one X-ray laser might destroy 50 RVs, but, using more realistic assumptions, the laser could destroy only 1 RV.[23] Even the optimistic estimate would not be attractive if the resulting hundreds or thousands of X-ray laser nuclear explosions interfered with the communication and sensor satellites necessary to manage the battle. Thus, X-ray lasers do not appear to be a promising defensive technology.

On the other hand, X-ray lasers could be very effective offensive weapons. Because of their small size and weight, X-ray lasers could be stationed inconspicuously in space or "popped-up" into space on a few minutes notice by ICBMs or SLBMs. A handful of X-ray lasers could preemptively destroy key defensive satellites just before an attack. Sensor and battle-station satellites would be much softer, less numerous, and more costly than RVs, making them far more attractive targets for X-ray lasers. Even without strategic defenses in place, U.S.

forces depend on a few high-altitude satellites for attack warning and communications; the development of a weapon that could instantaneously destroy these satellites would be extremely destabilizing.[24] Because the offensive potential of X-ray lasers as antisatellite weapons may outweigh their defensive potential, a nuclear test ban would be a logical step toward eliminating the threat that would be posed if the Soviets developed these weapons.

Similar arguments can be made for other NDEWs, since each would be able to destroy satellites long before it would be able to destroy boosters or RVs. The hypervelocity pellet weapon, for example, may be an ideal space mine weapon. Moreover, there are other avenues of nuclear research that are purely offensive. Special warheads could be developed to enhance blackout effects by producing a long-lived plasma in the atmosphere, thereby making radar tracking of incoming RVs difficult. If the Soviets do not now possess warheads as light and efficient as U.S. warheads—a matter of dispute—then continued testing would allow them to double the number of RVs or greatly increase the number of decoys without the construction of additional missiles. The Soviets would benefit because missiles are much more expensive to build than warheads. Nuclear testing would be valuable in designing rugged warheads that resist the effects of defensive weapons. And the development of sophisticated maneuvering reentry vehicles designed to evade terminal defenses could be facilitated by using custom-designed warheads: again, requiring continued nuclear testing.

It is sometimes claimed that nuclear testing would be vital in testing the vulnerability of defensive systems to nuclear weapon effects. While it is obvious that defensive systems must be invulnerable to these effects, it is much less obvious why additional restrictions on nuclear testing would interfere with this goal. The most interesting and relevant nuclear effects—EMP, blackout, redout, etc.—occur only when a weapon is exploded above ground, and such testing is already banned by the Limited Test Ban Treaty.

In view of these considerations, proponents of strategic defense should be skeptical about the sacrifices that a test ban would entail. Test ban supporters and SDI advocates may be unlikely bedfellows, but both groups claim to oppose the same thing: usable offensive nuclear capability. Advocates of strategic defense should realize that continued nuclear testing makes the job of the defense harder, not easier. A refusal by SDI supporters to adopt this point of view would cast doubt on their intentions and may indicate that their real interest in SDI is offensive — creating the shield that would allow one to wield the nuclear sword — and not defensive. Indeed, this is consistent with the views of those who believe that in order to deter the Soviet Union, the United States must be able to strike without fearing the possibility of unacceptable damage.

Relocatable Targets

"Relocatable targets" is a euphemism for mobile missiles and command posts. There are two basic ways to destroy mobile targets: track them in real-time and guide the warhead to the moving target, or increase the destructive range of a weapon so that it will destroy everything within the probable area of the mobile target. The first approach requires large advances in sensor technology, but probably does not require a special nuclear weapon. The most commonly mentioned weapon for the second approach is a nuclear-driven microwave weapon. Since electronic circuits are thought to be vulnerable to very low fluences of microwaves, a nuclear-driven microwave weapon might damage even hardened electronics within a 10-km radius. This would represent a hundred-fold increase in the lethal area of a strategic warhead against the proposed U.S. hardened mobile launcher.[25]

It is not known if such a weapon can be built or if electronics could be hardened to resist its effects. Continued testing might allow the Soviets to develop a weapon to threaten mobile targets. A central point of American strategic doctrine has been that U.S. forces should be invulnerable to preemptive attack; this is the rationale behind U.S. development of mobile missiles. Moreover, many deterrent strategies advocate that Soviet forces should be invulnerable as well: the United States would not want the Soviet Union to be forced to launch its missiles to avoid their destruction in a preemptive strike. According to this view, to the degree that a CTB prevents either the United States or the Soviet Union from developing a capability to destroy relocatable targets, it is a positive contribution to the security of both nations. On the other hand, critics of this analysis believe that the best way to deter war is the ability of the United States to destroy the Soviet Union while sustaining only limited damage in the process. Destroying mobile forces is a vital part of this strategy. Implicit in this argument is the belief that the risks of an arms race to gain strategic superiority would be outweighed by gains in deterrent capability once superiority was achieved.

Other Missions

Clever people have thought of many new and different ways to use nuclear weapons. For example, weapons have already been designed to enhance the electromagnetic pulse (EMP), presumably to destroy unhardened enemy equipment and to disrupt communications. This innovation is of dubious value to our security, however, since EMP effects are not known well enough to be relied on for a given military mission. Some strategists are in favor of developing warheads with insertable nuclear components (INCs) so that conventional weapons could be rapidly converted into nuclear weapons if necessary. Although this would increase the safety and security of nuclear forces, it is unlikely that INCs would be cost-effective compared to separate conventional and nuclear warheads. In addition, it is almost universally agreed that dual-capable weapons create a nightmare for arms control agreements that seek to place numerical limits on nuclear weapons. There undoubtedly are many other possible missions for nuclear weapons that would depend on future testing, but these examples give a good idea of the marginal net contribution that these developments would make to our security.

Undiscovered Weapon Technology

Opponents of a CTB sometimes overstate the importance of weapon technology that remains undiscovered. They imply that discoveries lying just ahead may prove to be our salvation from the nuclear threat or the ultimate weapon against our enemies, or, that our enemies have already found or may find by clandestine testing, some new secret that would radically change the strategic balance without our knowledge. CTB proponents sometimes fall into this trap by believing that our damnation, not salvation, may lie just around the technological corner and that we had best close the door before these horrors are discovered.

Such predictions are not new, and they have almost always been wrong in the past. Pure fusion weapons that would eliminate fallout never materialized (relatively clean bombs were developed, but never deployed), nor did hand-grenade-sized weapons with yields of a few tons. No one can foresee what may lie ahead and predict whether it will be good or bad for humanity, but it seems foolish to take any action—for or against a CTB—based on the specter of future technology. Some observers have interpreted the proposed abolition of nuclear testing as the beginning of an assault on scientific inquiry of all kinds. But there is no good reason that societies should not restrict paths of research thought to be disadvantageous, if not ultimately self-destructive. Furthermore, the probability of Soviet cheating resulting in a great advantage is unlikely. If a discovery is really just around the corner, the United States could quickly duplicate it; if it is not, a large (and probably detectable) Soviet effort would be required to discover it.[26]

WEAPON EFFECTS

Yet another rationale for nuclear test explosions is to subject various types of military equipment to the effects of nuclear weapons to determine how they would function in the harsh environment of nuclear war or how lethal our weapons would be against Soviet equipment. Nuclear warheads themselves are probably the most common subjects of these tests, to verify that an RV can penetrate nuclear ABM defenses. Nuclear effects testing is also valuable for testing C^3 and BMD components or systems, as well as to verify the survivability of basing modes for nuclear weapons.

Since the Limited Test Ban Treaty (LTBT) was signed in 1963, all nuclear testing has been performed underground. This greatly limits the types of nuclear effects experiments that can be done. For example, one can test a warhead for its vulnerability to the X-rays, neutrons, and blast produced by an explosion, but one cannot test C^3 or ABM systems for the effects that are produced only by atmospheric explosions. Understanding these effects is crucial for building C^3 and ABM systems that would be effective during nuclear war, but the existing LTBT already prohibits gaining such understanding; a CTB would not change anything in this respect. The LTBT also prevents nuclear experiments to determine the hardness of silos or other basing modes. To explore these effects the United States would have to abrogate the LTBT, a move that would be extremely unpopular because of the resulting radioactive pollution. A CTBT would only eliminate nuclear weapons as test sources of X-rays, gamma rays, neutrons, and ground shock, and there are other ways to generate these phenomena.

A promising method for generating the X-rays and neutrons produced by nuclear weapons is inertial-confinement fusion (ICF). In ICF, tiny pellets of deuterium and tritium are illuminated by intense laser or particle beams; the pellets implode, producing a small thermonuclear explosion with a yield of up to 1 ton. An object located a few meters away from a 1-ton ICF microexplosion would experience large X-ray fluxes. Roger Batzel, former director of Lawrence Livermore National Laboratory, has stated that ICF may substantially augment, and in some cases substitute for, nuclear vulnerability, lethality, and effects tests now done underground.[27] More vulnerable equipment, such as communications satellites, can be tested by using existing X-ray machines or accelerators. It has also been suggested that very-low-yield nuclear testing (e.g., up to 10 or 100 tons) would be permitted by a CTB if the explosion could be fully contained in permanent, above-ground facilities within, say, 30 meters of personnel. Explosions of these yields would be very valuable for effects testing.

A CASE STUDY: THE MORATORIUM

To further illuminate the points made above, suppose that the LTBT had banned explosions in all environments; what would have been the effect of forgoing many of the modernizations that have occurred from 1964 up to the present time that required nuclear testing? Even though the present situation is different from that of the early 1960s, and even though one can never be sure of what might have happened if a CTB had been negotiated at that time, analyzing the past can provide useful insights into our current predicament.

It will be assumed here that all U.S. warhead designs whose full-scale production began before 1964 would have been available for use in future delivery vehicles if the LTBT had been comprehensive.[28] In addition, the SADM, SUBROC, and Polaris A3 warheads would probably have been available since full-scale production of these warheads started five to ten months after the LTBT entered into force, and since nearly all of the required nuclear tests for these warheads had been performed by the end of 1963.[29] Herbert York, director of Lawrence Livermore National Laboratory and of defense research and engineering in the Department of Defense during this period, maintains that the Polaris A3 warhead would have been available.[30]

Safety and Security

Great advances have been made since the early 1960s in increasing the safety and security of nuclear weapons. Although the degree of nuclear safety in early designs was not as high as it is now, there was an acceptable margin of safety.[31] More impressive are the improvements in plutonium-dispersal safety gained by using IHE. Modifying designs to use IHE requires nuclear testing; therefore, if a CTBT had been negotiated in the early 1960s, no nuclear weapons could have used IHE. Before the introduction of IHE, accidents were prevented by changing deployment patterns and operational procedures, such as keeping alert bombers on the ground instead of in flight. Although the United States has had no reason to keep bombers constantly aloft since then, lack of IHE may have forced the United States to abandon other promising basing modes, such as ground-mobile ICBMs or cruise missiles. Although there is no known instance of an accident that was prevented by IHE, a plutonium-dispersal accident in Europe might have had serious political consequences among U.S. allies.

Delivery Systems

During the late 1940s and early 1950s, the long-range bomber was the only strategic delivery system. By the early 1960s, the United States had deployed a wide range of nuclear bombs with varying yields on several aircraft. The B36, B39, and B41 bombs were deployed on the now retired B-36, B-47, and B-58 bombers; and the B28, B43, and B53 bombs were (and some still are) deployed on the B-52 bomber. The B28 has five yields between 70 and 1,450 kilotons, the B43 has a yield of about 1 megaton, and the B53 has a yield of 9 megatons. The yield-to-weight ratio of these old bombs compares favorably with that of the newer B61 and B83 bombs.[32] The only significant advance in bomb technology that has occurred since the moratorium and that required nuclear testing (other than the use of the IHE mentioned above) is the ability to deliver bombs at high speeds at extremely low altitudes (50 to 150 feet). This capability makes aircraft less vulnerable to air defenses and allows for high accuracy, but there were other ways that this capability could have been achieved without nuclear testing.

Even though bomb technology has not changed much, the role of bombers has changed with the introduction of the ALCM. Cruise missiles were invented before the LTBT, but the Matador, Regulus, and Snark cruise missiles developed during the 1950s were much less accurate and reliable than the ballistic missiles that became available later that decade. Snark, for example, had a range of about 10,000 kilometers and carried a high-yield nuclear warhead (about 20 megatons), but it was very heavy (60,000 pounds) and therefore expensive.[33] The ALCM, on the other hand, is the most accurate of all strategic weapons, has enough range (about 2,500 kilometers) to allow bombers to attack from outside Soviet air defenses, yet is light enough (about 3,000 pounds) to allow two dozen to be carried by a B-52 or B-1B bomber.[34] The miniaturization of engine and guidance systems that made this possible could have happened under a CTB, but there may not have been a small and efficient nuclear weapon available. The W80 warhead deployed on ALCM is estimated to weigh 270 pounds and have a yield of 150 kilotons. The W58 warhead developed for the Polaris A3 missile, which weighed about 250 pounds and had a yield of 200 kilotons,[35] could have been used. The only other warheads of about this weight that would have been available had yields less than 15 kilotons.[36] Except for the W58, other available high-yield warheads weighed significantly more, and their use would have decreased the range of the ALCM by about 500 kilometers.[37] Of course, one could have compensated for a heavier warhead simply by designing a somewhat larger cruise missile.

The moratorium coincided with the development of the first ICBMs and SLBMs. The Atlas and Titan I ICBM and Polaris A1 SLBM missiles had just been tested, and the Titan II and Minuteman I ICBM and Polaris A2 and A3 SLBMs were under development.[38] Except for the Polaris A3 warhead, all ballistic missile warheads had high yields, ranging from the 800-kt Polaris A1/A2 warhead to the 9-Mt Titan II warhead, and were produced well before the LTBT. The lightest of these high-yield warheads probably weighed around 900 pounds, or roughly two to four times more than modern ICBM and SLBM warheads.[39]

Progress in propellant and guidance technologies could have continued unimpeded during a CTB, allowing the development of more advanced missiles such as Poseidon, Trident I, Trident II, Minuteman III, and MX. But instead of designing a custom warhead for a given missile design, the missiles would have been designed to use an existing nuclear warhead. There is no technical reason that MIRVs could not have been developed without nuclear testing. Using the W58 warhead for the Polaris A3 warhead, it would have been possible to deploy MIRVs on small missiles like Poseidon and Minuteman.[40] Using other high-yield warheads, the United States could have deployed MIRVs on large missiles such as the Trident II, Titan II, or MX. Even without improvements in nuclear design, miniaturization of guidance and warhead electrical systems would have reduced throw-weight requirements. At worst, the U.S. ICBM force would have resembled the current Soviet force.

As important as the development of MIRVs has been the increasing accuracy of ballistic missiles. Although the early Atlas and Titan ICBMs had an accuracy of about 1,300 to 1,600 meters, the MX is reported to have a CEP (circle of equal probability) of about 100 meters. Most of this increase in accuracy is due to improvements in inertial guidance systems that could have taken place under a CTBT. The accuracy of RVs may have suffered somewhat, however, owning to reentry errors that depend on the design of the nuclear weapon. The shape and size of the weapon influence the shape and size of the RV and its center of mass. Without access to detailed RV and warhead designs, it is difficult to estimate how accurate RVs could have been made using the larger warheads developed before 1964, but rough estimates indicate that ballistic RVs would probably have been limited to Minuteman-like accuracy.[41] Although lower accuracy combined with lower MIRVing ratios would have alleviated counterforce concerns, it might also have spurred the development of precision-guided RVs.

New Concepts

Since the development of modern, high yield-to-weight thermonuclear weapons in the late 1950s, there have been no quantum leaps in nuclear weapon technology. Even the stunning increase in the capabilities of ballistic missiles to destroy hardened military targets was made possible by a continuous stream of evolutionary improvements, many of which would have been possible under a CTB. There are no weapons in the current stockpile that operate on different physical principles than those deployed twenty-five years ago. If a CTBT had been signed in 1963, the fundamental character of the strategic arsenal would probably be the same as it is today, since further nuclear testing was not essential for the development and refinement of ICBMs, SLBMs, or bombers.

This was not the prediction of many CTB opponents in the late 1950s and early 1960s, however. In the test ban debates of this time, some weapon designers held out the promise of new missions for nuclear weapons that would require nuclear testing to perfect. Two such weapons — very-high-yield bombs and antiballistic missile warheads — dominated the congressional debate on the LTBT. Opponents of the test ban argued that very-high-yield bombs (100 megatons) with high yield-to-weight ratios would have unique military advantages, but no military requirement for these weapons ever materialized. When the retirement of the Titan II missile system is completed next year, the largest weapon in the U.S. arsenal will have a yield of about 1 megaton. Although an ABM system was deployed with custom-designed warheads, the system was retired after only a year of service for reasons that had nothing to do with nuclear testing. A CTB would not have affected this final outcome.[42]

Some may consider the neutron bomb to be a recent invention, but its origins go back to the 1950s. Although it has been advertised as a weapon that kills people but leaves buildings intact, it merely enhances the radiation effects of a given yield weapon, thereby allowing the yield (and collateral damage) to be reduced. The CTB would have prevented its development, but it does not appear that this would have had a significant effect on deterrence; in fact, these weapons have not yet been deployed for political reasons. Many weapon scientists argued that the development of a pure-fusion weapon, which would be free of fallout and which could lead to a revolution in nuclear warfare, would be prevented by a CTB. The consensus today is that pure-fusion weapons are impossible. As was noted above, devices were invented that had greatly reduced fission yields, but apparently they had no military advantages for they were never deployed. Exotic uses of nuclear devices were proposed: digging a sea-level canal across the Isthmus of Panama, mining the moon, space propulsion, and so forth. None of these proposals bore fruit.

Weapon Effects

Many of the most interesting effects of nuclear weapons cannot be studied in underground tests; therefore, the LTBT debate is especially illuminating about the importance of effects testing. CTB opponents focused on two weapon-effects problems: missile-site survivability, and blackout for ABM defenses. In the first case, it was argued that the inability to test the hardness of our silos would somehow weaken deterrence through the existence of unknown vulnerabilities. Despite the fact that our silos have never been tested against actual nuclear explosions, few analysts appear to be worried today. In the second case, it is true that a thorough understanding of blackout would increase the efficacy of an ABM defense. It was argued at the time that past test data combined with computer simulations and additional radars could compensate for the lack of atmospheric tests. The ABM system was abandoned in the end not because of any shortage of nuclear testing, but because the radar vulnerability problem could not be solved.

Conclusions

Based purely on technical reasoning, the U.S. nuclear arsenal might not look very different today if a CTBT had been negotiated in 1963. This undercuts the arguments of CTB proponents, who claim that a CTB would have been a major step toward ending the arms race: "It is sobering to consider how the state of the world would differ if a full test ban had been achieved in 1963. The number of nuclear weapons has grown tremendously since then and is now estimated at from 50,000 to 100,000. The loss of life and the social damage that would be inflicted in a major nuclear exchange are vastly greater than they were in 1963."[43]

This analysis undercuts the arguments of CTB opponents as well, who insist that nuclear testing has been essential in modernizing our forces. The two most important developments that have occurred since 1963 — MIRVs and increased accuracy — could have happened despite a CTB, though they would have been constrained by the clumsiness of existing nuclear warheads. I am not saying that a CTB *would not* have made a difference in the arms race, only that it *need not* have made a great difference. If the Polaris A3 warhead had not been available, today's ICBM force might have been composed of Minuteman II missiles and MX-like missiles carrying three to five 1-Mt weapons. The SLBM force might have had Poseidon and Trident I missiles with two 800-kt warheads each, or Trident II missiles with four warheads each. The bomber force might have had more emphasis on penetration, since cruise missiles would have been somewhat less capable. If the Polaris A3 warhead had been available and freely used (as it most probably would have), then most of these shortcomings would have been removed. There is no evidence that the potential for destruction would be much less than it is today.

Moreover, there is little reason to believe (again based on purely technical reasoning) that deterrence would be substantially more or less stable if a CTB had been signed at that time. On the positive side, the number of warheads per ICBM launcher might have been lower and ballistic missiles would have been less accurate, resulting in decreased incentives for preemption. On the other hand, the submarine and bomber forces, which are usually considered more stabilizing than ICBMs due to the invulnerability of the former and the slowness of the latter, would have been somewhat less capable of retaliation. In addition, the total yield of the stockpile would probably have been much greater, which would have increased collateral damage in the event of war. On the whole, these considerations are minor perturbations on an otherwise stable deterrent relationship. One should remember that the technical effects of a CTBT signed today would be considerably smaller than if the treaty had been negotiated twenty-five years ago.

SUMMARY

Although a ban on nuclear testing would affect the modernization of nuclear forces, the connection between testing and the missions that forces could perform is weaker than both proponents and opponents of a CTB have maintained. Except for the most exotic possibilities, more capable nuclear weapon systems can be designed around the existing stockpile of proven warheads and bombs, though perhaps at additional cost and with a modest loss of military effectiveness. Whether this loss of effectiveness is an important cost or benefit is determined by nuclear strategy, not by technical analysis. A CTB would prevent the development of exotic weapons such as EPWs or NDEWs, but these are unproven technologies that, even if technically feasible, may fail to serve any useful or beneficial military goal.

NOTES

1. Thomas B. Cochran, William M. Arkin, and Milton M. Hoenig, *Nuclear Weapons Databook*, vol. I: *U.S. Nuclear Forces and Capabilities* (Cambridge, Mass.: Ballinger Publishing Company, 1984), p. 67.

2. J. Carson Mark, personal communication, 27 April 1987, and Paul S. Brown, "Nuclear Weapon R&D and the Role of Nuclear Testing," *Energy and Technology Review*, September 1986, p. 9.

3. Fitting nuclear warheads into artillery shells is a challenging technical feat, and, at least for 155-mm shells, probably requires the use of conventional high explosives because of their greater energy density. The design of the W82 155-mm warhead, for example, did not incorporate IHE, even though IHE was available at the time. Cochran, et al., *U.S. Nuclear Forces*, p. 309.

4. Brown, "Nuclear Weapon R&D," p. 9.

5. Ibid., p. 12. Also see Cochran, et al., *U.S. Nuclear Forces*, p. 14, and Thomas B. Cochran, William M. Arkin, Robert S. Norris, and Milton M. Hoenig, *Nuclear Weapons Databook*, vol. II: *U.S. Nuclear Warhead Production* (Cambridge, Mass.: Ballinger Publishing Company, 1987), p. 17.

6. Brown, "Nuclear Weapon R&D," p. 7.

7. William M. Arkin, Andrew S. Burrows, Richard W. Fieldhouse, Thomas B. Cochran, Robert S. Norris, and Jeffrey I. Sands, "Nuclear Weapons," in Frank Blackaby, ed., *World Armaments and Disarmament: SIPRI Yearbook 1985* (London: Taylor and Francis, 1985), p. 45.

8. Cochran, et al., *U.S. Nuclear Forces*, p. 125.

9. I am grateful to Richard Garwin for this splendid analogy.

10. Cochran, et al., *U.S. Nuclear Forces*, p. 36.

11. See Matthew Bunn, "Technology of Ballistic Missile Reentry Vehicles," in Kosta Tsipis and Penny Janeway, eds., *Review of U.S. Military Research and Development, 1984* (Washington, D.C.: Pergamon-Brassey's, 1984), p. 71. Modern reentry vehicles have betas greater than 2,000 lb/ft^2, beyond which reentry errors decrease only slowly with increasing beta. Additional decreases in reentry error are better achieved by equipping warheads with inertial guidance and maneuvering capability.

12. Art Hobson, "Missile Vulnerability: Theory, Practice, and Arms Control Implications," *Physics and Society* 16, no. 1 (January 1987): 2.

13. Cochran, et al., *U.S. Nuclear Forces*, p. 76.

14. Department of Defense, *Soviet Military Power* (Washington, D.C.: U.S. Government Printing Office, April 1984), pp. 20–22.

15. D.G. Hoag, "Ballistic-missile Guidance," in B.T. Feld, T. Greenwood, G.W. Rathjens, and S. Weinberg, eds., *Impact of New Technologies on the Arms Race* (Cambridge, Mass.: MIT Press, 1971), p. 81.

16. Chapter 3 gives a simplified equation for the probability of kill. More complicated formulae take into account the fact that the hardness of hard structures is better described by the maximum impulse they can withstand rather than the maximum overpressure, since larger weapons generate a greater impulse for a given overpressure. This can be accounted for by making the hardness a function of yield. For the hypothetical silo in the text, an approximate equation might be

$$H = 4,000[B + B^2 + 0.3)^{1/2}]^2$$

where H is the hardness in psi, $B = 0.95Y^{-1/3}$, and Y is the yield in kilotons. Bruce Bennett, "How to Assess the Survivability of U.S. ICBMs," 2578-FF (Santa Monica, Calif.: Rand Corporation, June 1980), p. 9.

17. The thirty-fold decrease comes from the observation that no structure can survive within the crater formed by a nuclear explosion. The largest possible crater radius, which, depending on the geology of the target area, is 2.6 to 3.1 times greater than that formed by a surface burst, occurs when the explosion takes place at the so-called optimum depth of burst (DOB). Since the crater radius is proportional to (yield)$^{0.3}$, the yield of a surface burst would have to be 20 to 40 times larger than that of a weapon detonated at the optimum DOB to achieve equal crater radii. An overpressure of 10 psi occurs 90 to 170 meters from a 10-kt buried explosion, compared to about 2.3 kilometers from a 300-kt surface burst. Samuel Glasstone and Phillip J. Dolan, *The Effects of Nuclear Weapons* (Washington, D.C.: U.S. Department of Defense and U.S. Department of Energy, 1977), pp. 253–59.

18. George H. Miller, Paul S. Brown, and Milo D. Nordyke, "Facing Nuclear Reality," *Science* 238 (23 October 1987): 455. Also see George H. Miller, Paul S. Brown, and Carol T. Alonso, "Report to Congress on Stockpile Reliability, Weapon Remanufacture, and the Role of Nuclear Testing," UCRL-53822 (Livermore, Calif.: Lawrence Livermore National Laboratory, October 1987), pp. 8–9.

19. For example, a cruise missile could almost certainly have been designed to use the SRAM warhead. The SRAM is deployed in the same circumstances as ALCM (indeed, the SRAM's STS is more stressing in many ways than that of the ALCM), and the mass and yield of the SRAM warhead are about equal to those of the ALCM.

20. D.D. Gries, letter to U.S. Representative E.J. Markey, 23 May 1986.

21. There is some question as to whether a MaRV would need a new warhead, because many existing warheads may not be able to withstand the large accelerations that a MaRV experiences as it maneuvers in the atmosphere. Of course, old warheads could be modified and the necessary nuclear tests done before a CTBT was negotiated. A first-generation MaRV, the Mk-500, complete with warhead, "is essentially ready for deployment on the Trident I missile should a rapid change in Soviet ABM capabilities occur." Cochran, et al., *U.S. Nuclear Forces*, p. 110.

22. Lynn R. Sykes and Dan M. Davis, "The Yields of Soviet Strategic Weapons," *Scientific American* 256, no. 1 (January 1987): 36.

23. Assume that an impulse of 10 ktaps is needed to destroy an RV, and that this requires a fluence of 1 keV X-rays of about 25 kJ/cm². A hypothetical X-ray laser pumped by a 100-kt explosion that converted 1 percent of the energy into 1 keV X-rays with a divergence of 10 microradians could destroy 50 targets at a distance of 1,000 kilometers. Ten microradians is the diffraction limit for a lasing rod diameter of 0.1 centimeters. If either the beam divergence or the required impulse was 7 times greater (or if both were just 2.7 times greater), only one target could be destroyed. If the laser is only 100 kilometers away, 50 targets could still be destroyed with the wider beam and/or harder RV, but the offense could spread out the attack in space and time enough to deny this possibility. An X-ray energy of 10 keV could also compensate for the wider beam and/or harder RVs, but this would be much more difficult to achieve than 1 keV. A spiral angled foil could protect an RV against a single X-ray laser shot, which would halve the number of RVs that could be destroyed by a given number of X-ray lasers. See "Report to the American Physical Society of the Study Group on the Science and Technology of Directed Energy Weapons," *Reviews of Modern Physics* 59, no. 3, pt. II (July 1987): S62–S63, S136–S140.

24. See Steve Fetter, "Protecting Our Military Space Systems," in Edmund S. Muskie, ed., *The U.S. in Space: Issues and Policy Choices for a New Era* (Washington, D.C.: Center for National Policy Press, 1988).

25. U.S. strategic warheads have a yield of about 300 kilotons, and mobile launchers can be hardened to about 30 psi. A 300-kt weapon will cause a 30 psi overpressure roughly 1 kilometer from ground zero.

26. Some analysts argue that this is not necessarily true, since Soviet nuclear research could be proceeding along a very different path from U.S. research, or since capabilities may erode asymmetrically during a CTB. These arguments are unpersuasive because these effects rarely have happened in the past. The Soviet Union, for example, has duplicated nearly every major U.S. achievement in nuclear weapon development with a lag time of just a few years.

27. Roger Batzel, letter to Admiral Sylvester R. Foley, Jr., 22 July, 1986.

28. This would include all warheads and bombs with designator numbers less than 54, plus the W54, the W56, the B57, and the W59. See Cochran, et al., *U.S. Nuclear Warhead Production*, pp. 10–11.

29. Ibid.

30. Herbert F. York, "The Great Test-Ban Debate," *Scientific American* 227, no. 5 (November 1972): 21.

31. Herbert York and G. Allen Greb, *The Comprehensive Nuclear Test Ban*, Discussion Paper No. 84 (Santa Monica, Calif.: The California Seminar on Arms Control and Foreign Policy, June 1979), p. 21.

32. Cochran, et al., *U.S. Nuclear Forces*, p. 36.

33. Norman Polmar, ed., *Strategic Air Command: People, Aircraft, and Missiles* (Annapolis, Md.: Nautical and Aviation Publishing Co., 1979), p. 217.

34. The CEP of the ALCM is 10 to 30 meters, compared to ICBM, SLBM, or bomb accuracies of 100 to 200 meters. Cochran et al, *U.S. Nuclear Forces*, p. 66, 118, 121, 145, 177.

35. Robert S. Norris, "Counterforce at Sea," *Arms Control Today* 15, no. 7 (September 1985): 9.

36. ALCM yield from Robert S. Norris and William M. Arkin, "Nuclear Notebook," *Bulletin of the Atomic Scientists*, 43, no. 5 (June 1987): 56. The only pre-1963 weapons with weights of about the 270-lb W80 (and whose weights can be found in the open literature) are the W33 (240 pounds), W44 (less than 280 pounds), and the W45 (less than 365 pounds). The maximum yield of these warheads is 15 kilotons. Warhead yield and weight data from Cochran et al., *U.S. Nuclear Forces*, p. 47, 52.

37. The only pre-1963 warhead with a yield similar to the W80 (and for which yield and weight estimates appear in the open literature) was the W50, which had selectable yields of 60, 200, and 400 kilotons, and which weighed about 700 pounds. Allowing for weight reductions due to miniaturization of the warhead electrical system, the warhead might weigh about 400 pounds more than the W80. Assuming that this extra mass displaced fuel and that the ALCM has an average velocity of 500 mph, a thrust of 600 pounds, and a specific fuel consumption of 1.0 lb fuel/lb thrust/h (a rough average for small turbojets at this velocity), the reduction in range would be about 350 kilometers. More sophisticated calculations in which fuel efficiency is a function of fuel weight might result in range reductions of up to 500 kilometers. Data on warhead weights and ALCM characteristics are taken from Cochran, et al., *U.S. Nuclear Forces*, p. 56, 174.

38. The Atlas was first deployed in 1959, the Titan I probably in 1960, the Titan II and Minuteman I in 1962, and the Minuteman II in 1965. The Polaris A1 was first deployed in 1961, the Polaris A2 in 1962 or 1963, and the Polaris A3 in 1964. The next generation of ballistic missiles — the Minuteman III and the Poseidon — were not deployed until the early 1970s. Cochran, et al., *U.S. Nuclear Forces*, pp. 102–107, 111–18, 136.

39. See, for example, warhead weights for SLBMs given in Norris, "Counterforce at Sea," p. 9.
40. York, "The Great Test-Ban Debate," p. 21.
41. It is estimated that the ballistic coefficient, or beta, of RVs deployed before 1964 was below 1,000 lb/ft^2, which would result in reentry errors exceeding 600 meters, or five or six times greater than that attainable with modern RVs (Bunn, "Technology of RVs," p. 71, and Matthew Bunn, "U.S. Ballistic Missile Reentry Vehicles: A Research Note," unpublished, August 1986). Most of the decrease in reentry errors was due to the development of better materials, which could have happened under a CTB. If the half angle, nose-tip radius, density, relative center of mass, fusing, and RV materials are held constant, heavier RVs would be more accurate, since beta would then be roughly proportional to the one-third power of the RV mass. It is likely, however, that newer, smaller warheads are not simply scaled-down versions of their heavier predecessors, and that the warhead radius has become disproportionately smaller in order to minimize the half-angle. According to Bunn, the half-angle of the Mk-21 MX RV is 8.2°; if this is increased to 10° and the total volume and mass doubled to accommodate, for example, the Polaris A1/A2 W47 warhead, and everything else is held constant, beta would decrease from about 3,000 to about 2,700 lb/ft^2. Frank J. Regan, *Re-Entry Vehicle Dynamics* (New York: American Institute of Aeronautics and Astronautics, Inc., 1984), p. 230. Even if the half-angle is 12.5° — the same as that given by Bunn for the Mk-6 Titan II RV — the beta would still be greater than 1,600 lb/ft^2, resulting in overall CEPs of about 200 meters. For comparison, the CEP of the Minuteman III is about 180 meters.
42. Some analysts believe the "bargaining chip" argument that the U.S. deployment of a superior ABM system catalyzed the negotiation of an ABM treaty. There is some truth to this, for if there had been no interest in ABM systems, then there would have been no need to ban such systems. It cannot be argued, however, that the development of a superior ABM system, made possible in part by the development of custom warheads, catalyzed the ABM treaty. First, it was widely recognized that the U.S. ABM system could not have provided an effective defense, which made it very difficult to argue that the ABM system was vital to the national security. Second, the goal of the ABM treaty was to prevent the adverse effects that are caused by the deployment of even inferior, ineffective systems: a worst-case analysis of defensive capabilities by the other side, resulting in the inability to negotiate restraints on offensive forces.
43. Lynn R. Sykes and Jack F. Evernden, "The Verification of a Comprehensive Nuclear Test Ban," *Scientific American* 247, no. 4 (October 1982): 55.

3 STOCKPILE CONFIDENCE

Throughout the test ban debate, proponents of continued testing have argued that test restrictions inhibit improvements in nuclear warheads that would increase the safety, security, survivability, and effectiveness of weapon systems. When the Carter administration opened negotiations on a CTB in the fall of 1977, the nuclear weapon establishments in the United States and the United Kingdom raised a new objection: confidence in the reliability of existing nuclear weapons could not be maintained without nuclear testing. This argument helped to unify the bureaucratic opposition to a CTB, forcing President Carter to place a five-year and then a three-year limit on the length of the proposed treaty. Most recently, stockpile confidence objections have been a central premise in the Reagan administration's refusal to consider additional restrictions on testing.

The stockpile confidence objection has two parts: (1) to forgo nuclear testing would significantly undermine confidence in the stockpile, and (2) this would threaten the national security by weakening nuclear deterrence. To avoid many of the difficulties of definition that have muddied the debate on this issue, stockpile confidence is defined here as a reasonable assurance that the stockpile of nuclear weapons already deployed at the time a CTBT is negotiated would continue to perform with existing delivery systems, with the degree of reliability necessary for deterrence.

Stockpile confidence is not the same as stockpile reliability. Reliability is an objective measure of the average fraction of weapons that would perform properly. Reliability can be measured to any given degree of accuracy by performing a sufficient number of tests. Confidence, on the other hand, is a subjective measure based on the perception of those people responsible for the stockpile that the weapons are reliable. The amount of testing affects the likelihood that this perception is correct.

The difference between confidence and reliability could become extreme in the absence of continued nuclear testing. One could have perfect confidence in weapons that would be unreliable if used, or one could lose confidence in weapons that were perfectly reliable. Therefore, proving that nuclear weapons could be kept reliable during a CTB is not the same as proving that confidence could be maintained. Confidence would be based mostly on scientific experience and non-nuclear techniques, but it would also be subject to political and psychological distortions.

This is not a trivial point, since deterrence is more a matter of perception (confidence) than reality (reliability). If American leaders are convinced of the reliability of their weapons, and Soviet officials, observing this confidence, are also convinced of the potency of the U.S. arsenal, then the requirements of deterrence are satisfied independent of the actual reliability of the weapons. The difference between confidence and reliability would only be revealed on the fateful day that deterrence failed. The consequences of warhead unreliability would then depend on the degree to which nuclear weapons could defend a nation by limiting to some meaningful extent the damage wreaked by opposing forces.

The likelihood of problems with complex technologies is chronically underestimated by experts. Nuclear reactors said to have unsurpassed reliability suffer meltdowns. The Space Shuttle, which knowledgeable engineers and program managers claimed was extremely reliable, exploded after two dozen flights. One particularly relevant example is the high confidence of U.S. weapon designers in modifications made to stockpiled weapons during the 1958–1961 moratorium on nuclear testing—such high confidence, in fact, that the modified designs were not tested immediately after the moratorium ended. One nuclear weapon that was modified during the moratorium, the W52 warhead for the Sergeant surface-to-surface missile, entered the stockpile in 1962 without further testing. When the warhead was tested in 1963, it gave only a small fraction of its expected yield.[1] Of course, weapon designers, looking back on this experience, might begin to err in the other direction, losing confidence in reliable weapons during a CTB. But designers could be expected to perform every nonnuclear test possible to determine the reliability of a weapon. If all the results were positive, it would be difficult to conclude that the weapon was unreliable. It is at least as likely that, as with the Space Shuttle, weapons would be assumed reliable unless strong evidence to the contrary was presented. This suggests that those people responsible for the stockpile may be more likely to maintain confidence in unreliable weapons than to lose confidence in reliable ones.[2] Although lives depend on the reliability of nuclear reactors, it is not clear whether having confidence in unreliable nuclear weapons would be good or bad, because there are great differences of opinion about what nuclear weapons are supposed to do. Some strategists claim that nuclear weapons should never actually be used and that they would be of little benefit in defending the country that did use them; others maintain just the opposite.

The first section of this chapter focuses on the question of whether the nuclear arsenal can be kept sufficiently reliable without nuclear testing. Beliefs about this question will naturally have a strong influence on one's confidence in the stockpile during a CTB. The chapter then describes past instances of unreliability; techniques to detect, assess, and resolve reliability problems without nuclear testing; and the degree of reliability necessary for nuclear weapons. Finally, the chapter returns to the subject of the implications of decreased confidence.

MAINTAINING RELIABILITY WITHOUT NUCLEAR TESTING

The problem of maintaining nuclear weapons without nuclear testing is a sensitive issue because many of the arguments bear on details of weapon designs and techniques that are classified. The arguments cannot be resolved by simply referring to those individuals who in the past have been responsible for assuring the reliability of nuclear weapons, since they are often divided on this issue. For example, former Los Alamos National Laboratory (LANL) Director Norris

Bradbury, former Lawrence Livermore National Laboratory (LLNL) Director Herbert York, and former weapon designers J. Carson Mark, Richard Garwin, and Hans Bethe maintain that nuclear testing is not necessary to insure the reliability of the stockpile, but former LLNL Director Roger Batzel and former LANL Directors Harold Agnew and Donald Kerr contend that testing is essential.[3] Nevertheless, insight into this question can be gained by the careful application of common sense to unclassified historical examples.

Past Examples of Unreliability

Many problems with nuclear weapons have been detected in the past, not only in the development phase but also at various times after deployment. Some, but not all, of these problems would have resulted in a greatly reduced yield or no yield at all. Fourteen of the forty-one types of nuclear weapons introduced into the U.S. stockpile after 1958 developed stockpile confidence problems; of these, 75 percent were discovered and/or corrected by nuclear testing.[4] These fourteen problem warheads, along with two others described by Rosengren,[5] are listed in Table 3–1. One might be tempted to conclude that about one quarter of the stockpile would have been unreliable if testing had not been available, but the reliability problems do not lend themselves to such a simple interpretation.[6] The twenty-three problems described in Table 3–1 can be grouped into six categories: tritium decay, one-point safety, corrosion of fissile material, deterioration of high explosive, low-temperature performance, and other problems.

Tritium Decay.   During the moratorium, weapon designers began to suspect that the performance of weapons with aged tritium might have been overestimated. Tritium is radioactive and decays with a half-life of twelve years. This fact was known before the moratorium, of course, but weapons were stockpiled without testing for this effect because it was thought to be well understood. When the moratorium ended, nuclear tests confirmed that a problem existed. Seven nuclear weapons were tested in 1962 to assess and resolve problems of this type: the B28, B43, and B57 bombs; the W44 warhead for the antisubmarine rocket; the W45 warhead for the Little John, Terrier, and Bullpup tactical missiles and the medium atomic demolition munition; the W50 warhead for the Pershing I missile; and the W59 warhead for the Minuteman I intercontinental ballistic missile (ICBM).

Table 3–1. Nuclear Weapon Types Known to Have Had Stockpile Confidence Problems.[a]

Weapon System	Production Period	Problem	Year Problem Resolved
B28 (bomb)	1958–66	Inadequate one-point safety	1962
		Inadequate performance with aged tritium	1962
B43 (bomb)	1961–65	Inadequate one-point safety	1962
		Inadequate performance with aged tritium	1962
W44 (ASROC)	1961–68	Inadequate performance with aged tritium	1962
W45 (Little John, Terrier, MADM, and Bullpup)	1962–66	Corrosion of fissile material	1963
		Inadequate performance with aged tritium	1964
		Deterioration of high explosive	1965
W47 (Polaris A1)	1960–64	Neutron vulnerability	1962
		Corrosion of fissile material	1963
		Inadequate one-point safety	1963
W50 (Pershing I)	1963–65	Inadequate performance with aged tritium	1962
W52 (Sergeant)	1962–66	Poor high-explosive safety	1963
W56 (Minuteman II)	1963–69	Inadequate one-point safety	1963
B57 (ASW bomb)	1963–67	Inadequate performance with aged tritium	1962
W58 (Polaris A3)	1964–67	Corrosion	1970s
W59 (Minuteman I)	1962–63	Inadequate performance with aged tritium	1962
B61 (bomb)	1979–present[b]	Poor low-temperature performance	1981
W68 (Poseidon)	1970–75	Deterioration of high explosive	1980
W79 (8″ AFAP)	1981–83	Poor performance with new gas fill when original reservoir could not be manufactured	1982
W80 (ALCM)	1981–present	Poor low-temperature performance	1981
W84 (GLCM)	1983–present	Poor low-temperature performance	1981
		Differences in stockpile hardware	1984

a. Except for the W56 and W58, these problems are taken from Frederick Reines, Lew Allen, Edwin L. Goldwasser, Andrew J. Goodpaster, Arthur K. Kerman, M. Brian Maple, Kenneth McKay, William G. McMillan, Herbert F. York, and Rochus E. Vogt, "Nuclear Weapons Tests: The Role of the University of California–Department of Energy Laboratories," Report to the President and the Regents of the University of California by the Scientific and Academic Advisory Committee, July 1987, p. 35. The W56 and W58 are from J.W. Rosengren, "Some Little-Publicized Difficulties with a Nuclear Freeze," RDA-TR-122116-001 (Arlington, Va.: R&D Associates, October 1983), pp. 18–20. Production dates are from Thomas B. Cochran, William M. Arkin, Robert S. Norris, and Milton M. Hoenig, *Nuclear Weapons Databook*, vol. II: *U.S. Nuclear Warhead Production* (Cambridge, Mass.: Ballinger Publishing Company, 1987), pp. 10–11.

b. Six different modifications of the B61 have been produced since 1966, but the modification that experienced the low-temperature problem has not been specified. Because of the nature of the problem and its timing, the most likely candidates are the B61-3 or the B61-4, which were manufactured beginning in 1979.

One-point Safety. Nuclear weapons are designed to be "one-point safe," which means that only a trivial nuclear yield will result if the high explosive is detonated accidentally.[7] In the past, four nuclear weapons experienced problems related to one-point safety: the B28 and B43 bombs; the W47 warhead for the Polaris A1 submarine-launched ballistic missile (SLBM); and the W56 warhead for the Minuteman II ICBM. Of these, only the problems with the W47 and the W56 have been described in detail. In the case of the W47, a test just before the moratorium indicated that the warhead was not inherently one-point safe. Since further testing was not permitted, a mechanical safing device was added to the weapon. With time, however, this safing mechanism jammed. In the first version of the warhead (W47Y1), this problem was resolved without requiring nuclear testing. When the second version (W47Y2) developed similar problems after the moratorium ended, the decision was made to modify both versions, with the aid of testing, to make them inherently one-point safe, thus eliminating the need for mechanical safing. The W56 warhead was also developed without enough tests to ensure inherent one-point safety. It too was fitted with a mechanical safing mechanism that jammed after a few years. In this case, however, the problem was eliminated with a small design change that did not require nuclear testing.

Corrosion of Fissile Material. In two cases, the W45 tactical warhead and the W47 Polaris warhead, the normal stockpile surveillance program discovered that the fissile material was corroding. A nuclear test of an extremely corroded W47 indicated that warhead performance was not very sensitive to the effects of corrosion. Extremely corroded units were removed from the stockpile based on this test, and a slight design change prevented further similar deterioration in both warhead types. The W58 warhead for the Polaris A3 SLBM is also known to have developed a corrosion problem. This problem was evaluated by nonnuclear techniques, which indicated that the observed deterioration had little effect on warhead performance. No nuclear tests were done.

Deterioration of High Explosive. The stockpile surveillance program discovered dimensional changes in the high explosive of the W45 tactical warhead. This problem was resolved by modifying the high explosive and its packaging and by testing the modified warhead. After several years in the stockpile, the high explosive in the W68 warhead for the Poseidon SLBM also began to deteriorate. Fortunately, the W68 had been tested during development with another high explosive that did not have this problem. The switch was made and a modified warhead was tested successfully.

Low-temperature Performance.   After deployment, the W80 warhead for the air-launched cruise missile (ALCM) failed when it was tested for the first time at the low-temperature limit of its operating environment.[8] The warhead was modified, with the aid of nuclear testing, to remove this deficiency. Nuclear tests were then done on two other stockpiled weapons with features similar to the W80: the B61 bomb and the W84 GLCM (ground-launched cruise missile) warhead. Both worked satisfactorily.

Other Problems.   Four other problems have been mentioned in the unclassified literature. First, the W47 Polaris warhead was found to be unacceptably vulnerable to neutrons from nearby nuclear explosions. Nuclear tests were done to evaluate solutions to this problem. Second, the W52 warhead for the Sergeant surface-to-surface tactical missile was designed with a very sensitive high explosive. Two fatal accidents occurred during the first production of the weapon, killing four people. A decision was made to change the high explosive, but the moratorium prevented testing the modified weapon. As mentioned above, scientists were confident that the weapon would perform satisfactorily, but a nuclear test after the moratorium gave only a small fraction of its rated yield. The weapon was then redesigned and tested. Third, the design of the W79 warhead for the 8-inch artillery-fired atomic projectile (AFAP) had to be modified when a certain component could not be manufactured. Fourth, the W84 for the GLCM warhead was stock-piled using slightly different hardware than the test versions. When a stockpiled version of the warhead was subjected to a nuclear test the yield was low. Nuclear tests were done to resolve this problem, but the cause of the yield reduction is still not understood.

These reliability problems resulted either from design errors that were not revealed by the normal testing program during the development phase of a weapon, or from the unexpected aging and deterioration of weapon components after deployment. This distinction is important because most of the examples of past failures, presented as proof that testing is essential for stockpile reliability, in fact reflect an incomplete testing program. Known failures of this type need never be repeated if they are eliminated during development.

The difficulties with one-point safety, for example, are a mixture of design and aging problems. Although it is true that the mechanical safing device in the W47 jammed due to corrosion, this device would not have been required in the first place if enough tests had been done to ensure inherent one-point safety. But, in its haste to deploy new weapons before the moratorium took effect, the U.S. stockpiled warheads such as the W47 after a truncated development and testing program. The W52 was modified, but not tested because of the moratorium, to correct flaws discovered during the first production of the warhead. Future problems of this type can be prevented by resisting the temptation, should a CTB become a reality, to stockpile the latest designs or modify existing weapons in ways that cannot be certified without nuclear tests.

Other problems occurred simply because weapon designers did not appreciate certain aspects of weapon design or the behavior of the weapon in its stockpile-to-target sequence (STS). The problems with tritium decay, for example, were not due to unexpected aging per se, but to a lack of understanding about the effects of this aging on weapon performance. Because of this lack of understanding, nuclear tests were not done during weapon development to assess the consequences of tritium decay. Similarly, because of a lack of theoretical understanding and because nonnuclear tests at low temperature did not produce obviously suspicious results, nuclear tests were not done at the low-temperature limit. Little information is available on the neutron vulnerability problem of the W47, but it is likely that the warhead was not subjected to a nuclear effects test before depolyment; otherwise, this problem would have been discovered.

There may be additional shortcomings in design and testing practices that are yet to be identified, but, as with most other technologies, the number of such problems decreases as the technology becomes more mature. Although no testing program can be complete in the sense that all possible design flaws are anticipated, it should be noted that all of the flaws mentioned above were discovered soon after the first production of a warhead. Of the eighteen examples of design flaws mentioned above, six were discovered and corrected in the same year that quantity production of the warhead began; six were resolved one year after first production; three, two years later; one, three years later; and two were corrected within four years of first production. In the past twenty-five years, all design flaws were discovered within two years of first production. By relying only on warheads that have been tested, produced, and deployed for a few years, it appears that problems due to design errors can be substantially avoided.

Problems caused by aging and deterioration are more difficult to deal with because they cannot be eliminated by a thorough testing program during the development phase. Unexpected aging and deterioration is likely to be the major stockpile confidence problem under a prudently implemented CTB. By their very nature, nuclear weapons must contain reactive materials such as plutonium and high explosive. Warheads are routinely tested after undergoing simulated accelerated effects of aging, but this does not catch all the problems that can crop up during the lifetime of a weapon. Three warheads – the W45, the W47, and the W58 – experienced corrosion problems. None of these problems were detected by nuclear tests, and only one nuclear test was done to evaluate the problems (a successful test of an extremely corroded W47 warhead). In two cases – the W45 and the W68 – the high explosive deteriorated. Nuclear tests did not detect these problems, although tests were done to certify the modified warheads. In the three cases where mechanical safing devices deteriorated – the W47Y1, the W47Y2, and the W56 – two were resolved without nuclear testing. Therefore, nuclear tests were done to resolve four of the eight cases of unexpected aging and deterioration described in the open literature. Since all four of these tests were successful, nuclear tests were not necessary to maintain the actual reliability of the stockpile. They were done to maintain the confidence of those people responsible for the stockpile.

Demonstrating that nuclear testing was instrumental in resolving past problems does not prove that testing would be required in the future, however. First, the fact that nuclear tests were *done* does not indicate that tests were *necessary*, since the problems were resolved in a context in which nuclear testing was permitted. If testing had not been permitted, confidence might nevertheless have been sufficient in some warheads (e.g., the W68 had already been tested with the substitute high explosive), or alternate approaches might have solved the problem without nuclear testing (e.g., safing mechanisms in the W47Y2 could have been repaired often or a jam-free mechanism developed). Second, most of the past problems in the stockpile appeared around the time of the moratorium, when the technologies being deployed were new. The key concepts for reliable, high yield-to-weight thermonuclear warheads had just been invented, as had intercontinental and submarine-launched ballistic missiles. It is not surprising that these young technologies exhibited growing pains. But now that the technology of modern nuclear weapons is more mature and well understood, problems should be less likely in the future. It is sometimes said that new designs are less reliable because they are more complex, but reliability is influenced more by technological maturity and production expertise than by complexity per se.

Detecting Problems without Nuclear Testing

Although some analysts claim that nuclear testing is necessary to detect reliability problems, this is questionable for two reasons. First, the only reliability problems that were detected by nuclear testing in the past were caused by design flaws, not by aging and deterioration. Except for the W52, nuclear tests were not used to detect even these design problems, but instead have been used to assess recognized possible problems, as in the case of tritium decay in the W47. Second, the rate of nuclear testing for these purposes has been very low. In recent years only 8 percent of all tests were done for stockpile confidence purposes, and few of these were of old weapons.[9] Even if two old warheads were tested every year, this would allow only one stockpile confidence test every fifteen years for each weapon type, since there are twenty-five to thirty-five types of nuclear weapons in the stockpile at any given time. Furthermore, a single successful stockpile confidence test gives little information about the reliability of the weapon; even a weapon 50 percent reliable would give a successful test half of the time. The normal stockpile surveillance program, which consists of the careful disassembly, inspection, and testing of components from many weapons, is far more effective than nuclear testing for detecting deterioration.

Evaluating Problems without Nuclear Testing

A nuclear test is often the simplest way to determine if a deteriorated warhead will perform properly. Even so, testing for these purposes is relatively rare: only 8 of nearly 300 tests since 1970 were done to evaluate defects in stockpiled weapons.[10] There are many tools and techniques other than nuclear testing that can be used to assess the reliability of old weapons. First, nonnuclear testing of weapons can be done by substituting inert materials for the special nuclear materials (SNM) and detonating the high explosive. This type of test would be useful in evaluating the aging of a high explosive, for example. Small amounts of fissile material could be used in the experiment, as was done during the moratorium, resulting in a very small nuclear yield (e.g., less than a pound of high explosive equivalent).[11] Second, the operation of nuclear weapons is routinely simulated and studied with elaborate computer programs running on the fastest computers in the world. These programs have been adjusted to give correct results for past nuclear tests and may therefore be more valuable in assessing the performance of old weapons than in predicting the performance of new warheads (which is currently their most common use). Computer simulations might determine if a slight change in the composition or shape of certain components would affect the yield of a weapon, for example. Although these techniques have not spotted every problem in the past, they were instrumental in solving problems with many warheads. Moveover, the power of these techniques has increased consistently with the passage of time. Even though they cannot by themselves guarantee proper operation of a weapon, past experience gives a good indication of the range of problems for which they can be trusted to give reliable advice.

Correcting Problems without Nuclear Testing

Laboratory techniques are best at indicating whether deterioration problems are serious and at suggesting minor changes that have been verified by testing experience. To solve serious reliability problems without nuclear testing, one must either remanufacture the warhead or find an acceptable substitute. These approaches are discussed below.

Remanufacturing. If deterioration occurs and laboratory procedures indicate that the weapon may no longer be reliable, the weapon could be remanufactured to the original specifications. Only one U.S. warhead has been remanufactured; the production line was closed for three years in the early 1970s, and the remanufactured weapon was not proof-tested.[12] Remanufacturing has been rare because weapons usually are replaced by newer designs before the end of their lifetime. The main objection to remanufacturing is that it rebuilds old problems into new warheads; designing new weapons would solve aging and deterioration problems, improve warhead safety and military effectiveness, and save money. But if the advantages of a CTB outweigh the marginal benefits of these modernizations, and if the warhead to be rebuilt had a reasonably long shelf life, then remanufacturing can be an effective solution. Three difficulties with replicating nuclear weapons have been raised: (1) materials, fabrication techniques, equipment, and workmanship quality change in subtle ways over time, with unpredictable results for weapon performance; (2) the production process requires trained weapon designers, who will become less and less skilled under a CTB; and (3) remanufacturing old warheads is less cost-effective than building new, state-of-the-art warheads.[13] These are not insoluble problems.

Changes in Materials and Techniques. The difficulty of remanufacturing nuclear warheads has been compared with that of rebuilding a 1950s television set: even if one had the schematic diagram, where would one find the proper parts? In the United States, warheads typically are manufactured during a five- to ten-year period, after which the production line is closed. Since nuclear weapons are designed to have a shelf life of about twenty-five years, fifteen to twenty years could elapse between the original manufacture of the warhead and its remanufacture. Although this might be the case with warheads that are already out of production when a CTBT takes effect, the production lines for warheads currently under production could be kept open indefinitely to minimize the possibility of changes in materials and techniques. At present, the B61, W76, W80, B83, and W87 strategic nuclear weapons are being produced, and in the next few years, the W88 and the warhead for the new short-range attack missile (SRAM II) will be produced (see Table 3–2). Furthermore, warheads that are out of production but are planned to be part of the long-term stockpile, such as the W78, could be brought back into production before a CTB took effect.

Rebuilding the 1950s television might not be difficult if during the original manufacture one had taken special precautions to minimize the problems of replication. The composition and structure of materials can be specified with extreme accuracy, as can the techniques used to produce a material. Chemists sometimes complain that they do not know all the variables to specify in order to replicate some substances, or the deviations that can be permitted without affecting weapon performance. But studies can and should be undertaken to resolve these issues. If questions remain about the possibility of

Table 3–2.   Bomb and Warhead Types in the Strategic Arsenal of the Late 1980s and Early 1990s.[a]

Warhead Type	Production Period
W56 (Mk-11C Minuteman II warhead)	1964–69
B61 (Gravity bomb)	1969–present
W62 (Mk-12 Minuteman III warhead)	1969–78
W68 (Mk-3 Poseidon warhead)	1970–78
W69 (SRAM warhead)	1970–76
W76 (Mk-4 Trident I/II warhead)	1977–present
W78 (Mk-12A Minuteman III warhead)	1979–83
W80 (ALCM and ACM warhead)	1979–present
B83 (Gravity bomb)	1983–present
W87 (Mk-21 MX and Midgetman warhead)	1985–present
W88 (Mk-5 Trident II warhead)	To be produced

a. Thomas B. Cochran, William M. Arkin, Robert S. Norris, and Milton M. Hoenig, *Nuclear Weapons Databook*, vol. II: *U.S. Nuclear Warhead Production* (Cambridge, Mass.: Ballinger Publishing Company, 1987), pp. 10–11.

duplicating a material, it could be produced without interruption or stockpiled. Fabrication techniques can also be specified with great precision, using the computer-aided design and engineering systems that are already in use at these facilities.[14] Warhead components from the original production line could be stored for direct comparison with remanufactured components. While it is often argued that tightening occupational health and safety standards may prevent the industrial use of certain key materials, this need not prevent the use of the same materials in weapons; the cost of additional protection for personnel should not be an issue if national security was at stake.

Admiral Foley, then assistant secretary of energy for defense programs, agreed with this analysis: "Assuming, therefore, that vendor-supplied materials and components are still available at the time desired for remanufacture (and this will not necessarily be the case), the remanufacture of existing, well-tested warheads is possible."[15] Assuring the supply of the required materials should not be an impossible task for a country as large and advanced as the United States.

Even so, many analysts claim that nuclear tests of remanufactured weapons would be required, since nothing complex can be relied on without testing. But some systems, such as nuclear artillery or com-munication satellites, are considered sufficiently reliable without crit-ical nuclear tests. The United States has not fired a live, modern nuclear artillery shell because above-ground tests are banned and underground tests would be too expensive. The new and expensive MILSTAR and Navstar satellite systems are intended to provide critical command and control communications during a nuclear war, even though they cannot be tested under these conditions. If there is no crisis of confidence about systems that have not been thoroughly tested, why should one lose confidence in thoroughly tested weapon designs that have been remanufactured?

Designer Skill. The stock of weapon scientists with nuclear testing experience would gradually diminish under a CTB, and the cessation of testing and weapon development may accelerate the loss of trained scientists and make the recruitment of high-quality personnel more difficult. This raises several interrelated questions.

First, would it be difficult for the weapon laboratories to keep experienced scientists and hire high-quality personnel under a CTB? If weapon scientists are motivated solely by the desire to design and test weapons that will go into the stockpile, then a CTB would lead to a complete loss of personnel. But individual motivations are much more complex and include the desire to discover and publish, the freedom to think creatively, recognition by one's peers, access to state-of-the-art equipment, and the desire to contribute to the national security. The fact that weapon laboratories would no longer be stock-piling new types of warheads would undoubtedly lead some of the more zealous people to leave, but many motivations for weapon-related work would not change significantly under a CTB. Much work would remain that is challenging and creative, laboratory equipment could still be first-rate, and the contribution to the national defense just as important. Scientists wanting a new challenge could move to nonwea-pon programs at weapon laboratories, where they would still be available for consultation about stockpile problems.

Second, even if reasonably good scientists are available, can they keep the stockpile reliable without the skills and practical experience that nuclear testing can give? Although tests are essential to confirm predictions about designs that extend the state of the art, they are not necessary to maintain established designs. Experienced weapon de-signers must be involved in the production of a warhead, but only in the initial phases when it is uncertain whether the production processes can match the specifications of the designer. After these initial phases, there is little designer involvement. Furthermore, every activity other than nuclear testing that contributes to design expertise would be available under a CTB. Besides exploring the theoretical aspects of weapon design, weapon scientists could investigate many aspects of weapon physics by using the nonnuclear testing and computer simulation techniques mentioned above or by improving the ability of computer simulations to predict the behavior of stockpiled weapons for comparison with existing test data. Experiments in a wide variety of areas could be done using the small fusion explosions created in the laboratory with inertial-confinement fusion (ICF). ICF would train technical people in the unique disciplines of direct relevance to nuclear weapons and would retain and attract talent to the weapon laboratories.[16] The design of advanced conventional explosives would also help to maintain skills of direct relevance to nuclear weapon design. Of course, if some level of nuclear testing is allowed under a CTBT or low-yield threshold test ban treaty, this would also help to maintain skills. Even though direct experience in nuclear testing is unlikely to be important for maintaining the stockpile, some scientists with testing experience would still remain twenty years after a CTBT was negotiated.

Third, will those people responsible for maintaining the stockpile have confidence in their own work without recourse to nuclear testing? Will decisionmakers have confidence in the judgment of these people? These questions underscore the difference between confidence and reliability. Well-trained, competent people who make correct decisions could lose confidence, and incompetent people could nevertheless be completely self-confident. Many of today's weapon designers say that they would be much less self-confident without access to nuclear testing, even if they were only responsible for maintaining old designs. Although perhaps true, it is hard to find examples of a similar loss of self-confidence in other technical fields. The individuals responsible for the stockpile during the moratorium were self-confident, and those responsible for the satellite systems mentioned above do not express doubts (if they have any) about those systems working as intended in a harsh environment in which they have never been tested. There may be a perverse effect at work here: without experimental data to prove them wrong, scientists become more confident in their theoretical judgment. This effect might be exaggerated if those who are most comfortable with experimental proof leave the laboratories.

It is not clear that the actions of decisionmakers would have much to do with the self-confidence of scientists or the adequacy of their training. Decisionmakers are usually in no position to judge the adequacy of a scientist's training or the quality of his or her judgment. If doubts about the stockpile were expressed, decisionmakers may believe that the scientists were being overly cautious or that the risks of a problem are not outweighed by the benefits of ignoring it. This was the case with the Challenger disaster, where the worries of engineers were overridden by program managers concerned about long delays. Although weapon designers would have built-in motivations to exaggerate confidence problems, a technical community, even one as exclusive as the nuclear weapon community, is rarely unanimous in its advice. It is likely that decisionmakers will be influenced primarily by political considerations and that they will choose the technical analysis they want to hear. For example, decisionmakers who were against a CTBT in the first place may use a perceived technical problem to catalyze a decision to abrogate the treaty. On the other hand, those who do not want to upset the international political equation may choose to ignore the problem.

Fourth, it is often said that a CTB would lull the United States into a false sense of security and that budgetary support for the weapon laboratories would evaporate, since their primary mission, the development and testing of new weapons, would have been effectively banned. In the past, however, excessive fear of a lulling effect has stimulated actions that reduced the value of the treaties signed.[17] It is unlikely that a CTBT would be ratified by the U.S. Senate without considerable support from the defense community, and especially the Joint Chiefs of Staff. This support, in turn, is unlikely without certain assurances, or safeguards, from the president that would partially compensate for the loss of nuclear testing. In the case of the LTBT, these safeguards included well-funded weapon laboratories, a vigorous underground testing program, and maintenance of the capability to resume atmospheric testing should the Soviets violate the treaty.[18] In the case of a CTBT, the safeguards might include excellent funding for laboratories, a vigorous nonnuclear testing program, and maintenance of the capability to resume underground testing at short notice. It is true that the United States allowed its ability to promptly resume atmospheric testing to lapse ten years after the treaty was signed. Some analysts claim that this is evidence that safeguards cannot be maintained. But the United States has only let this safeguard lapse because of the realization that nearly all important tests can be done underground (which was not thought to be true in 1963) and that prompt resumption of atmospheric testing is not critical to protect national security if the Soviets abrogate the LTBT.

Finally, it has been argued that the Soviet Union would develop a relative advantage over the United States in the quality of weapon scientists, since the Soviet Union can force trained scientists to continue in weapon-related work. Creative thinking cannot be forced, however, and Soviet scientists would also live under the constraint of a test ban. Without new data, they would make little progress. One could just as well argue that U.S. scientists would have an advantage, since U.S. tests probably have been performed with better instrumentation and diagnostics, and since the computers available for weapon simulations are vastly superior to those in the Soviet Union. Hence, the loss of trained personnel does not favor the Soviet Union if both parties abide by the treaty. But if the Soviet Union did test clandestinely at low yields and at a small but steady rate, this could give them an advantage in expertise if the treaty collapsed at a later date.

Cost-Effectiveness. There will be additional costs incurred if remanufacturing is necessary to restore confidence in aging weapons that would have remained in the stockpile had testing been available. Although modern nuclear weapons are designed to have a shelf life of about twenty-five years, a shorter lifetime might be more appropriate under a CTB. A stable stockpile might consist of 10,000 to 20,000 weapons of 10 to 20 different types. If the weapon lifetime was twenty years, for example, 500 to 1,000 weapons would be manufactured each year, or an average of 50 weapons of each type. This rate of manufacture is well below the current capacity.[19] Assuming that an average nuclear weapon costs roughly one million dollars, this remanufacturing program would cost less than one billion dollars per year, or less than one-sixth the amount now spent on nuclear weapon research, development, testing, and production activities.[20] Most of the cost of a warhead is probably accounted for by special nuclear material, fabrication, and assembly costs.[21] Funds may also be required to assure the availability of commercially produced materials, either by subsidizing the vendor or by government production, but this should not be exorbitantly expensive.

Interchangeable Warheads.   If laboratory techniques and remanufacturing are not sufficient to restore confidence in an aged warhead, there is often an alternate warhead that could be used on the delivery vehicle. Table 3–2 lists the warheads that will constitute the U.S. strategic arsenal during the late 1980s and early 1990s. It is not usually recognized that many warheads have a natural backup already in the stockpile. Consider, for example, the ICBM force. If the new and sophisticated W87 warhead used in the Mk-21 reentry vehicle (RV) for the MX (and probably Midgetman) missile should develop serious stockpile confidence problems, then the Minuteman III W78 warhead/Mk-12A RV combination could be substituted. The MX has been successfully flight-tested with Mk-12As.[22] Even though the W78 warhead lacks the insensitive high explosive and more sophisticated fusing mechanisms of the W87, the military effectiveness of the MX would not be significantly affected by this change. The decrease in accuracy of the MX missile resulting from use of the Mk-12A warhead would probably reduce the probability of destroying hard targets by a few percent.[23] This hardly represents a fatal flaw in deterrence, unless one believes that deterrence is weak now because the MX is not yet fully deployed. Similarly, if the W78/Mk-12A failed, one could use the other Minuteman III warhead/RV, the W62/Mk-12, which is functionally identical to the W78/Mk-12A except for having only half the yield. One could even guard against undiscovered failures by initially deploying a mix of warheads on each missile type, so that the complete failure of a particular warhead would not disable an entire missile system. Note that these substitutions do not involve repackaging the warhead or subjecting the warhead to a very different stockpile-to-target sequence; therefore, nuclear testing is unnecessary.

Similar arguments can be made for the other legs of the triad. Consideration of the SLBM force is somewhat more complicated because of the anticipated reliance in the long term on a single missile — the Trident II — and the fact that details about the warhead payload have not been made public. One author speculates that 75 percent of the Trident II missiles will be armed with 8 of the new W88/Mk-5s now under development, with the remainder carrying 12 to 14 of the older W76/Mk-4s.[24] These warheads could substitute for one another, although the yield of the W76 is only about one-fifth that of the W88. Against soft targets, 14 W76s would be about 60 percent as effective as 8 W88s in causing blast damage. Against hard targets, 14 W76s would be about as effective as 8 W88s,[25] although avoiding fratricide effects would complicate targeting. One could also consider using ICBM warheads on Trident II. Since the W78 and the W87 were considered as warheads for the Trident II, it is likely that they could also substitute for the W88 (and vice-versa).[26]

In the case of the bomber force, the B61 and B83 gravity bombs would be natural substitutes for each other; if confidence lessened in one, greater reliance could be placed on the other. The short-range attack missile (SRAM), which uses the W69 warhead, is soon to be replaced by the SRAM II with a new warhead. If this new warhead develops problems, one could resort to the old warhead and missile. The same cannot be said for the cruise missiles, since both the ALCM and the new advanced cruise missile (ACM) being developed use the W80 warhead. It is likely, however, that the W84 GLCM warhead or the SRAM II warhead could be used with ALCM, since they are deployed in similar circumstances and have about the same yield as the W80.

Although many of these substitutions should be straightforward, it is conceivable that a nuclear test would be desired in some cases. This possibility should be investigated, and, if necessary, nuclear tests performed, *before* a CTB took effect. Warheads could be tested for the accelerations, vibrations, and temperature extremes that might be expected with other delivery vehicles. The delivery vehicles may have to be flight-tested with the new warheads, but a CTB does not prevent this. Such a program would undoubtedly be expensive, but it is an option for those analysts who believe that, for unforeseen reasons, remanufacture may not always work.

Super-Reliable Warheads.   Modern U.S. warheads are designed close to many technological edges: for a given task, the overall volume or mass of the weapon, or the amount of SNM in the weapon, is minimized. Many of the failures that happen during the development of a weapon occur because the yield of the primary (or fission component) is not large enough to cause the secondary (or fusion component) to ignite. Since the secondary accounts for most of the yield of a weapon, the resulting failure is nearly total. In many cases, this is overcome by adding more SNM to the primary, which increases the cost (but not necessarily the weight or size) of the warhead.

If priorities were changed so that weapon designers strove for maximum reliability instead of the most "bang for the buck," it is likely that weapons could be made more robust than is the case at present. An active program could begin before a CTB took effect to design super-reliable warheads that are as far from known technological edges as possible, are easy to remanufacture, and use the most deterioration-resistant materials available. For example, three super-reliable warheads could be designed to substitute directly for critical warheads in the stockpile: the W80 or the SRAM II warhead, the B61 or the B83, and the W87 or the W88. The super-reliable warhead need not be larger or heavier than the original, but it may cost considerably more (because of the increased use of SNM), its yield may be lower (because of the greater volume of high explosive), or it may be less safe (because of the lack of insensitive high explosive or a modest relaxation of the one-point safety criterion). The development and testing of three super-reliable weapons probably could be completed in about five years. Note that these warheads need not be stockpiled in large quantities; the designs could simply be an insurance policy against potential catastrophic failures in the regular stockpile.

If such a development program is deemed too costly, there are still many alternatives short of developing entirely new warheads. For example, each stockpiled warhead could be tested with two different types of high explosive, so that if the material of choice deteriorated, reliability could be reestablished without nuclear testing, as was the case with the W68. Alternate materials could be developed for several critical weapon components, or tests done for the effects of extreme deterioration. Experienced weapon designers could doubtless think of many other ways to prepare for a CTB, if time and money were allocated for this purpose.

Warhead Performance in Context

Weapon reliability is often stated in the most simplistic terms: either every weapon of a given type gives its full rated yield, or every weapon is a dud. Although an entire stockpile of duds could conceivably result from serious design or manufacturing errors, as happened with the W52 warhead, it is an unlikely consequence of weapon deterioration. Indeed, for two reasons, most of the deterioration problems in the past would not have resulted in a stockpile of duds. First, deterioration, which is by nature a random process, only affects a fraction of the stockpile at a given time. Only a fraction of the mechanical safing devices in the W47 and the W56 jammed; only a fraction of the W45,

W47, and W58 warheads experienced severe corrosion of the fissile material; and only a fraction of the W58 and W68 warheads experienced deterioration of the high explosive. It may take years after a problem is first spotted for a significant fraction of the stockpile to be affected, and this time can be used to formulate an acceptable solution to the problem. Second, many aging problems result in a reduced yield, not a complete failure. Corrosion resulted in only a slightly reduced yield for the W47, and an aged W45 gave half its rated yield. Many military missions can still be accomplished with a reduced yield.

Reliability.   Current levels of testing are insufficient to determine the actual reliability of a particular type of weapon with a high degree of certainty. Even if ten confidence tests were performed and all were successful, there would still be a 30 percent chance that the weapon would be less than 90 percent reliable and a 10 percent chance that it would be less than 80 percent reliable.[27] To be 95 percent sure that the weapon is at least 95 percent reliable would require nearly sixty tests, all successful. This number of tests is, of course, out of the question and has never been performed. One could argue that a small number of tests for individual weapon types is sufficient because all weapons have many things in common, but this would only be true if the failure modes of weapons due to deterioration were similar, predictable, and well understood, which is not the case.

In spite of this statistical reasoning, some weapon designers continue to insist that nuclear weapons are either 0 percent or 100 percent reliable. This may be true at the theoretical design level, but it is unlikely to be true of aging effects. The simultaneous failure of every unit in use is unheard of in commercial technologies. Imagine all blenders failing at the same time because a rubber gasket cracks or every light bulb burning out after the same amount of use. It is difficult to understand why nuclear weapons should be thought to exhibit this pattern of catastrophic failure due to aging. Indeed, it appears paradoxical for weapon designers on the one hand to claim that nuclear weapons are such delicate devices that seemingly harmless variations in the manufacturing process can have remarkable effects on weapon performance, yet on the other hand to maintain that weapons are so uniform in behavior that they all could completely fail at the same time.

Weapon designers insist that nuclear weapons should be extremely reliable — nearly 100 percent reliable — even though this very high degree of reliability is excessive when it is put in the context of the many other much greater uncertainties that exist when using nuclear forces. Consider the events that must occur to use an ICBM effectively: (1) the National Command Authority (NCA) must issue the command, (2) the command must be received by the launch crew, (3) the launch crew must execute the order, (4) the missile and its guidance system must perform correctly, and (5) the nuclear warhead must explode. The reliability of each of the first four steps is far from perfect. Missile reliability is commonly assumed to be about 75 to 90 percent.[28] No one knows what missile reliability would be during an attack, nor does anyone know what fraction of the launch crews actually would obey orders. The communications systems — including the critical satellite systems — used to transmit the order have never been tested under wartime conditions, in which nuclear weapons may be exploding at a rate of ten per second. Even the survival of the NCA is not certain. Seen in this context, a warhead reliability of, for example, 98 percent greatly exceeds reasonable system requirements. There is no logical reason to insist on such a high reliability. There should be little cause for immediate alarm if one finds that 5 or 10 percent of a given type of weapon are showing signs of deterioration. This level of unreliability has a small effect on military effectiveness, and several years are likely to elapse before uncertainties about the unreliability of the warhead overwhelm the large uncertainties in the rest of the military system. The reliability of the MX warhead could decrease by 25 percent and still have the same probability of destroying a typical silo as a Minuteman III warhead.[29] One should also remember that no single warhead design bears the whole weight of deterrence. There are currently eleven major strategic nuclear warheads spread among three classes of delivery vehicles: the SLBM force, with three warhead types and the ICBM and bomber forces, with four types each. The most numerous strategic warhead planned, the W80, will account for less than 20 percent of the total.[30]

Yield.   The uncertainties in yield measurements are typically about 5 percent, and a nuclear test generally is considered successful if the estimated yield falls within 10 percent of the predicted yield.[31] Many tests have failed to meet the predicted yield, but few tests have resulted in no yield at all, because the primary almost always detonates even though its yield may not be great enough to ignite the secondary.

Similarly, aging and deterioration problems seldom result in zero yield. In the case of the W45 warhead for the Little John missile, the stockpile confidence test gave half the rated yield. Although this was considered an awful failure by weapon scientists, the military effectiveness of the weapon would not have been seriously affected by this reduction in yield.

Consider the effect that reductions in yield have on the probability of destroying hardened military targets such as missile silos or command bunkers. The probability that the target will be destroyed depends mainly on four variables: the yield and accuracy of the weapon, the hardness of the target, and the combined reliability of the command, missile, guidance, and warhead systems. A simplified equation for the probability of kill is given by

$$P_k = R\{1 - 2^{-(EY/CEP^3H)^{2/3}}\}$$

where Y is the yield in megatons (Mt), CEP the circle of equal probability in nautical miles (nmi), H is the hardness in pounds per square inch (psi), R is the system reliability, and E is a constant that determines the overpressure at a given distance from the explosion; for surface bursts and high overpressures, E is about 16.4 nmi³psi/Mt.[32] If more than one weapon is used against the target, then the probability of kill is

$$P_k(n) = 1 - [1 - P_k]^n$$

where n is the number of weapons. (This equation assumes that the warheads are delivered by different missiles, that their reliabilities are independent, and that there are no fratricide effects.)

Figure 3–1 shows the decrease in the kill probability as a function of warhead yield for a two-on-one attack of MX and Minuteman missile warheads against a target hardened to 2,000 psi (a typical silo). The MX is assumed to have a CEP of 0.05 nmi and a yield of 300 kilotons, and Minuteman to have a CEP of 0.1 nmi and a yield of 335 kilotons.[33] Both missiles are assumed to be 85 percent reliable. Note that decreases in yield have very little effect on the kill probability of the MX. Even if the yield of the MX warhead drops by 85 percent, the kill probability would be the same as that of Minuteman III. The results for the Midgetman and Trident II missiles should be similar to those for the MX, since they are expected to have approximately the same yield and accuracy. Unless one is prepared to argue that counterforce capability on the order of that provided by the MX, and not much less, is essential for deterrence, then even large ($<50\%$) yield

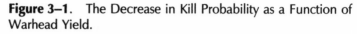

Figure 3–1. The Decrease in Kill Probability as a Function of Warhead Yield.

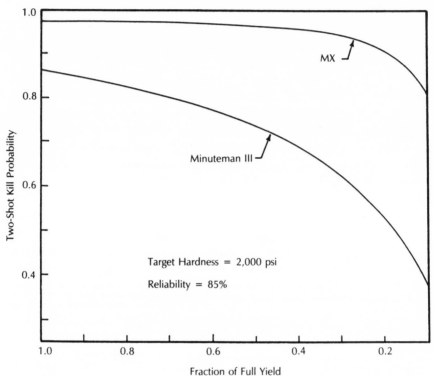

Fraction of Full Yield

reductions do not matter for accurate warheads (CEP < 0.05 nmi) on hard targets (H < 10,000 psi).

Modest increases in accuracy and overall system reliability can compensate for decreases in yield. For example, a 21 percent decrease in CEP or a 4 percent increase in system reliability would compensate for a 50 percent reduction in the yield of the MX warhead. If the weapon yield were only one tenth of its expected value, this could be offset by halving the CEP. Another consideration is "bias," or the possibility that the actual wartime flights of ballistic missile RVs might be deflected from their targets because of unanticipated systematic errors. Former Secretary of Defense James Schlesinger stated that abias of 0.1 to 0.2 nmi might be possible for the Minuteman III system;[34] if this is true, then reducing the bias by half would compensate for a 20 to 60 percent reduction in yield of that system.[35]

Stockpile confidence problems caused by aging may simply result in a greater uncertainty about yield, rather than a certainty of reduction. Figure 3–2 shows the increase in the relative uncertainty in the kill probability as a function of the relative uncertainty in weapon yield for the MX and Minuteman III systems. Note that uncertainties in yield have no effect on the uncertainty in kill probability for the MX and that large yield uncertainties can be tolerated for the Minuteman III. For example, increasing yield uncertainties from 10 to 50 percent increases the uncertainty in kill probability by only 0.3 to 1 percent for MX and 10 to 39 percent for Minuteman, depending on the size of uncertainties in yield, CEP, hardness, overpressure, and reliability.

There is already great doubt that some missions — such as destroying a large percentage of an opponent's ICBM force — could be carried out at all, and absolute reductions in yield or increases in uncertainty about yield are unlikely to change that situation much. Many aging problems would result in a probable reduction in yield or increased yield uncertainty, but they would not result in a total weapon failure. For attacks against moderately hard targets with accurate warheads, yield reductions of at least 50 percent could be tolerated. Moreover, the uncertainty in the yield could be many times greater than that allowed now, without significantly increasing the uncertainty in the kill probability.

For attacks against urban-industrial targets, yields reduced by 95 percent would still cause tremendous devastation. Although many people find countervalue attacks repugnant or implausible since they would invite a similar response, the possibility of such attacks is the foundation of virtually all formulations of deterrence. A force of only 1,000 strategic warheads (7 percent of the current force) each with a reliability of only 10 percent and a yield of only 10 kilotons (1 to 10 percent of current strategic warhead yields), if used in such a manner as to maximize deaths, could kill at least ten million people.[36] "Before, however, we become too bemused with megatons and multimegatons," Bradbury said in testimony to Congress in 1963, "I would urge one to look again at the pictures of Hiroshima and Nagasaki in 1945 after 15 or 20 kilotons — kilotons, not megatons."[37]

Figure 3–2. The Increase in the Relative Uncertainty in the Kill Probability as a Function of Yield Uncertainty.[a]

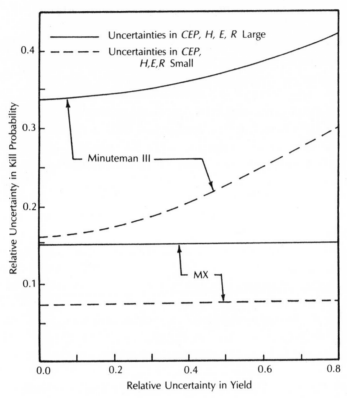

a. The uncertainty in kill probability, σ_P, is given by

$$\sigma_P^2 = \sigma_R^2(\partial P/\partial R)^2 + \sigma_C^2(\partial P/\partial C)^2 + \sigma_H^2(\partial P/\partial H)^2 + \sigma_Y^2(\partial P/\partial Y)^2 + \sigma_E^2(\partial P/\partial E)^2$$

where σ_R, σ_C, σ_H, σ_Y and σ_E are the uncertainties in reliability, CEP, hardness, yield, and overpressure. Substituting for $(\partial P/\partial R)$, $(\partial P/\partial C)$, $(\partial P/\partial H)$, $(\partial P/\partial Y)$ and $(\partial P/\partial E)$, which are the partial derivatives of the equation for the kill probability with respect to reliability, CEP, hardness, yield, and overpressure, we have

$$\delta_P = aR\{9\delta_C^2 + \delta_H^2 + \delta_Y^2 + \delta_E^2 + [(1 - e^f)/a]^2\delta_R^2\}^{1/2}$$

where δ_P, δ_C, δ_H, δ_Y, δ_E, and δ_R are the fractional uncertainties in kill probability, CEP, hardness, yield, overpressure, and reliability, and $a = 2fe^f/3$, where $f = -ln(2)\,(EY/H)^{2/3}\,CEP^{-2}$. Using the value of E given in the text and assuming a target hardness of 2,000 psi gives $a = 0.022$ for the MX ($Y = 0.30$ Mt, $CEP = 0.05$ nmi) and $a = 0.31$ for the Minuteman III ($Y = 0.34$ Mt, $CEP = 0.10$ nmi). The reliability is given by $R = R_cR_mR_w$, where R_c is the reliability of the C^3 system, R_m is the reliability of the missile, and R_w is the reliability of the warhead. The uncertainty in the reliability is given by $\delta_R = (\delta_{R_c}^2 + \delta_{R_m}^2 + \delta_{R_w}^2)^{1/2}$.

For the curve labeled "other uncertainties small," $\delta_C = 0.1$, $\delta_H = 0.2$, $\delta_E = 0.2$, $R_c = R_m = 0.95$, $R_w = 0.98$, $\delta_{R_c} = \delta_{R_m} = 0.05$, and $\delta_{R_w} = 0.02$; for the curve labeled "other uncertainties large," $\delta_C = 0.2$, $\delta_H = 0.4$, $\delta_E = 0.5$, $\delta_R = 0.15$, $R_c = R_m = 0.90$, $R_w = 0.98$, $\delta_{R_c} = \delta_{R_m} = 0.10$, and $\delta_{R_w} = 0.02$. The fractional uncertainty in kill probability for two RVs/target is equal to $\delta_P(1 - P)/(1 - P/2)$.

IS DECREASED CONFIDENCE GOOD OR BAD?

The degree of confidence required in the stockpile depends on how one plans to use nuclear weapons. Advocates of limited nuclear use, escalation dominance, and the extended, war-fighting, or war-winning variants of deterrence demand more confidence in the stockpile than those who espouse minimum deterrence, simply because they envision that nuclear weapons may actually be used at some future date to achieve a rational goal of national policy. In this view, demonstrations of military might, such as nuclear tests, are also essential to maintain the psychology of deterrence — that is, to make the opponent fearful that nuclear weapons would be used in a conflict, thus deterring actions that might lead to conflict in the first place. Advocates of minimum deterrence, on the other hand, generally feel that the destructiveness of nuclear weapons is so great and that control over their use during war is so difficult that their use can serve no rational goal. They also feel that brandishing weapons is more likely to provoke hostility than to deter conflict. If the specter of turning Washington or Moscow into a radiating ruin is sufficient for deterrence, then deliberations about stockpile confidence are mostly irrelevant. This section makes some general observations about stockpile confidence without attempting to take sides on the more fundamental issue of what deterrence is all about.

Gradual Erosion of Confidence

Many analysts talk about a decline in stockpile confidence in much the same way as they would talk about a decline in reliability: a gradual erosion that takes place over years or decades. But there are many reasons for believing that no matter what happened to warhead reliability, confidence would remain high until a case of serious unreliability was discovered, after which confidence would plummet. A catastrophic decline in confidence has happened several times with other technologies. For the sake of argument, however, let us first assume that a gradual decline is possible. Estimates of warhead reliability might decline from essentially 100 percent to, say, 90 percent, then 80 percent, then 70 percent, and so forth, over a number of years. What effect would this gradual erosion of confidence have on deterrence, crisis stability, and arms race stability?

At one extreme are those analysts who argue that a gradual decline in confidence would threaten the very foundation of U.S. nuclear strategy, since the United States depends on nuclear weapons for more than simple deterrence. They argue, for example, that declining confidence would weaken extended deterrence because it would reduce the credibility of nuclear use in situations short of general nuclear war. As the credibility of nuclear use diminishes, both countries may be more likely to escalate crises or engage in conventional warfare. This, in turn, may raise the risks of nuclear war, as the losing conventional forces turn to nuclear weapons. Although there is some truth to this argument, it is overstated, for it assumes that the current arsenals — and not much less — are required to deter a Soviet attack on Europe. This argument also ignores the fact that battlefield nuclear weapons are important primarily because they raise the probability of strategic nuclear war, not because they could achieve a tactical goal.[38] Tactical nuclear weapons much less reliable than current forces are sufficient to pose the risk of escalation, and strategic weapons much less reliable than current forces are sufficient to pose the risk of devastating retaliation. It is difficult to believe that nuclear deterrence is so fragile that a gradual loss of stockpile confidence would make either country more willing to start a large conventional war or less determined to avoid a nuclear war.

Related to this argument is the concern that declining stockpile confidence would weaken the security guaranties of allies and compel each to strengthen its own forces, conventional or nuclear. This is less than convincing. How could other countries know more about the U.S. stockpile than the United States would know? The United States simply would not allow the stockpile to deteriorate to such an extent that it would worry allies or embolden other countries; corrective action would be taken long before this point was reached. Furthermore, it is highly unlikely that the stockpiles of the superpowers would degrade so much that the significance of the arsenals of a third party would increase markedly as a result.

In regard to arms race stability, the superpowers might increase the size of their nuclear arsenals in the wake of a CTB to compensate for a perceived decrease in the reliability of their weapons. Although this would be a temptation, vertical proliferation could be constrained by limiting the numbers of weapons with SALT- or START-like treaties, which most CTB proponents hope would accompany (and many feel must precede) a CTBT. Even if these efforts failed and the number of warheads did increase, this would not necessarily lead to arms race instability or a higher risk of war. Many observers feel that the increasing military effectiveness of new weapon systems, which continued nuclear testing makes possible, creates a greater danger in the arms race than an increase in the number of weapons per se.

At the other extreme are those analysts who try to make declining confidence into a virtue. The main argument here is that declining U.S. stockpile confidence would reduce the incentives for the United States to launch a preemptive strike during a crisis, since it would make a successful first strike more difficult to achieve. Similarly, crisis stability would be enhanced if Soviet confidence in their stockpile eroded. Ironically, a similar argument is made by members of the Reagan administration regarding the Strategic Defense Initiative (SDI): even a partially effective defense would be desirable because it would hopelessly complicate a first strike. The main difference is that with a CTB the uncertainties would be accepted voluntarily, and no arms race or countermeasures (short of violating or abrogating the treaty) could change the symmetry of the situation, but with SDI the uncertainties would be forced on the other side, and a race for countermeasures could quickly alter the situation. Moreover, while an opposing defense may create anxiety about the effectiveness of a second-strike force, it is difficult to see how modest decreases in warhead reliability would have this effect.

Even if the argument in favor of decreasing confidence is technically sound, it would be unwise from the standpoint of U.S. domestic politics to stress this point. A CTB is only possible with the support (or at least without the organized opposition) of the military, which is unlikely to be convinced that unreliable equipment is somehow better than reliable equipment. Nevertheless, there is an important connection between decreasing stockpile confidence and the goals of a CTB that should not be missed: the less confident one is that nuclear weaponry will work as predicted, the less one will depend on it for limited military objectives; and the less confident one is in the design of new weapons, the less valuable new weapons become. Most CTB proponents *want* the superpowers to become less dependent on nuclear weapons for keeping the peace. Whether decreased reliance on nuclear weapons will enhance or degrade the national security or make war more or less likely is, of course, debatable.

Some strategists argue that the Soviet Union would have more stockpile confidence than the United States has, even if the Soviet Union did not cheat. If this is true, some of the effects of confidence erosion would not be felt by the Soviet Union, which might leave the United States at a relative disadvantage. It has often been pointed out that the Soviets are more cautious and conservative in developing technologies than Americans. Their designs tend to advance in an evolutionary way, rather than by exploiting the latest improvements in technology. Supported by evidence that the yield-to-weight ratio of Soviet weapons is less than that of U.S. weapons[39] (which can permit more robust designs), some analysts have argued that their designs would be more reliable under a CTB. Still, the stability of deterrence rests largely on perceptions. If the Soviets do not design near the technological edge, it is probably due to a simple lack of confidence, not to a conscious desire to build super-reliable warheads. The Soviet Union, respecting the technological prowess of the United States, may fear that U.S. designs are more reliable than Soviet designs. This is the case in satellite technology, where the Soviets, for all their technological caution and lack of sophistication, still have equipment that is far less reliable.

Catastrophic Weapon Failure

Suppose that the worst happened: an ingredient in the arsenal that was judged to be essential for deterrence deteriorated, and nothing short of nuclear testing could make it right again. The weapon had been diagnosed to have a reliability or yield insufficient to achieve its military mission. Laboratory testing and computer modeling were unable to support an adequate modification that could be trusted without testing. Remanufacturing was for some reason problematic. An acceptable substitute could not be found, or the substitute experienced reliability problems as well. A super-reliable replacement warhead was not designed. What would happen then?

Theoretically, deterrence would only be harmed if the Soviet Union shared the United States' perception that the stockpile was unreliable. But how could the Soviets ever be sure that American confidence in the U.S. stockpile had really declined? Laboratory directors might testify before Congress to this effect, but would the Soviets believe it?

Or would the Soviets fear that it was merely a ploy to resume testing? Even if they were sure that American confidence had declined, how could they know that the actual reliability of the weapons had decreased, when even Americans would not know this for sure? Furthermore, how could the Soviets extract any military or political benefit from an American lack of confidence?

No matter what the Soviets thought, and no matter what the theoretical implications for the stability of deterrence, the hysteria about a "confidence gap" *would* adversely affect the American-Soviet relationship. If the Joint Chiefs of Staff joined with the weapon laboratories in stating that the deterrent force was crippled, the president would be under tremendous pressure to withdraw from the treaty. Even though a CTBT would almost certainly contain an escape clause that allowed a party to withdraw if its vital interests were threatened, the political ramifications of abrogation would be enormous.

The adverse consequences of a confidence gap are great, but the risk depends on the probability that the scenario will occur, which the foregoing analysis suggests is small. To demonstrate how unlikely this scenario is, let us assign hypothetical probabilities to each failure that must occur before a catastrophic failure results. Based on the past thirty years' experience, the probability that a warhead (i.e., one that has been in the stockpile for a few years before the start of a CTB) will experience a serious deterioration problem (i.e., one that would result in an ineffective weapon) is about 10 percent.[40] The probability that the problem could not be resolved without nuclear testing might be 25 to 50 percent.[41] For the sake of argument, assume a 10 to 20 percent probability that remanufacturing the warhead is for some reason difficult or impossible. The likelihood that a suitable substitute could not be found or that the substitute would fail as well, might be 10 to 20 percent.[42] Also assume that the United States has not been prudent enough to design a super-reliable warhead or to test substitutes for the deteriorating component. Using these conservative assumptions, the probability that one of the eight critical strategic warheads (B61, W76, W78, W80, B83, W87, W88, and SRAM II) would experience a problem during a twenty- to thirty-year period that could not be resolved without nuclear testing is no more than 1 percent. If two warhead types must fail catastrophically for a crisis of confidence to occur, then the odds would be very much smaller. To be a net advantage to the United States, the advantages of a CTB must outweigh this small risk.[43]

NUCLEAR TEST QUOTA: A SOLUTION TO THE CONFIDENCE PROBLEM?

As a final measure to remove even the small risk of catastrophic failure, one could allow infrequent proof-tests of stockpiled weapons. One test every year or two might be enough for stockpile confidence, but not for significant modernization. Even if every allowed test were used for the development of new nuclear weapons instead of for the proof-testing of old weapons, this low rate of testing would greatly increase the time necessary to develop a new and significantly different type of weapon, which requires about ten tests. Exotic nuclear weapons such as the X-ray laser would require many more than ten tests before even a development decision could be made. Thus, insurance against the small risk of catastrophic failure might be gained while still constraining modernization.

There is one glaring technical problem with a test quota: how does one know how many weapons have been exploded during a single event? It has usually been assumed that multiple explosions would be permitted under a test quota treaty, but this could allow modernization. If, for example, the total yield of the allowed event was 150 kilotons, then ten 15-kt devices could be detonated simultaneously, thus allowing the development of new nuclear weapons. Weapon development would be more awkward than is now the case, as one could not simply iterate the process of testing and modification until the final design is derived. One would instead have to try many different ideas at once, pick the one that worked best, and try several modifications of that design next year. In this way, it should be possible, though awkward and slow, to develop even advanced weapons such as an X-ray laser, since several directed-energy experiments can be done with a single nuclear test.

One solution to this problem might be to lower the maximum yield of such tests to the lowest yield consistent with verifying stockpile reliability. Since the primary is the most unreliable part of a nuclear weapon, this maximum yield might be about 15 kilotons.[44] Muffling the seismic signals to allow greater yields could be prevented by allowing on-site inspection of the test, such as is specified in the Peaceful Nuclear Explosion Treaty (PNET). The number of devices being tested might be determined without gathering sensitive data. A treaty of this kind would be at least as detailed as the PNET, which took eighteen months of intense negotiations to conclude.

SUMMARY

Although there are valid reasons for worrying about the reliability of the nuclear stockpile under a CTB, there are many methods other than nuclear testing by which the confidence of those people responsible for the stockpile can be maintained. Regular inspections would provide assurance that problems do not exist. If a weapon is found to have deteriorated, extensive laboratory techniques and computer simulations can assess the consequences of the problem and possibly suggest minor modifications. If this is not satisfactory, and if the weapon has enjoyed a reasonably long lifetime, the weapon can simply be remanufactured to its original specifications. If this proves difficult, adequate substitutes exist for most warheads. Super-reliable warheads could be designed and tested before a CTBT is negotiated as an insurance policy against catastrophic failures. Lastly, stockpile problems resulting in reduced weapon reliability or yield, or increased uncertainty in the reliability or yield, may not significantly affect the military effectiveness of the weapon system or of the strategic deterrent as a whole.

If estimates of weapon reliability decrease only slowly, this does not appear to harm deterrence, crisis stability, or arms race stability. If the Soviet Union abided by the treaty, there is no reason that significant asymmetries would develop. But if the United States were to suffer a catastrophic failure of a critical weapon system, the president would be under great pressure to withdraw from the treaty—an action which would have enormous domestic and foreign policy implications. Fortunately, the probability of a catastrophic failure is very small, but it is a danger that must weigh in the balance between the risks and benefits of a CTBT. Allowing one 15-kt test every one or two years would nearly remove this risk, but at the expense of making the test ban less than comprehensive and sacrificing some of the political rationale for a test ban.

To date, the nuclear weapon establishment in the United States has been far more imaginative about the problems a CTB might pose than about possible solutions to these problems. This seems to be changing somewhat, since in 1982 the military characteristics (MCs) or specifications for nuclear warheads were expanded to include maximizing warhead lifetime, maximizing the ability to replicate the warhead at a future date, and maximizing the ability to incorporate the warhead into other delivery systems.[45] Even though these developments are reassuring, one might legitimately ask why these considerations were not included during the more than two decades this country held a CTB as a goal of national policy, and why they are not accorded a higher priority now. If stockpile confidence is a real concern of weapon designers, a vigorous program to solve these problems should be started well before a CTB is negotiated. Since the Reagan administration maintains that a CTB is a long-term goal, now would be an especially appropriate time to begin planning for one.

NOTES

1. Paul S. Brown, "Nuclear Weapon R&D and the Role of Nuclear Testing," *Energy and Technology Review*, September 1986, p. 13.
2. York has felt that the opposite is more likely. Herbert F. York, letter to Norris Bradbury, Richard Garwin, and J. Carson Mark, 21 September 1978.
3. See letter to President Jimmy Carter from Norris Bradbury, Richard Garwin, and Carson Mark, 15 August 1978, in House Armed Services Committee Report No. 95–89, "Effects of a Comprehensive Test Ban Treaty on United States National Security Interests," 14, 15 August 1978, Appendix 3, p. 181. Also see letter to Representative Dante Fascell from Hans Bethe, Norris Bradbury, Richard Garwin, Spurgeon M. Keeney, Jr., Wolfgang Panofsky, George Rathjens, Herbert Scoville, Jr., and Paul Warnke, 14 May 1985, and letter to Representative Henry J. Hyde from Roger E. Batzel and Donald M. Kerr, 7 June 1985, in Hugh E. DeWitt and Gerald E. Marsh, "Weapon Design Policy Impedes Test Ban," *Bulletin of the Atomic Scientists* 41, no. 10 (November 1985): 11–13. For Harold Agnew's views, see interview in *Los Alamos Science* 152 (Summer/Fall 1981): 152. The position of Herbert York, as expressed in his letter to Norris Bradbury, Richard Garwin, and J. Carson Mark, 21 September 1978, is somewhat more complicated. York believes that reliability can be maintained, but doubts that the current leadership of the nuclear establishment could maintain confidence in this reliability. He therefore suggests beginning with a nuclear test quota treaty allowing no more than two tests per year yielding no more than 10 kilotons to settle the nerves of the leadership.
4. Paul S. Brown, "Nuclear Weapons R&D and the Role of Nuclear Testing" (paper for American Physical Society meeting, San Francisco, Calif., 28 January 1987).
5. J.W. Rosengren, "Some Little-Publicized Difficulties With a Nuclear Freeze," RDA-TR-122116-001 (Arlington, Va.: R&D Associates, October 1983).
6. Details about problems with the W45, the W47, the W52, the W56, the W58, and the W68 have been brought out in the on-going debate between Jack Rosengren and Ray Kidder. See J.W. Rosengren, "Some Little-Publicized Difficulties"; Ray E. Kidder, "Evaluation of the 1983 Rosengren Report from the Standpoint of a Comprehensive Test Ban," UCID-20804 (Livermore, Calif.: Lawrence Livermore National Laboratory, June 1986); Jack W. Rosengren, "Stockpile Reliability and Nuclear Test Bans: A Reply to a Critic's Comments," RDA-TR-138522-001 (Arlington, Va.: R&D Associates, November 1986); and Ray E. Kidder, "Stockpile Reliability and Nuclear Test Bans: Response to J.W. Rosengren's Defense of His 1983 Report," UCID-20990 (Livermore, Calif.: Lawrence Livermore National Laboratory, February 1983). Also see George H. Miller, Paul S. Brown, Carol T. Alonso, "Report to Congress on Stockpile Reliability, Weapon Remanufacture,

and the Role of Nuclear Testing," UCRL-53822 (Livermore, Calif.: Lawrence Livermore National Laboratory, October 1987); R.E. Kidder, "Maintaining the U.S. Stockpile of Nuclear Weapons During a Low-Threshold or Comprehensive Test Ban," UCRL-53820 (Livermore, Calif.: Lawrence Livermore National Laboratory, October 1987); and Brown, "Nuclear Weapon R&D," pp. 13–14.

7. The formal definition of one-point safety requires that "in the event of a detonation initiated at any one point in the high-explosive system, the probability of achieving a nuclear yield greater than 4 pounds of TNT equivalent shall not exceed one in one million." Thomas B. Cochran, William M. Arkin, and Milton M. Hoenig, *Nuclear Weapons Databook*, vol. I: *U.S. Nuclear Forces and Capabilities*, (Cambridge, Mass.: Ballinger Publishing Company, 1984), p. 67.

8. Miller, et al. "Report to Congress," p. 21.

9. Robert S. Norris, Thomas B. Cochran, and William M. Arkin, "Known U.S. Nuclear Tests: July 1945 to 16 October 1986," Nuclear Weapons Databook Working Paper 86-2 (Washington, D.C.: Natural Resources Defense Council, October 1986), p. 10.

10. Ibid., p. 11.

11. Robert N. Thorn and Donald R. Westervelt, "Hydronuclear Experiments," LA-10902-MS (Los Alamos: Los Alamos National Laboratory, February 1987).

12. Paul S. Brown, Lawrence Livermore National Laboratory, personal communication, 13 October 1986.

13. Letter from Batzel and Kerr in DeWitt and Marsh, "Weapon Design Policy," pp. 12–13. Also see letter from Frank J. Gaffney to Representative Edward J. Markey, 21 January 1986, in Hugh E. DeWitt and Gerald E. Marsh, "An Update on the Test Ban," *Bulletin of the Atomic Scientists* 42, no. 4 (April 1986): 10–12.

14. William H. Hubbell, Jr., "The Weaponization Program," *Energy and Technology Review*, September 1986, p. 33.

15. Admiral Sylvester R. Foley, responses to questions for *Department of Energy Budget Hearing before the Subcommittee on Procurement and Military Nuclear Systems, Armed Services Committee*, U.S. House of Representatives, 19 February 1986.

16. Roger Batzel, letter to Admiral Sylvester R. Foley, Jr., 22 July 1986.

17. Ivo H. Daalder, "The Limited Test Ban Treaty," in Albert Carnesale and Richard N. Haass, eds., *Superpower Arms Control: Setting the Record Straight* (Cambridge, Mass.: Ballinger Publishing Company, 1987). See also, in the same book, Sean M. Lynn-Jones, "Lulling and Stimulating Effects of Arms Control."

18. U.S. Congress, Senate, Committee on Foreign Relations, *Nuclear Test Ban Treaty, Hearings on Executive M*, 88th Cong., 1st sess., 1963, "Letter to Senator Russell from the Chairman of the Joint Chiefs of Staff re: safeguards recommended by the JCS," p. 982.

19. Thomas B. Cochran, William M. Arkin, Robert S. Norris, and Milton M. Hoenig, *Nuclear Weapons Databook*, vol. II: *U.S. Nuclear Warhead Production* (Cambridge, Mass: Ballinger Publishing Company, 1987), p. 12.

20. Nuclear warheads cost 10 to 15 percent of total system costs (Brown, "Nuclear Weapon R&D," p. 7). Total system costs per deployed warhead (in current dollars) range from $6 million for Minuteman III to $13 million for Trident (Cochran, et al., *U.S. Nuclear Forces*, pp. 119–40). The projected 1987 expenditures for weapon research, development, testing, and production are $4.4 billion, and another $2.6 billion will be spent on weapon materials production and waste management. Cochran, et al., *U.S. Nuclear Warhead Production*, p. 21.

21. There are also "virtual costs" of remanufacture, because the same money could have bought more effective, custom-designed warheads for new delivery vehicles. From the viewpoint of CTB proponents, however, this is one of the main

advantages of a test ban: to the degree that nuclear testing is important in developing "more effective" (i.e., counterforce) weapons, a ban on testing would have a stabilizing effect on the arms race in general.

22. William M. Arkin, Andrew S. Burrows, Richard W. Fieldhouse, Thomas B. Cochran, Robert S. Norris, and Jeffrey I. Sands, "Nuclear Weapons," in Frank Blackaby, ed., *World Armaments and Disarmament: SIPRI Yearbook 1985*, (London: Taylor and Francis, 1985), p. 45.

23. The accuracy of ballistic missile reentry vehicles is primarily determined by the inertial guidance system of the missile, the fusing system of the RV, and the aerodynamic properties of the RV. The Mk-21 and Mk-12A RVs have slightly different aerodynamic properties, arising from differences in the ballistic coefficient (a measure of atmospheric drag) and the symmetry of the ablation of the RV. A discussion of guidance errors is found in Matthew Bunn, "Technology of Ballistic Missile Reentry Vehicles," in Kosta Tsipis and Penny Janeway, eds., *Review of U.S. Military Research and Development: 1984* (Washington, D.C.: Pergamon-Brassey's, 1984), pp. 67–116. Inertial guidance errors limit the CEP to no less than about 30 meters (D.G. Hoag, "Ballistic-missile Guidance," in B.T. Feld, T. Greenwood, G.W. Rathjens, and S. Weinberg, eds., *Impact of New Technologies on the Arms Race* [Cambridge, Mass.: MIT Press, 1971], p. 81). Assuming that this has been achieved in the guidance system of the MX missile and that the CEP of the MX is about 100 meters, the CEP due only to reentry errors would be 95 meters (the total error is the square root of the sum of the squares of the individual errors). Assuming a ballistic coefficient of 3,000 lb/ft^2 for the Mk-21 and 2,200 lb/ft^2 for the Mk-12A (Matthew Bunn, "U.S. Ballistic Missile Reentry Vehicles: A Research Note," unpublished, August 1986), then, according to the figure on page 71 of Bunn, the reentry error of the Mk-12A is about 1.3 times greater than that of the Mk-21. The CEP of the MX using the Mk-12A would therefore be roughly 25 meters greater than when using the Mk-21. Assuming a 300-kt yield for the Mk-21 and a 335-kt yield for the Mk-12A, the probability of destroying a target hardened to 2,000 psi would be decreased by about 5 percent by using the Mk-12A instead of the Mk-21 on the MX. Even if the CEP was 40 meters greater, the kill probability would be decreased by 9 percent, although the decrease would only be 3 percent for a two-on-one attack, assuming a reliability of 85 percent. The accuracy of the Mk-12A probably could be improved by using advanced fusing and nose-tip technology developed for the Mk-21.

24. Robert S. Norris, "Counterforce at Sea: The Trident II Missile," *Arms Control Today* 15, no. 7 (September 1985): p. 7.

25. Reentry errors for SLBMs RVs are less than for ICBMs RVs due to the greater angle of reentry. Even if the W76/Mk-4 had a CEP 15 percent greater than the W88/Mk-5, the hard-target-kill capability of the two systems would be equal, assuming 14 W76s with 100-kt yield, 8 W88s with 475-kt yield and a CEP of 100 meters, a Trident II missile reliability of 85 percent, and a target hardness of 2,000 psi.

26. Cochran, et al., *U.S. Nuclear Forces*, p. 145.

27. The probability of m successes out of n tests of a weapon with reliability r is $C_{n,m} r^m (1 - r)^{n-m}$ where $C_{n,m} = n![m!(n - m)!]^{-1}$. If all the tests are successful ($m = n$) and all reliabilities have the same a priori probability, then the probability P that $r \geq R$ is $(1 - R^{n+1})$, and the number of tests required for given values of P and R is $\log(1 - P)/\log(R) - 1$. Weapon designers implicitly assume a very low a priori probability for values of the reliability other than zero or one, so for them a single test is enough to tell whether a warhead type is perfect or a dud. The reason most often given for this assumption is that warhead performance is highly

nonlinear (i.e., small changes in a certain parameter can induce large changes in yield). But since modern warheads are designed close to the technological edge, and since the variations induced by aging are random and are often in the parameter space where the yield varies rapidly, a reliability between zero and one is quite possible. The only way to find out for sure is to test.

28. Some analysts argue that warhead reliability is more important than missile reliability because launch failures can be instantly compensated for, while weapon failures cannot. In fact, retargeting reserve missiles to execute the attack plans of launch failures is a time-consuming process. In principle, one could compensate for weapon (or guidance) failures by having the warhead radio back that the mission was a success (see Richard Garwin, "Bombs that Squeak: Nuclear Explosion Location During Nuclear War," unpublished, November 1981) or by monitoring the targets with nuclear-burst-detection systems aboard satellites.

29. Assume here that the MX has a yield of 300 kilotons and a CEP of 0.05 nmi and Minuteman III has a yield of 335 kilotons and a CEP of 0.10 nmi (Cochran, et al., *U.S. Nuclear Forces*, pp. 116–21) and that both are used against a target hardened to 2,000 psi (a typical silo). If the target is twice as hard, then the MX reliability can be reduced by 40 percent; if only half as hard, then by 12 percent.

30. The number of ALCMs and ACMs planned is 3,150. The total number of strategic weapons is about 16,000. Robert S. Norris and William M. Arkin, "Nuclear Notebook," *Bulletin of the Atomic Scientists* 43, no. 5 (June 1987): 56.

31. Paul S. Brown, personal communication.

32. Kosta Tsipis, *Arsenal: Understanding Weapons in the Nuclear Age* (New York: Simon and Schuster, 1983), pp. 305–308. More complicated formulae take into account the height of the burst and the fact that the hardness of hard structures is better described by the maximum impulse they can withstand rather than the maximum overpressure, but these differences are small for the examples given in the text.

33. Cochran, et al., *U.S. Nuclear Forces*, p. 75, 118, 121, 126.

34. In testimony before the Arms Control Subcommittee of the Senate Foreign Relations Committee on 4 March 1974, Schlesinger gave examples of 0.1 to 0.2 nmi for the Minuteman missile, which is 100 to 200 percent of the CEP. Quoted in Matthew Bunn and Kosta Tsipis, "Ballistic Missile Guidance and Technical Uncertainties of Countersilo Attacks," PSTIS Report No. 9 (Cambridge, Mass.: Program in Science and Technology for International Security, Massachusetts Institute of Technology, August 1983), p. 66.

35. The effect of bias is calculated from data in Bunn and Tsipis, "Ballistic Missile Guidance," p. 63.

36. The bomb dropped on Hiroshima had a yield of 12.5 kilotons (Cochran, et al., *U.S. Nuclear Forces*, p. 32) and an effective lethal area of 8.5 km² (Samuel Glasstone and Philip J. Dolan, eds., *The Effects of Nuclear Weapons* [Washington, D.C.: Department of Defense and U.S. Department of Energy, 1977], p. 544). For comparison, about 7.2 million people live in the city of New York, which has a land area of 786 km². The use of 100 10-kt warheads to destroy the most densely populated areas in the United States would result in at least 10 million deaths.

37. U.S. Congress, *Nuclear Test Ban Treaty*, p. 580.

38. Thomas C. Schelling, *Arms and Influence* (Yale: Yale University Press, 1966), pp. 107–116.

39. Lynn R. Sykes and Dan M. Davis, "The Yields of Soviet Strategic Weapons," *Scientific American* 256, no. 1 (January 1987): 29–37.

40. As mentioned earlier, most of the past stockpile problems resulted from design flaws that were detected within a year or two of first warhead production. By relying on warheads that were first produced five years before the start of a CTB,

these problems would be substantially eliminated. Only five of the warheads listed in Table 3–1 experienced aging and deterioration problems: the W45, the W47, the W56, the W58 and the W68. This represents 12 percent of the 41 warheads deployed since the moratorium. The problem rate in newer warheads can be expected to be lower, since the mechanical safing devices and materials-compatibility problems so troublesome in the past have been eliminated.

41. Seventy-five percent of past stockpile problems used nuclear tests for their resolution, but many of these problems were design flaws (see note 40). Four of the eight warhead aging problems described here (50 percent) were resolved without nuclear tests. If nuclear testing had not been available, a greater fraction of these problems would have been resolved without testing. Specifically, it is likely that the W68 would have been accepted as reliable without further tests, and it is also likely that with additional time and effort a nonnuclear solution to the mechanical safing problem would have been formulated.

42. Some CTBT opponents are very skeptical of remanufacture and feel that the probability that it would not work would be much higher (e.g., 50 percent instead of the 10 to 20 percent assumed here). On the other hand, the probability that a substitute would not work may be much lower than the 10 to 20 percent given here, especially since no cases where a substitute is unavailable for a strategic warhead have been identified. The probabilities used in the text are for illustrative purposes only, but I do not believe that they underestimate the likelihood of a catastrophic failure.

43. This simple analysis ignores common-mode failures (i.e., one problem that would affect several warhead designs at once), but very little can be said about this without a detailed examination of specific warhead design features, which is beyond the scope of this book.

44. Frank von Hippel, Harold A. Feiveson, and Christopher E. Paine, "A Low-Threshold Nuclear Test Ban," *International Security* 12, no. 2 (Fall 1987): 135–51.

45. Brown, "Nuclear Weapons R&D," p. 8.

4 VERIFICATION

Verification has been the most contentious technical issue of the test ban debate. Difficulties with verification ostensibly were responsible for the failure of the Eisenhower and Kennedy administrations to negotiate a CTBT, despite their strong support for a test ban. The principal reason for the first official meeting between the United States and the Soviet Union on a possible test ban (the Conference of Experts in 1958) was to study the issue of verification. At that time, it was assumed (perhaps naively) that if this issue could be resolved, a test ban would be achieved quickly. The Conference of Experts concluded that above-ground explosions greater than 1 kiloton could be monitored effectively. It also concluded that underground explosions greater than 5 kilotons could be detected and identified reliably, but new data on underground tests and theories on how verification might be made less efficient cast doubt on this conclusion. President Kennedy decided to adapt the treaty to these concerns by banning only those explosions that were considered to be adequately verifiable. Verification continues to play a role as a reason—and some people would say as an excuse—for failing to pursue negotiations to ban all nuclear tests or even to limit further the yield of permitted tests.

THE RATIONALE FOR VERIFICATION

Three reasons are often given for verification: (1) to build confidence between parties by verifying treaty compliance, (2) to deter cheating by raising the risks and lowering the benefits of cheating, and (3) to detect militarily significant cheating early enough to protect the national security. Groups on both sides of the CTB issue often stress only one of these functions, but each plays an important role in treaty verification.

Building Confidence.   The role of verification in building confidence between parties is often emphasized by the Soviet Union and many advocates of a CTB, who claim that parties will abide by their treaty obligations as long as the treaty serves their interests. In this view, a party will formally abrogate — not clandestinely violate — a treaty that no longer serves its interests. If parties therefore assume that cheating probably would not occur, a verification system would only need to be capable of collecting information that would dispel any residual suspicions of noncompliance by, for example, demonstrating that a seismic signal had not been generated by a nuclear explosion. This effort could be cooperative, since parties would have strong incentives to demonstrate that they were observing the terms of the treaty. A verification system designed to perform this function must have a low false alarm rate, otherwise it might have the opposite effect of decreasing mutual confidence.

Deterring Cheating.   Past Soviet behavior (or at least the U.S. perception of it) has led many Americans to doubt that the Soviets would automatically comply with a CTBT. They believe that if nuclear tests up to a certain yield could be conducted without the risk of detection, and if cheating up to this yield promised to provide benefits, then the Soviets would probably cheat. They therefore require a verification capability that would reduce the yield at which undiscovered testing could take place to below that at which a net benefit could be obtained. Such a capability should act as a deterrent to cheating.

It is difficult, however, to define such a verification capability because Soviet assessments of the value of testing at a given yield and of the penalties for being found cheating are not known. Some analysts in the United States feel that low-yield testing can be valuable and that the Soviets are indifferent to world opinion; others believe that the benefits of low-yield testing are negligible and that the Soviets are sensitive about their reputation. The crucial choice is whether the United States should have high confidence that clandestine explosions could be detected, or whether the United States must merely deny the Soviet Union high confidence that it could cheat without discovery. The former requires a much more effective system of verification than the latter.

Detecting Cheating. Lastly, a verification system can detect cheating if it occurs. Although some analysts feel that any cheating, no matter how trivial, is significant because it indicates dishonesty, the majority feel that it is most important to be able to detect militarily significant cheating soon enough so that the nation's security would not be jeopardized. This is the most common standard against which verification systems have been measured in the past. But what level of testing has military significance?

MILITARY SIGNIFICANCE OF CLANDESTINE TESTING

For security reasons, government officials avoid discussing the significance of nuclear testing at various yields. To determine the degree of cheating that is militarily significant, one must estimate the level of testing that could result in a given military capability and decide how significant this capability could be in altering the military balance. The first of these steps is mostly objective (though uncertain), while the second is more subjective since it depends on untested theories of deterrence and nuclear warfare. The military capabilities that clandestine nuclear testing could provide would be the same as the capabilities that testing provides now: modernization and stockpile confidence.

Very-Low-Yield Tests. The lowest level of testing imaginable would be occasional tests having very low yields (less than 0.01 kiloton). There are no U.S. warheads deployed with yields less than 0.01 kiloton, so evidently such explosions are not deemed to have great military utility. Very-low-yield explosions could be used to test the effects of nuclear weapons on military hardware, to explore weapon physics, or to maintain the skills of weapon designers so that confidence could be better maintained in the stockpile. Some analysts claim that maintaining skills would be especially valuable if a party intended to abrogate a CTBT by surprise, since they could resume full-scale testing with better trained scientists and engineers. One analyst has suggested that a test ban treaty should allow nuclear explosions that could be completely contained in permanently occupied above-ground buildings, which would probably permit unlimited testing at these yields.[1] A CTB would almost certainly allow inertial-confinement fusion experiments and near-zero-yield (i.e., a few pounds of TNT equivalent) nuclear testing, which would provide some of the advantages of very-low-yield clandestine tests. Clandestine testing below 0.01 kiloton appears to have very little military significance.

Low-Yield Tests. Next, consider a program of low-yield testing: several tests per year with yields between 0.01 and 1 kiloton. In addition to the capabilities mentioned above, this level of testing would permit the proof-testing of many tactical weapons (or at least their low-yield options) and the development of new tactical weapons. In the past, many types of nuclear weapons with yields in this range have been deployed by the United States in tactical systems such as air-to-air, surface-to-surface, and surface-to-air missiles; artillery; antisubmarine warfare; and atomic demolition munitions.[2] (Little is known about the yields of Soviet tactical warheads.) The development of a new type of tactical warhead would be militarily significant only if it resulted in a capability that could not have been obtained using existing warheads. Improving the yield-to-weight ratio of low-yield warheads, for example, might be valuable if it allowed smaller missiles to deliver warheads of equal yield, but substantial progress here is unlikely, even without restrictions on testing.

The presence of tactical nuclear weapons can be important in changing the tactics of conventional armies in ways that benefit the defense (by threatening a large build-up of armored forces, for example). But many strategists (especially those in Europe) believe that these weapons are more important for the signal their use, or the threat of their use, sends to the opponent than for any effect they might have on the battlefield.[3] In this view, tactical nuclear weapons deter war primarily because they increase the probability of escalation to strategic nuclear war, not because they might achieve a tactical goal. Innovation in tactical weapons gained by clandestine testing may improve their effectiveness on the battlefield somewhat, but it is doubtful that this would make theater forces more effective at deterring war. Even those strategists who emphasize the battlefield utility of nuclear weapons do not generally claim that future advances in low-yield warhead technology are critical to success. Enhanced radiation warheads ("neutron bombs"), for example, have already been designed for most major battlefield nuclear weapon systems.

To discover things that new low-yield warheads might do that old warheads cannot, one must consider more unusual possibilities. Spectacular advances in guidance technology could make low-yield weapons capable of performing strategic missions, but it is very unlikely that warheads with yields less than 1 kiloton will be useful for strategic missions in the foreseeable future. The probability that an X-ray laser could be developed at this level of testing is extremely small, because it is more difficult to pump X-ray lasers at the lower energy densities achievable with low-yield devices, and because many years of testing at yields a hundred times greater have produced no practical results. Nuclear-driven microwave weapons may be possible at low yields, but it is highly uncertain whether such weapons would have an important military application. Although a program of low-yield testing is unlikely to change the military balance, a verification system should be capable of detecting such testing (especially in the 0.1- to 1-kt range) with moderate probability.

Moderate-Yield Tests.   Lastly, consider tests with yields from 1 to 10 kilotons. While such yields are small compared to those of most strategic weapons, they are large enough to test the most critical part of modern thermonuclear warheads: the primary, or fission "trigger." Von Hippel estimates that most primaries have yields of 5 to 15 kilotons and that the threshold for the physical process that makes small primaries possible (boosting) is about 1 kiloton.[4] A successful test of a primary can go a long way toward assuring the proper functioning of a complete weapon, especially if the secondary had been tested previously at or below the yield of the primary. A single test of 5 to 15 kilotons could therefore provide reassurance about the reliability of a much higher yield strategic warhead or could verify that minor modifications in warhead design (as necessitated by, for example, a new stockpile-to-target sequence) do not affect its performance. Several tests per year at yields greater than a few kilotons could support research and development of new boosted warheads. This would make the development of advanced tactical weapons possible, and it would also allow weapon effects testing. By accepting a moderate degree of technical risk, these new primaries could be incorporated in weapons yielding tens (if not hundreds) of kilotons. New low-yield strategic warheads could be militarily significant if incorporated in new types of delivery vehicles, such as earth-penetrating or maneuvering reentry vehicles. The development of nuclear directed-energy weapons (especially microwave weapons) could continue with nuclear tests of a few kilotons. A verification system should therefore be capable of detecting a single test in this yield range with moderate probability and a series of such tests with high probability.

Figure 4–1, which shows the rate of U.S. and Soviet testing as a function of yield, illustrates these distinctions. Note that no U.S. test during this period had an expected yield of less than 0.01 kiloton, which reflects the insignificance of very-low-yield tests (at least in the presence of a 150-kt threshold). Only about 5 percent of U.S. tests had expected yields between 0.01 and 1 kiloton, and most of these tests were not for warhead development. Note the rapid rise in testing at yields greater than 1 kiloton. Over 40 percent of all tests had yields between 5 and 15 kilotons, which probably corresponds to the yields of primaries. The yields of Soviet tests estimated from seismic measurements show a similar pattern. Although Figure 4–1 seems to indicate that a larger fraction of Soviet tests had yields in the 0.5- to 5-kt range, one should note that a plot of seismically measured yields for American tests would also show more tests in this range because the peak in the testing rate at 10 kilotons would be broadened due to variations in weapon performance and in the generation and propagation of seismic waves. Moreover, seismic yield estimates are not very accurate for yields less than a few kilotons.

To summarize, nuclear tests with yields less than 0.01 kiloton are not militarily significant. A series of tests with yields of 0.01 to 1 kiloton might be significant since it would allow the proof-testing of some old tactical warheads, development and testing of some new tactical warheads, and somewhat limited nuclear-effects testing, but it is unlikely that these developments would change the military balance. A single test of 5 to 15 kilotons could be important since it would allow the most important features of an aged or slightly modified weapon to be evaluated. A series of tests at yields at or above a few kilotons would be significant because it would permit the development of new boosted fission weapons. Such a testing program could support the development of new strategic weapons and the exploration of new weapon concepts. Translating these estimates of military significance into verification procedures is the subject of the remainder of this chapter.

Figure 4–1.   The Cumulative Fraction of U.S. Nuclear Tests as a Function of Expected Yield and USSR Weapon Tests as a Function of Seismic Yield, 1980–1984.[a]

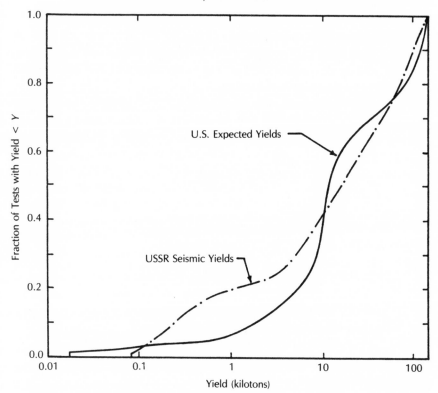

a. Values for U.S. testing rates as a function of predicted yield are adapted from Ray E. Kidder, "On the Degree of Verification Needed to Support a Comprehensive Test Ban," UCRL-95155, (Livermore, Calif.: Lawrence Livermore National Laboratory, August 1986), p. 11; values for Soviet testing rates as a function of measured seismic yield are taken from Lynn R. Sykes and Steven Ruggi, "Soviet Underground Nuclear Testing: Inferences from Seismic Observations and Historical Perspective," Nuclear Weapons Databook Working Paper NWD 86-4 (Washington, D.C.: Natural Resources Defense Council, November 1986), pp. 53–65.

SEISMIC MONITORING

The Limited Test Ban Treaty of 1963, which banned all nuclear weapon test explosions in the atmosphere, in space, and underwater, was acceptable primarily because explosions in these environments were considered to be adequately verifiable and because underground testing was allowed. Since then, most test ban verification research has focused on characterizing underground testing. The most effective way to characterize underground explosions is to collect and analyze the seismic waves they emit. The most common problems with seismic methods are detecting low-yield explosions and discriminating between nuclear explosions and other seismic events, such as chemical explosions and earthquakes. A measure of the strength of a seismic event is m_b, which is related to the logarithm of the amplitude of the compressional seismic wave (the P-wave) measured at a frequency of 1 Hz. Earthquakes and explosions emit many other types of seismic waves (e.g., shear waves, Rayleigh waves, Love waves), but because the P-wave propagates to long distances, m_b is most commonly measured and reported.

Seismic Magnitude vs. Yield

Figure 4–2 shows the relationship between m_b and the yield of an underground nuclear explosion. The top set of curves are for tamped explosions in hard or water-saturated rock, circumstances that result in the largest seismic signal for a given yield. Explosions of a given yield at the Nevada Test Site (NTS) produce smaller seismic signals than those at the Soviet Kazakhstan test site because of differences in the underlying geology (the strata under Kazakhstan are older and more stable and transmit seismic energy more efficiently). Explosions tamped in rock at most locations in the Soviet Union will generate larger signals than those from similar explosions at NTS.

It is possible to reduce the seismic signal from an explosion. If a weapon is detonated in a thick layer of dry, porous rock (e.g., alluvium or tuff), m_b is reduced by about one magnitude unit; for example, a 1-kt explosion in hard or water-saturated rock and a 10-kt explosion in dry alluvium will generate seismic signals of about equal magnitude. Thick layers of dry alluvium exist at NTS, but it is thought that such conditions are rare in the Soviet Union and that the maximum yield that could be muffled by firing in the thin layers that do exist is less than 1 to 2 kilotons.[5] The seismic signal from an explosion also can be reduced by detonating the explosive in a cavity. This technique is known as "cavity decoupling." It has been estimated that a 300-kt

Figure 4–2.   Seismic Magnitude, m, as a Function of Yield for Tamped Explosions in Hard Rock at NTS and Kazakhstan, and for Decoupling Factors of 10 and 50.[a]

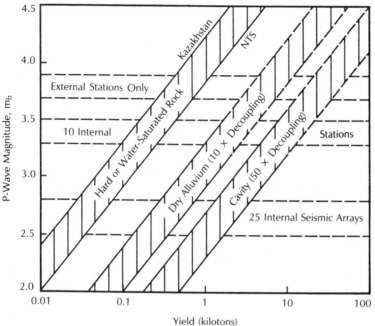

Yield (kilotons)

a. The curve for explosions in hard rock at NTS is a composite of values given by Charles B. Archambeau, "A Time and Threshold Limited Nuclear Test Ban," in Jozef Goldblat and David Cox, eds., *Nuclear Weapon Tests: Cessation or Limitation?* (Oxford: Oxford University Press, 1988), W.J. Hannon, "Seismic Verification of a Comprehensive Test Ban," *Science* 227 (18 January 1985): 255, and David W. Cheney, "Monitoring Nuclear Test Bans," CRS Report No. 86-155 SPR (Washington, D.C.: Congressional Research Service, 23 September 1986), p. 10. The m_b generated by a given yield is thought to be 0.3 to 0.4 magnitude units higher for tests at the Soviet Kazakhstan test site. The broken lines for decoupling at high yields indicates the limits of the feasibility of these methods.

explosion, decoupled by a sufficiently large cavity, would generate a seismic signal at a frequency of 1 Hz of the same magnitude as a 1-kt explosion tamped in hard or water-saturated rock.[6] The extent of the reduction in seismic estimates of the yield is called the "decoupling factor." At higher frequencies, the decoupling factor is lower; as a practical matter, decoupling factors much greater than 50 are unlikely.[7] The magnitude-yield curves for explosions in dry alluvium and in cavities (assuming a decoupling factor of 50) are also shown in Figure 4–2.

Seismic Detection

The ability of seismic networks to detect events in a given region depends on many factors: the number of stations in the network, the geographic distribution of the stations relative to the seismic event, the quality of the seismic equipment, background noise, and so forth. Increasing the number of regional stations increases the probability that an event will occur close to a station, resulting in a higher signal-to-noise ratio (SNR) and greater high-frequency content in the signal. A seismic network completely external to the Soviet Union could have a 90 percent probability of detecting an event inside the Soviet Union with an m_b of about 4, which corresponds to a tamped explosion of about 1 kiloton.[8] To detect decoupled explosions this small, however, stations inside the Soviet Union are required. In the CTB negotiations of the late 1970s, the Soviets agreed in principle to accept ten seismic stations on their territory. Ten internal stations, combined with external stations, would have a 90 percent chance of detecting events with an m_b as low as 3.3 to 3.5, which corresponds to tamped explosions of a few tenths of a kiloton and decoupled explosions of about 10 kilotons (assuming a decoupling factor of 50).[9] Increasing the number of internal sites from ten to twenty-five and using seismic arrays instead of single stations would lower the detection threshold to an m_b of 2.5 to 2.8.[10] This corresponds to tamped explosions of only a few tens of tons. Charles Archambeau estimates that at least one station in a network of twenty-six internal seismic arrays could detect 1-kt decoupled explosions anywhere in the Soviet Union (assuming a low-frequency decoupling factor of 200) and that at least four stations would detect explosions in 95 percent of the Soviet Union, assuming frequencies up to 30 Hz could be detected.[11]

In the following analysis, it is assumed that a seismic network similar to that described by Archambeau would be used to verify a CTBT. It is not clear whether the Soviet Union would accept twenty-five seismic arrays, each of which might contain two dozen seismometers spread over ten square kilometers. The cost of such a network might be about $250 million.[12] If the Soviet Union is willing, it appears possible to detect militarily significant underground testing. It would not be sufficient, however, merely to detect seismic signals. It is essential to be able to identify whether the detected signals have been generated by a nuclear explosion or by some other event such as an earthquake or a chemical explosion.

Seismic Identification

A regional seismic network would not only be capable of detecting very small nuclear explosions, it would also detect tens of thousands of earthquakes and chemical explosions each year. Most earthquakes can be distinguished from explosions on the basis of several discriminants: location, depth, and the distribution of energy in the various seismic waves generated.

Location. With the advances in signal processing that have been made in the last few years, one should be able to estimate to within 10 kilometers the location of most events detected with high SNR by two or more seismic arrays. It will be assumed here that nearly all regional events with m_b > 2.5 could be located to within 25 kilometers by a network of twenty-five internal seismic arrays. Assuming that clandestine tests would not be conducted in foreign countries or under the seabed in deep water, all events more than 25 kilometers from Soviet borders and shores could therefore be eliminated. This rules out thousands of earthquakes that occur under the Pacific Ocean and the Sea of Okhotsk near Kamchatka and the Kurile Islands. Although little is known about the seismicity at low magnitudes in the Soviet Union, extrapolations from data at higher magnitudes (m_b > 4) predict that roughly 2,000 earthquakes (give or take a factor of 2, and ignoring earthquake aftershocks) would be detected within the Soviet Union by a network of twenty-five internal seismic arrays.[13] About half of these earthquakes would be located in the southern tectonic belt, which runs along the southern Soviet border from the Black Sea to Siberia, and the rest would be near land in the Kamchatka/Kurile region, with a small fraction sprinkled throughout the large stable area of the Soviet Union. Unfortunately, the transmission of seismic waves in tectonic regions is inefficient; thus, many events in these regions would be detected by only a few stations in the network. For the network proposed by Archambeau, perhaps one quarter of the events in the southern tectonic belt would be detected by fewer than four stations, and a few events would be detected by only one station.[14]

More earthquakes could be eliminated on the basis of location, because an underground nuclear test requires human activity at the test site. Verifying the absence of such activity with photo reconnaissance satellites is discussed below, in the section on non-seismic monitoring.

Depth. Most underground nuclear explosions are done at depths of 300 to 600 meters, and the deepest explosion has been at 2.6 kilometers.[15] Since almost no holes have been drilled more than 10 kilometers deep, it would be safe to conclude that events located deeper than that are not explosions.[16] Only about 10 percent of large Soviet earthquakes occur within 10 kilometers of the surface, but it is difficult to determine the depth of an event with this accuracy.[17] There is a consensus that the depths of events detected at several stations can be estimated accurately enough so that those deeper than 50 kilometers could be ruled out as possible explosions. The number of ambiguous earthquakes would then be reduced to roughly 1,000 per year (if low-magnitude earthquakes have the same depth distribution as high-magnitude earthquakes). This figure is consistent with estimates made by the National Academy of Sciences.[18] As depth estimation becomes more accurate, the number of ambiguous earthquakes could eventually be reduced by one quarter to one half.

Spectral Discriminants. The only seismic method of identifying the shallow earthquakes that occur within the Soviet Union is to analyze the energy and frequency content and radiation pattern of the various seismic waves emitted. Differences between explosions and earthquakes are expected, because explosions are point sources of energy, whereas earthquakes result from the slipping of faults over large distances. Problems with spectral discrimination often arise, however, because very small earthquakes can behave like point sources of energy, and because explosions sometimes result in earthquake-like releases of tectonic stress.

The most powerful discriminant that has been developed depends on the difference between the magnitudes of the compressional P-wave, m_b (measured at about 1 Hz), and the Rayleigh surface wave, M_s (measured at about 0.05 Hz). For a given amount of energy released, explosions generate smaller Rayleigh waves than earthquakes. Figure 4–3 shows a plot of the M_s and m_b values for earthquakes and explosions recorded by a single low-noise, high-quality station located 400 kilometers from the average seismic event. Note that the earthquakes and explosions separate into two distinct populations, with a small overlap in the middle. This overlap creates a tradeoff between verification effectiveness and false alarm rate. For example, if a high verification effectiveness, or probability of correctly identifying a clandestine explosion, is desired, then the decision line in Figure 4–3 would be set so that almost all of the explosion population lies to the

Figure 4–3. The (m_b − M_s) Discriminant for Populations of NTS Explosions and Earthquakes in the Western United States.[a]

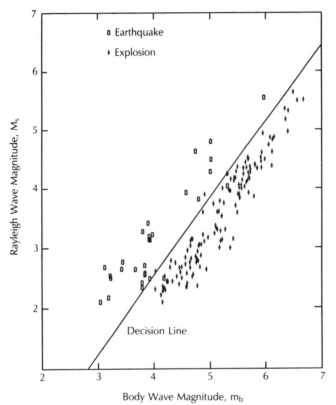

a. Data from Marvin D. Denny, Steven R. Taylor, and Eileen S. Vergino, "Investigation of m_b and M_s Formulas for the Western U.S. and their Impact on the m_b : M_s Discriminant," UCRL-95103, (Livermore, Calif.: Lawrence Livermore National Laboratory, August 1986), and from Ronald Glaser, Lawrence Livermore National Laboratory, personal communication, May 1987. The data are for the Elko station only and represent 141 explosions and 29 earthquakes.

right of the line. This procedure would, however, increase the false alarm rate, or the number of earthquakes misclassified as explosions. Similarly, if the false alarm rate is made small, the verification effectiveness inevitably decreases. A seismic identification system would be successful if, for an agreed-upon level of verification effectiveness, the false alarm rate was small enough so that nonseismic means, such as on-site inspection, could identify those events not identifiable by seismic means. Otherwise, unidentified but suspicious-looking events would erode confidence in treaty compliance.

Figure 4–4 shows a plot of $p(x|q)$, the probability of misclassifying an earthquake, as a function of $p(q|x)$, the probability of misclassifying an explosion. In the terminology commonly used in detection analysis, $p(q|x)$ is the probability of a "type one" error (i.e., a failure to recognize a signal), and $p(x|q)$ is the probability of a "type two" error (i.e., an incorrect interpretation of noise as a signal). The seismic verification effectiveness is given by $p_d[1 - p(q|x)]$, where p_d is the probability of detection. For events with magnitudes above the 90 percent detection threshold of the network, p_d is essentially equal to one.[19] The seismic false alarm rate is equal to $p(x|q)$. The data for $(m_b - M_s)$ in Figure 4–4 is derived from Figure 4–3 by moving the decision line to the right or left while keeping the slope constant.[20] Consider the usual assumption that the verification effectiveness should be very high—at least 90 percent. According to Figure 4–4, this would imply a false alarm rate of at least 10 percent; that is, at least 100 of 1,000 shallow earthquakes would be misclassified as potential explosions by the $(m_b - M_s)$ discriminant. Nonseismic means would not be able to cope with such a large number of false alarms. If, on the other hand, the number of false alarms is limited to a more manageable number (e.g., less than 1 percent, or roughly ten per year), then the probability of correctly classifying a single clandestine explosion would fall to less than 50 percent. It is not clear whether a 50 percent probability of identifying a single explosion would satisfy those analysts who believe that the Soviet Union is untrustworthy.

Although the preceding analysis gives an impression of statistical precision, there are a number of considerations that tarnish this image:

Station Performance. The data in Figure 4–3 were taken from the station with the lowest noise (Elko). Two of the other three stations in the seismic network had reasonably low noise levels, but at the fourth station (Landers), noise was so high that $(m_b - M_s)$ discrimination was very poor. It is usually assumed that all of the seismic monitoring stations would be situated in low-noise environments, but the possibility of a few stations performing poorly should be considered. The Soviets would know which sites are noisy, and they could even attempt to make some sites noisier; therefore, it can be argued that identification criteria should be based on the noisiest stations, because clandestine tests are more likely to be conducted near these stations. If, for example, the data from the Landers station were used in the above analysis, the false alarm rate would be unacceptable even at low verification effectiveness.[21]

Variations in Geology. The nuclear explosions all occurred at the same site (NTS), but the earthquakes were distributed over the

Figure 4–4.   The Probability of Misclassifying an Earthquake as a Function of the Probability of Misclassifying an Explosion for ($m_b - M_s$) and Multivariate Discriminants for Events in the Western United States.[a]

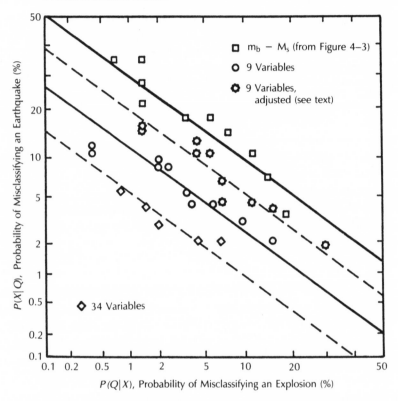

a. Data from Ronald Glaser, Lawrence Livermore National Laboratory, personal communication, May 1987.

western United States. Body waves travel through the interior of the earth and variations in geology are known to influence their transmission. Anne Suteau-Hanson and Thomas Bache state that the spectra from explosions in different areas are as different from each other as the spectra from earthquakes and explosions in the same area.[22] Although one can correct for transmission effects, calibration shots would be required and the correction factors would not be perfect. The fact that geological variations increase uncertainties in m_b may explain why the earthquake population in Figure 4–3 has a standard deviation in $(m_b - M_s)$ about 40 percent larger than that of the explosion population. Since clandestine nuclear tests could occur in a variety of geologies, the standard deviation for the explosion population should be greater. An upper limit is given by setting the standard deviation of explosion population equal to that of the earthquake population, which would nearly double the false alarm rate. A competing explanation is that earthquakes are more complex sources of seismic energy; therefore, one would expect the standard deviation of the earthquake population to be greater, regardless of variations in geology. For example, earthquakes do not radiate their energy isotropically, which creates variations in the received seismic signals, despite differences in geology. There has been insufficient seismic analysis to decide which of these effects is dominant.

Constant Scaled Depth.   Nearly all of the NTS explosions occurred at a constant scaled depth; that is, at a depth determined by the expected yield of the explosion so that complete containment could be assured. Some characteristics of the seismic signals from explosions have been observed to vary with scaled depth.[23] Since clandestine explosions could occur at very different scaled depths from those now used at NTS (e.g., either more shallow to minimize evidence of human activity or very deep to minimize the probability of a radioactive leak), this consideration may alter discrimination capability by an unknown amount.

Network Calibration.   Unless the seismic network is installed before the complete cessation of nuclear testing, or unless a CTB is accompanied by a large number of calibration shots, it will be impossible to determine experimentally the discrimination formulae for explosions at sites in the Soviet Union. Without calibration shots, one would have to assume that the distributions of discriminants are about the same in both countries. The Soviet Union, however, could have extensive data on the discrimination characteristics of particular sites and may be able to exploit differences.

Multivariate Discrimination.   The preceding analysis considered only one spectral discriminant (albeit probably the most efficient one), but many other discriminants have also been shown to be effective.[24] Even if these discriminants are not as effective as $(m_b - M_s)$, they could still greatly decrease the false alarm rate for a given verification effectiveness if they are statistically independent of $(m_b - M_s)$.

An extensive multivariate analysis has been performed by Ronald Glaser, Steven Taylor, Marvin Denny, and Eileen Vergino for data collected at the four stations mentioned above.[25] A combination of up to nine of thirty-six possible discriminants was chosen to yield the best discrimination for each data set. (See Table 4–1 for a list of discriminants.) The results for the Elko station, which are plotted in Figure 4–4, show that the false alarm rate is reduced by a factor of 3 to 5 over $(m_b - M_s)$ alone, for verification effectiveness greater than 75 percent. This indicates that it may be possible to maintain a moderately high verification effectiveness (about 75 percent) while suffering a reasonably low false alarm rate (about 1 percent). Figure 4–4 also indicates that if thirty-four of the thirty-six discriminants are used, the false alarm rate drops by an additional factor of 3. Table 4–1 summarizes these results.

The improvement in discrimination would be even better if large amounts of data had not been missing from the multivariate analysis. In the nine-variable analysis, most misclassified events were described by only one to three variables.[26] For example, of the 94 earthquakes and 248 explosions analyzed, $(m_b - M_s)$ data were available for only 29 earthquakes and 141 explosions. This is especially unfortunate since $(m_b - M_s)$ is often the single best discriminant. Indeed, the multivariate analysis perfectly discriminated between earthquakes and explosions for those events that had $(m_b - M_s)$ values.[27] Moreover, better path

Table 4–1. The Approximate Number of False Alarms per Year as a Function of Verification Effectiveness, Assuming 1,000 Ambiguous Events per Year, Extrapolated from Figure 4–4.

Discriminant(s)	Verification Effectiveness		
	50 percent	75 percent	90 percent
$(m_b - M_s)$	15	40	100
9 Variables[a]	2	8	30
9 Variables, adjusted[b]	6	20	60
34 Variables[c]	0.5	3	10

a. For the Elko station, the nine discriminants chosen were $(m_b - M_s)$, L_g/P_g and L_g/R_g amplitude ratios, transverse long-period Love-wave energy density, spectral ratio of Love to Rayleigh waves, third moment of frequency (radial L_g and transverse P_g), and Bakun-Johnson spectral ratios (radial P_n and transverse P_g).

b. Adjusted to include only those explosions with $m_b < 4.0$ and to account for the lack of low-magnitude earthquakes in the sample.

c. Additional discriminants include relative excitation of short-period SH waves, $(m_b - M_s^h)$, where M_s^h is the Forsyth higher mode surface wave, excitation of S_n, and Murphy-Bennett and Bakun-Johnson spectral ratios and third moment of frequency for vertical, radial, and transverse L_g, P_g, and P_n waves (27 ratios in all).

corrections, the use of negative evidence (i.e., the fact that a certain seismic wave was *not* received can be used profitably in the discrimination analysis), and improved discriminants — especially better spectral ratio discriminants of L_g and P-waves — may make multivariate discrimination much more powerful.[28] Definite conclusions will have to await the results of these studies.

Multistation Discrimination. The discriminants used above were based on data from a single station, but if an event is recorded by several stations, then random errors in measurement and systematic errors due to path effects can be greatly reduced. In other words, events that are misclassified by one station may not be misclassified by other stations. However, most earthquakes occur in tectonic regions, where the transmission of seismic waves is less efficient. As a result, many events in these regions will be detected by only a few stations. Moreover, in the four-station network described above, multistation discrimination performed no better than discrimination at the single best station, Elko.

Small-Magnitude Events. The magnitude distribution of earthquakes and explosions in the sample is not the same as one would expect in an actual monitoring situation. In particular, there are too few low-magnitude earthquakes and too many high-magnitude explosions. This affects discrimination capability, since misclassification has been observed to increase markedly with decreasing m_b in the multivariate analysis.[29] This increase occurs not only because data are less accurate at magnitudes near the detection threshold but also because earthquakes look more explosion-like in some ways as they become smaller. The seismic signals generated by clandestine explosions are likely to be much smaller than those generated by most NTS explosions; therefore, the misclassification rate for a hypothetical clandestine explosion population might be significantly larger than that indicated above. In addition, earthquakes with magnitudes near the detection threshold of the network were underrepresented in the sample earthquake population. From data at higher magnitudes, one can deduce that the sample should have contained about forty earthquakes with m_b between 3.0 and 3.5, but only twenty-six such earthquakes were in the sample.[30] Since the misclassification rate for earthquakes increases with decreasing m_b, a sample with a greater number of small earthquakes should have a higher misclassification rate.

A rough estimate of these effects was obtained by considering only those explosions in the sample with m_b less than 4.0 and by multiplying

$p(x|q)$ for each magnitude interval by the ratio of the expected number of earthquakes to the actual number in the sample. The results, which are shown in Figure 4–4 and Table 4–1, indicate that this increases the false alarm rate by a factor of 2 to 3 for the nine-variable discrimination analysis.

More sensitive stations or seismic arrays that are capable of reliably detecting long-period waves from small events may improve discrimination considerably. Jack Evernden and Charles Archambeau claim to have found a spectral ratio discriminant that works *better* at lower magnitudes not because the deviation in the distributions decreases but because the mean separation between the populations increases.[31] Preliminary results of Steven Taylor, Nevin Sherman, and Marvin Denny also indicate that some discriminants may be powerful at low magnitudes.[32] If this is true, identification of small magnitude events may be as easy as that of large magnitude events.

Chemical Explosions. The only seismic events considered in the above analysis were earthquakes and nuclear explosions, but large numbers of chemical explosions would also be detected by the network. There is little detailed information available on the use of chemical explosives in the Soviet Union, but one can assume that Soviet mining and earth-moving operations are similar in scale to those in the United States. Nearly two million tons of high explosive are used each year in the United States for commercial purposes.[33] Preliminary investigations indicate that chemical explosions with yields greater than 100 tons occur at least 500 times per year in the United States, although most of these occur at only a few mines.[34] A 100-ton chemical explosion generates about the same magnitude seismic signal as a 200-ton tamped or a 10-kt decoupled nuclear explosion.[35] Chemical explosions larger than 10 tons, which in some respects correspond to decoupled nuclear explosions with yields greater than 1 kiloton, occur at least 5,000 times per year in the United States.[36] The limited data available on chemical explosions in the Soviet Union are consistent with this estimate.[37] Thus, the number of chemical explosions that would be detected by a sensitive regional seismic network may exceed the number of earthquakes.

To limit the false alarm rate to a reasonable level, seismic methods are needed that can efficiently discriminate chemical from nuclear explosions. Photoreconnaissance satellites could detect the surface effects that would result from most large industrial explosions, but this would not be practical on a routine basis. Although seismic methods probably cannot distinguish between a single chemical explosion and a nuclear explosion, most industrial explosions in the United States are "ripple-fired," or composed of many small explosions detonated at intervals of a fraction of a second. Ripple-firing fractures rock more efficiently than single blasts and minimizes ground vibrations that could damage nearby structures. One-hundred-ton ripple-fired explosions take place over several seconds, and 10-ton explosions in coal mines typically last about one second.[38] Evidence of ripple-firing has been observed in the seismic waveforms of chemical explosions. The seismic waves from ripple-fired explosions have less high-frequency content than single explosions of the same yield because the high-frequency waves interfere with one another. In fact, ripple-fired chemical explosions look earthquake-like when analyzed by spectral ratio discriminants. Suteau-Henson and Bache, however, found that spectral ratios could not reliably discriminate between simulated decoupled nuclear explosions and actual chemical explosions.[39] This may be because some of the mines did not use ripple-firing, or because of variations in geology from site to site. If a large fraction of all chemical explosions with yields greater than 10 tons are ripple-fired, and if ripple-fired chemical explosions can be discriminated efficiently from nuclear explosions using seismic methods, then the false alarm problem posed by chemical explosions would be substantially solved. More research is needed to resolve this problem.

Summary. The uncertainties mentioned above make it difficult to summarize the capabilities of seismic identification. The numerical estimates in Table 4–1 indicate that a moderately high verification effectiveness (75 percent) can be achieved with a false alarm rate of less than a few percent. Three factors—the availability of more data in multivariate analyses, the use of better spectral ratio discriminants, and multistation discrimination—could decrease the false alarm rate. The potential for misclassifying chemical explosions, on the other hand, could greatly increase the false alarm rate. The other factors discussed above—increased noise at some stations, greater variance in the explosion population, and lack of extensive calibration—could also increase the false alarm rate, but probably only by a factor of two or so. Thus, the assertion by some seismologists that the technical problems of seismic identification have been solved is not true. The seismic techniques now available may be sufficient for monitoring a CTB, but more experimental evidence and operational experience is necessary to confirm that some factors, such as false alarms from routine industrial explosions, would not interfere with CTB verification. One may be more optimistic, however, about the ability of current techniques to verify a low-yield threshold test ban.

NONSEISMIC MONITORING

Seismic techniques are the most efficient way to monitor underground testing, but several nonseismic methods also deserve consideration. Some of these, such as photoreconnaissance or electronic intelligence satellites, are known as "national technical means" (NTM) since, unlike internal seismic stations or on-site inspections, they do not require the cooperation of the monitored party. Other methods, such as atmospheric or ionospheric monitoring, are most effective if conducted within the territory of the monitored party.

Photoreconnaissance

Probably the most powerful nonseismic means of test ban verification is provided by the photoreconnaissance satellites that orbit just above the earth's atmosphere. These satellites are capable of identifying objects with dimensions of less than one meter, which is more than sufficient for detecting the drilling or mining equipment and roads or railways necessary to conduct nuclear tests. As early as 1965, photoreconnaissance was recognized as a powerful supplement to seismic monitoring for test ban verification.[40]

A photoreconnaissance satellite is like a flashlight in the dark — it can only illuminate what it is pointed at, and this would be a tiny fraction of the entire Soviet Union. Seismic detectors would be used to point photoreconnaissance satellites at possible test sites, rather than the satellites simply hunting for testing activity at random. For example, the locations of suspicious seismic signals could be inspected to determine if there was evidence of testing activity. Sites showing no signs of human activity could be dismissed as earthquakes, while the remainder would be subject to further scrutiny and perhaps on-site inspection.

As mentioned above, a successful seismic identification system using a network of twenty-five internal seismic arrays may give tens of false alarms per year. Seismic methods should be able to locate most of these suspicious events to within 10 kilometers, and nearly all to within 25 kilometers. A single medium-resolution photoreconnaissance satellite with pointing capability, such as the French SPOT or the planned German Atlas-C satellites, could photograph at least 100 sites per year, usually within a few days of the event.[41] The 3- to 10-meter resolution of these satellites is sufficient to detect roads, railroads, and large vehicles or buildings.[42] If there is no evidence of human activity, the event could be safely ruled out as an explosion of significant size (i.e., greater than 1 kiloton). If human activity is present, then high-resolution satellites could be used to examine the site more closely. It is very difficult to hide significant human activity, especially when multispectral imaging is used. It would be virtually impossible, for example, to hide the construction of a large underground cavity in the wilderness.

A substantial fraction of seismic false alarms could thus be dismissed because the Soviet Union is, for the most part, an unsettled country. Over 75 percent of the Soviet population lives in European USSR, which constitutes about one quarter of the total land area, and the great majority of the nation's 1,400,000 kilometers of roads (only 400,000 kilometers of which are paved) and 140,000 kilometers of railroads are located there as well.[43] Most of the remaining population, roads, and railways are concentrated along a triangle-shaped corridor leading from the Ural Mountains to Lake Baikal. At least 30,000 kilometers of navigable waterways cross the vast expanse of Siberia, but half of the country remains more than 25 kilometers from any road, railroad, or navigable waterway.[44] Medium-resolution photoreconnaissance satellites could probably verify that 75 percent of the land area of the Soviet Union did not show signs of significant human activity.

One cannot immediately draw the conclusion that 75 percent of the seismic false alarms can be ruled out, however, because earthquakes are not uniformly distributed throughout the Soviet Union. As described above, about half of the shallow earthquakes occur near land in the Kamchatka-Kurile region, and half occur along the southern tectonic belt. The Kamchatka peninsula and the Kurile Islands are very sparsely populated and are crossed by few roads. The major economic activities are fishing, trapping, and lumbering, none of which would be confused with or camouflage nuclear testing. Virtually all of Kamchatka-Kurile earthquakes (e.g., 95 percent) that are detected but not identified by seismic means could be disregarded because a photoreconnaissance survey of the area would show no human activity near the location of the event.

The southern tectonic belt, on the other hand, contains areas of great human activity. Earthquakes occur in three major areas along the belt: the extreme southeast of European USSR along the Caucasus Mountains, in the states of Georgia and Azerbaijan; central Asia near the border with Afghanistan, Pakistan, and China in the Tien Shan Mountains, in the states of Kirghiz and Uzbek; and a narrow corridor that stretches along the Mongolian border in the Republic of Tuva, turns north along Lake Baikal, and reaches east in the Republic of Buryat. For convenience, these three regions will be referred to here as Caucasus, Tien Shan, and Baikal.

The Caucasus region contains the most economic activity, having a population density of 60/km^2 (about the same as that of California). Roughly half of the earthquakes associated with the southern tectonic belt occur in this region. As in the other regions, the seismicity is associated with an uplifting of the earth's crust, which makes the region rich in minerals. It is not surprising, therefore, that mining is one of the region's main economic activities. The major mineral resources are manganese, iron, molybdenum, copper, lead, zinc, and cobalt. Coal, lignite, and peat are also mined, and Azerbaijan contains some of the richest oil fields in the world. Since this is a highly developed area, and since much of the economic activity could be a disguise for nuclear testing, photoreconnaissance may not be able to confirm the absence of nuclear testing in much of this region. Detailed road maps of the region are scarce, but one can make rough comparisons with the United States, which, although it has six times more roads per square kilometer, has been settled for much less time. Only about 5 percent of the land area of California, for example, is more than 10 kilometers from a road. Even if all earthquakes occurred in the mountains, less than one third of the mountainous areas of California are more than 10 kilometers from a road.[45]

The remaining earthquakes in the southern tectonic belt are roughly equally distributed between the other two regions. The Tien Shan region has about the same population density as Maine (15/km^2) and is rich in antimony, lead, tungsten, mercury, uranium, coal, and oil. The Lake Baikal region is about as densely populated as Montana or Nevada (2/km^2). Iron, tungsten, molybdenum, gold, nickel, manganese, aluminum, and coal are mined there. It will be assumed that about 50 percent of the earthquakes in Tien Shan and 90 percent of those in the Lake Baikal region are located more than 10 kilometers from a road, railway, or navigable waterway.

When the estimates for each of these regions are combined, one finds that roughly three quarters of all shallow earthquakes in the Soviet Union occur more than 10 kilometers from a road, railroad, or waterway. If one assumes that seismic methods could locate most events within 10 kilometers and that low-resolution photoreconnaissance satellites could efficiently verify an absence of human activity, low-resolution photoreconnaissance could reduce the seismic false alarm rate by about a factor of 4.

High-resolution photoreconnaissance may be useful in reducing the number of false alarms still further, since many areas within 10 kilometers of a road or settlement would not show evidence of the mining or drilling activities required to support nuclear testing. Over 70 percent of Soviet roads are unpaved, and these would show signs of the movement of heavy equipment. High-resolution satellites could scan the site of ambiguous events no later than a week or two after they took place, searching for signs of testing activity. As a rough guess, perhaps half of the events within 10 kilometers of a road would not be located within 10 kilometers of a mine or drilling rig, or the site would show no evidence that the heavy equipment necessary for a test had ever been present. Thus, medium- and high-resolution photoreconnaissance satellites together may be able to reduce the seismic false alarm rate by about an order of magnitude. This would make a seismic false alarm rate of 1 percent more than adequate, and even a 10 percent rate might be acceptable.

Photoreconnaissance satellites also would be valuable in gathering evidence about actual clandestine nuclear testing activity that had been detected seismically. Seismic means might not be able to locate a test accurately enough for human inspectors to request a visit to the test site, but satellites would have a better chance. If a nuclear device is not buried deeply enough, the ground at the surface might collapse after the explosion; NTS is dotted with hundreds of such subsidence craters, which are easily visible from satellites. Craters occur especially after tests in dry alluvium. Presumably, a cheater would take precautions to avoid creating a crater, but such precautions (such as digging a deep hole) may actually *increase* the chance that testing activity would be detected by photoreconnaissance. Satellites might also detect the mining of a cavity intended to decouple explosions, especially if the cavity is constructed in hard rock rather than salt.

Atmospheric Monitoring

There is always a chance that a clandestine nuclear test would not be fully contained in the earth. Many underground tests in the United States and the Soviet Union have vented radioactive debris in the past, and on several occasions debris has been detected beyond national borders. Although radioactive debris could be most easily detected by special airplanes patrolling the eastern border of the Soviet Union, this would be very expensive. Ground-based monitoring stations, although less effective, would be far cheaper and could be collocated with internal seismic stations. The monitoring stations could be equipped with large fans to blow air through filters that would trap debris; the presence of radioactivity in the filters could be monitored remotely. A country that wished to cheat would then face a more difficult decision: quickly drill a shallow hole to minimize the chance that photoreconnaissance satellites would detect testing activity, or drill and carefully seal a deep hole to minimize the possibility of venting. A hole at least several hundred meters deep would be required to be confident that a 1-kt explosion would not vent or produce a subsidence crater.[46]

Ionospheric Monitoring

An underground explosion creates an acoustic wave in the atmosphere, which grows in amplitude as it propagates into regions of low density at high altitudes. When the wave reaches the ionosphere it disturbs the electron density there; these disturbances can be observed by monitoring the reflection of high-frequency radar waves from the ionosphere. This technique is still in the experimental stage, but the ionospheric disturbances produced by a 600-ton atmospheric chemical explosion in 1981 were observed and correctly predicted.[47] It should be noted that earthquakes and many other natural phenomena also produce ionospheric disturbances; therefore, even if this technique is proven to be sensitive to low-yield underground explosions, much work would remain on discriminating between nuclear explosions and other events. It is uncertain whether ionospheric monitoring will ever make a significant contribution to test ban verification.

Human and Electronic Intelligence

The Soviet Union and the United States routinely eavesdrop on the conversations of opposing military and political leaders. The United States, for example, claims to have a transcript of the conversations between Soviet pilots and ground stations during the recent incident that led to the destruction of a Korean airliner. It is difficult to keep a large covert operation completely secret, and although project managers would try to make sure that all communications were conducted in a secure manner, mistakes happen. Just the knowledge that certain individuals who are known to have been associated with the nuclear testing program have all moved to a new location could be evidence of a violation attempt. Both countries also work carefully to plant spies in high positions, and neither can be absolutely sure that a program is not compromised by a spy. Lastly, Soviet citizens defect, some of whom worked on secret projects. The Soviet government could not rule out the possibility that someone who was aware of clandestine testing might defect and reveal this information. The contribution of human and electronic intelligence to test ban verification may be low (it would be impossible to quantify its contribution in any case), but it certainly cannot be ignored by a potential cheater.

ON-SITE INSPECTION

All U.S. proposals for a CTBT have included provisions for U.S. personnel to inspect suspicious events in the Soviet Union. In the negotiations of the late 1950s and early 1960s, this took the form of mandatory on-site inspections (OSIs): any event that was not identified as an earthquake by agreed-upon seismic criteria would be inspected. The Soviet Union rejected the idea of mandatory OSIs, claiming that they would be used as an excuse for espionage. The Soviet Union saw OSIs as a means of building confidence by demonstrating that ambiguous events were earthquakes; in this view, OSIs should be performed only by mutual agreement. The two sides compromised on the idea of a quota of OSIs, in which each party could perform a fixed number each year, but they differed on the value of the quota. Khrushchev offered three OSIs per year, but the Kennedy administration insisted that at least seven were required. Although it may seem that these numbers were not far apart (in fact, Kennedy was prepared to accept six, and perhaps only five, inspections), great differences in the *nature* of OSIs remained (e.g., the nationalities of the inspectors, permitted inspection techniques, etc.).

In the CTB negotiations of the late 1970s, the United States and the Soviet Union made a significant compromise by agreeing to voluntary OSIs, in which one party could request to inspect a suspicious event and the other party could either grant or refuse the request. The refusal of a request for an OSI would not be a violation of the treaty, but it would be serious cause for concern. It would be up to the inspecting party to decide if the event, coupled with the refusal of an OSI, was so suspicious that it should act as if the treaty had been violated. The United States decided to change its position from mandatory to voluntary OSIs when it realized that the two approaches would be the same in practice, because an OSI request of a clandestine test that was not well hidden would be refused whether OSIs were "mandatory" or not. The cheater could always claim that the request for an OSI was frivolous or that the area to be inspected was near a sensitive military installation (the test could even be conducted near such a facility to ensure that this excuse would sound reasonable). An OSI would only detect an explosion if the cheater was foolish enough to allow an inspection of a test that could be discovered with the approved inspection techniques. Thus, it is extremely unlikely that either type of OSI would prove that a clandestine nuclear test had occurred, and the burden of abrogating the treaty would remain on the accusing party. OSIs should therefore be seen as a confidence-building or deterrent measure, not as a method for detecting violations.

Understanding this point is crucial because it has important consequences for defining the role of OSIs in verifying compliance. A party in compliance with a CTBT would have every incentive to prove that suspicious events were not nuclear explosions. If seismic analysis and photographic and geological surveys were not enough to convince the other party, then an OSI would be permitted. Suppose, on the other hand, that one party cheated and that the other party requests an OSI. If the proposed inspection area does not include the test site, the cheater might grant the request for an OSI because no evidence of cheating could be gathered. An OSI might even be permitted of the actual test site if the cheating party is sure that the test would not be discovered using the permitted inspection techniques. If an OSI revealed no conclusive evidence of a violation, then, no matter how suspicious the seismic and NTM data, the inspecting party would find it difficult to conclude that a violation had taken place. Therefore, the purpose of an OSI is to maximize the probability that a request for an OSI will be refused if a party has cheated. The possibility of an OSI request necessitating a refusal would act as a deterrent to clandestine testing, since the refusal would be widely interpreted as an admission of guilt. OSIs would also increase the costs of cheating because of the additional precautions that would be necessary to minimize the probability that an OSI would be requested at the correct location. The capabilities to locate an event as accurately as possible before requesting an OSI and to identify explosions during an OSI are crucial in maximizing the value of this deterrent.

Location.   Seismic signals detected by two or more seismic arrays can usually be located to within 10 kilometers, which corresponds to an area of three hundred square kilometers. This is much larger than the area of active search during an OSI, which would be at most a few tens of square kilometers.[48] Photoreconnaissance satellites would play an important role in selecting the area for the OSI request, but if an event occurs in a large mining district, this may be of little help. In fact, a sophisticated cheater could set up a decoy test site a few kilometers from the actual test site to divert attention from the actual location. The area selected for an OSI should include signs of significant human activity, including a road, railroad, or waterway that could have been used to transport mining or drilling equipment. Note that if the event was an earthquake, the area selected for the OSI is unlikely to include the fault along which the earthquake occurred.

Even an area of a few tens of square kilometers is too large to search at random for evidence of clandestine testing. Pinpointing the location of an event is made easier by the fact that some explosions and most earthquakes are followed by a series of small aftershocks. The frequency of aftershocks decreases exponentially with time, however, and measurements must be made within a few days or weeks, depending on the magnitude of the event. A local seismic network of one or two dozen sensitive seismometers could be deployed over the entire site, with more seismometers installed near the event as the location is better and better determined. Such a network may be able to locate an event within a few hundred meters.[49] Nearby mining activity may have to be suspended during this time. If the aftershocks occur along a fault or are located at a depth of many kilometers, this would indicate a probable earthquake. A geological survey of the site might also suggest corrections to the seismic analysis of the event, making it more or less suspicious.

Identification.   Once the event is located more precisely, an intensive search for artifacts of a nuclear test could begin. Magnetic techniques could detect the presence of buried metal objects, and geophysical techniques could detect the underground cavity or the rubble-filled chimney that would accompany an explosion. The only positive identification of a nuclear explosion, however, would be the detection of radioactive weapon debris. Even if the containment works properly, radioactive gas would seep to the surface along small fissures or would diffuse to the surface through the ground. Gas samples were collected at eight U.S. test sites from nine months to fourteen years after detonation, and krypton-85 was discovered at each site.[50] There may be a timing conflict between aftershock and radioactivity monitoring, however, since it may take longer than a few months for radioactivity to diffuse to the surface from a deep explosion, and it is unlikely that the treaty would grant more than two or three months to complete an OSI. There may also be a problem if the OSI takes place in an old nuclear test site, since radionuclides still seeping to the surface from prior tests could interfere with detecting a recent test.

The invasive, accusatory, expensive, and time-consuming nature of OSIs limits the number of inspections that could be performed to certainly no more than a few per year. Many analysts have argued that fewer than one per year should be sufficient for the purpose of building confidence. With roughly 1,000 shallow Soviet earthquakes detected annually by the seismic network, only a few tenths of a percent of all events could be inspected (and an even smaller percentage if chemical explosions are included). The remaining events would have to be identified by the seismic and nonseismic techniques outlined above, or simply ignored.

The efficiency of OSIs is hotly debated, but it is difficult to arrive at a meaningful definition of efficiency. Too much depends on un-known details to permit a prediction. But at least one can presume that an intelligent cheater would make a worst case assessment of the effectiveness of OSIs, because it would be much worse to have a test discovered than to refuse an inspection. The crucial variable is the likelihood that the inspecting party would choose the right location for an OSI. Although it is possible to determine beforehand if the permitted OSI techniques would be likely to discover the test, a cheater might be nervous that something had been overlooked or that the situation would change with time (e.g., the cavity might collapse or radioactive gas might leak to the surface after the OSI began). Because OSIs are extremely unlikely to turn up additional evidence of cheating if cheating actually occurred, some analysts recommend giving up the idea of OSIs altogether. Indeed, the burden of negotiating satisfactory OSI provisions may well outweigh their deterrent value. On the other hand, even if the evidence for cheating was strong without an OSI, many analysts would still prefer a Soviet refusal to permit an OSI before making an appropriate response. In addition, it may be worth considerable inconvenience in negotiating a treaty simply to turn OSIs from a symbol of mistrust between the United States and the Soviet Union into a symbol of cooperation and understanding, thus providing an opportunity for the Soviet Union to demonstrate graphically its willingness and ability to comply with arms control treaties.

EVASION

The term "evasion" as it is used here means obtaining a unilateral advantage by engaging in activities that are banned or limited by a treaty while other parties continue to abide by the terms of the treaty. In the case of a CTBT, it would mean conducting clandestine nuclear tests at yields high enough, at rates large enough, and for a period of time long enough to obtain a military advantage. Evasion does not necessarily require that the testing activities escape detection, but merely that the activities are sufficiently ambiguous so that other parties will not abrogate the treaty, thereby depriving the cheater of a unilateral advantage.

There are two basic ways to evade a CTBT: by preventing detection of clandestine tests or by preventing their identification. Most research on test ban evasion has focused on preventing detection and specifically on preventing seismic detection. The probability that an event will be detected by seismic means depends on the SNR at the site; thus, one can minimize detection by decreasing the signal or increasing the noise. The simplest way to cheat is to test below the detection threshold of the seismic network. For tamped explosions in hard or water-saturated rock, Figure 4–2 shows that only tests of a few tens of ton could escape detection by a network of twenty-five internal seismic arrays. To increase the yield while avoiding detection, one must decouple the explosion or test where the seismic network is less sensitive.

Decoupling

The magnitude of the seismic signal detected from an explosion of a given yield depends on the geology of the test site. Early results of the U.S. underground testing program showed that much less of the explosion's energy is coupled to the earth if the explosion takes place in dry, porous rock, such as alluvium or tuff. Although U.S. scientists lack detailed knowledge of Soviet geology, they think that thick layers of alluvium are rare in the Soviet Union and that the maximum yield that could be muffled in this fashion is 1 to 2 kilotons.[51] Muffled explosions with yields less than a few tenths of a kiloton may go undetected by a network of twenty-five internal seismic arrays, but the military insignificance of tests at these yields, combined with the risk of subsidence craters and venting of radioactive gases in dry alluvium, would make this an unattractive way to cheat.

The most effective way to decrease the seismic signal from an underground explosion is to explode the device in a large cavity. To achieve the full effect, the cavity must be large enough so that the walls respond elastically (i.e., they do not fracture or become plastic from the shock of the explosion). An explosion in such a cavity is said to be "fully decoupled," since the low-frequency seismic signal is reduced to the maximum extent. Theoretical calculations in the early 1960s showed that a 300-kt fully decoupled explosion could result in the same m_b as a 1-kt tamped explosion.[52]

The decoupling theory was tested in the 1966 Sterling experiment, in which a 0.38-kt nuclear device was detonated inside a cavity of 17-meter radius that was produced by an earlier 5.3-kt explosion in a salt dome. The observed decoupling factor at low frequencies was about 70.[53] One apparent reason that the decoupling factor was less than the theoretical maximum is that the salt was weakened by the first nuclear explosion, making the pressure the walls could withstand much lower, and thereby making the cavity too small to fully decouple the second explosion. If a cavity of the same radius had been mined instead of explosively formed, it is estimated that the decoupling factor would have been 120 to 200.[54] Another reason that the decoupling factor may be smaller in practice is that the initial pressure pulse from the nuclear explosion, which is much greater than the average pressure but lasts only a few milliseconds, may fracture the cavity walls. This effect might be overcome by evacuating the cavity and inserting thin foils to soak up the heat of the explosion, but this would undoubtedly add to the cost of the facility. Unless the Soviets had done extensive nuclear decoupling experiments before a CTBT took effect, it seems unlikely that they could be sure of achieving a decoupling factor greater than 50 in an evasion attempt.

The volume of the cavity required for full decoupling is proportional to the yield of the explosion and inversely proportional to the pressure that the cavity walls can withstand. Depending on the strength of the medium, a cavity with a radius of 17 to 27 meters is required to fully decouple a 1-kt explosion in salt.[55] Such a cavity might cost $8 to $20 million[56], which is not excessive when compared to the cost of a normal U.S. nuclear test ($20 to $30 million). Decoupling a 10-kt explosion would require a 37- to 58-meter radius cavity, at a cost of $60 to $120 million.[57] Actual costs would undoubtedly be higher, to assure containment of radioactive gases and to provide a "cover" operation so that the test site would look like a normal commercial enterprise. Cavities could also be constructed in crystalline rocks such as granite, which are more abundant than salt domes in the Soviet Union, but the mining costs would be much greater. In addition, the radius of a cavity in granite would be limited to perhaps 25 meters, and the tectonic stress and fractures normally present in such rocks may make even this impossible to achieve.

The variation of the decoupling factor with frequency has received attention recently, since the detection of high-frequency seismic waves is now believed to be possible at distances of several hundred kilometers. According to the standard theory, the decoupling factor for a fully decoupled explosion remains constant up to a certain characteristic frequency (the corner frequency) of a tamped explosion of the same yield. At higher frequencies the decoupling factor drops rapidly, eventually reaching a constant value for frequencies greater than the corner frequency of the cavity. The corner frequency of a 1-kt tamped explosion in salt is about 5 Hz.[58] Since m_b is measured at 1 Hz, full decoupling should be observed at this frequency. But at 20 Hz the theoretical decoupling factor is only 30, at 30 Hz it is about 15, and above 40 Hz it drops to only 6.[59] In the Sterling experiment, the decoupling factor was observed to decrease to about 7 at high frequencies.[60] Since it appears that the signal from a 1-kt fully decoupled explosion can be detected at frequencies of up to 20 to 30 Hz by a seismic network of twenty-five internal stations, fully decoupled explosions would have decoupling factors ten times less than the theoretical limit.[61] It should be noted that although these theoretical arguments are supported by the available experimental evidence, exceptions (i.e., explosions with little high-frequency and earthquakes with much high-frequency content) have been observed. These exceptions might make seismic discrimination more difficult, but without a reliable way to suppress high frequencies from explosions, they do not necessarily make evasion easier.

Increasing the size of the cavity beyond that necessary for full decoupling ("over-decoupling" the explosion) does not increase the decoupling factor below the tamped corner frequency, but it does decrease the cavity corner frequency and increase the decoupling factor above this frequency. For example, if the cavity radius is twice that necessary for full decoupling (i.e., the volume is eight times larger), then the theoretical decoupling factor does not fall below 20 at frequencies greater than 30 Hz; if the radius is three times greater (i.e., the volume is twenty-seven times larger), a decoupling factor of 50 can be maintained above 20 Hz.[62] An obvious drawback of this scheme is that the cost of the cavity increases with volume, so that doubling the cavity radius would cost at least four times more. Even with huge cavities that would cost hundreds of millions of dollars to build, or with high-frequency detection limited to only 15 Hz, real-world decoupling factors greater than 50 are unlikely. In addition, the maximum cavity size, even in salt, is probably limited to that which could fully decouple a 10-kt explosion.

It has been suggested that using an elongated cavity could impede identification of an explosion because seismic radiation in the direction of the long axis of the cavity would contain less high-frequency energy, and because shear waves would be generated.[63] Theoretically, if the long axis is pointed toward nearby stations, these stations would not detect the event at any frequency. Radiation in the direction of the small axis, however, would still be rich in high frequencies. If twenty-five stations are uniformly distributed throughout the Soviet Union, the maximum distance to a station along one axis is about 1,000 kilometers.[64] The locations for twenty-five internal seismic stations specified in an analysis by Jack Evernden, Charles Archambeau, and E. Cranswick, however, indicate that an elongated cavity constructed in granite about 500 kilometers west of Semipalatinsk with the long axis oriented east-west would be 1,500 kilometers from the nearest station in the north-south direction.[65] Elongated cavities would be easier to build than spherical cavities, and they could be constructed in bedded salt formations, which are much more common than salt domes, but the small axis of the cavity must still be large enough so that the walls respond elastically, which may increase the cavity volume by a factor of 3 to 5. Lastly, not enough shear waves would be generated to make an explosion look like an earthquake.

Although cavities make seismic detection more difficult, their construction may be detected with photoreconnaissance satellites. This is especially true for cavities constructed in granite, because a large amount of rock would have to be hauled from the site. Several thousand truckloads would be required to dispose of the spoil removed from even a small cavity. It would be difficult to hide this operation from intelligence analysts who would be on the lookout for cavity-building activities. Salt, on the other hand, can be removed much less conspicuously with solution mining techniques, in which water is injected into the cavity and brine is pumped out. The process of forming a large cavity would take at least several months and would be distinguishable from commercial salt mining by the high injection rates. One should also remember that thick salt deposits occur over only a few percent of the area of the Soviet Union and that seismic stations could be clustered about them to decrease greatly the detection threshold. Since salt domes are relatively aseismic, decreasing the detection threshold in these areas should not significantly increase the false alarm rate.

Seismic techniques complement nonseismic methods and present the potential cheater with a dilemma: should a large and expensive reusable cavity be built, or individual cavities for each test? A large, reusable cavity could have the advantages of a greater decoupling factor and lower overall costs, but the facility must withstand repeated nuclear tests. Repeated activity at the site might be more noticeable, and large cavities used several times would run a greater risk of collapse. Although it may be more difficult for photoreconnaissance to locate a single large, well-hidden facility than many small ones, there would be the risk of venting radioactive gas each time the cavity was reopened. And if small seismic signals were detected by the other party, several events occurring in the same location would be very suspicious. Even if an OSI was not requested, it would be very risky to reuse the cavity after an event was detected.

Testing in Third Countries

A less-mentioned evasion possibility is to test in other countries where the seismic network is not so sensitive. The detection threshold of the seismic network would probably be much lower in parts of the Southern Hemisphere. In one proposed network the threshold would be about 0.6 m_b units lower in Australia, Antarctica, and at the tips of South America and Africa, which would allow tests with yields five times larger to escape detection.[66] The Soviet Union has no close allies in these regions, however (remote possibilities might be Angola, Mozambique, or Madagascar), and even with the help of a third country, it would be a risky way to cheat. Betrayal or blackmail would always be possible; radioactive debris remaining in the third country would provide immutable evidence that a test had taken place, and an analysis of the debris would show that the device was the product of a country very knowledgeable in weapon design. It is unclear if nonseismic means would be effective in detecting such cases, since, like seismic networks, these would be concentrating on detecting activity in the Soviet Union.

Hiding in Noise

Decreasing the signal is not the only way to avoid seismic detection — one can also increase the noise. The estimates of the detection capability of seismic networks given above were based on statistical variations in normal microseismic noise. It is unlikely that periods of increased natural microseismic noise (microseism storms) could be systematically exploited to hide explosions, because the frequencies of microseisms are low compared with those emitted by explosions. An evader could, however, increase the high-frequency noise level artificially. It would be necessary to increase the noise at several stations — not just one station — and such behavior would certainly be interpreted as harassment possibly connected with an evasion attempt. A CTBT should contain a clause that allows the monitoring party to move seismic stations that become noisy.

Hiding in Earthquakes

A more serious worry is the possibility that an explosion of considerable size could be hidden in the noise created by an earthquake. This is called the "hide-in-the-earthquake" (HIE) evasion scenario. The requirements for HIE are demanding. The evader must detect earthquakes with a seismic network; accurately determine their location, depth, and m_b; decide in a few tens of seconds if they are capable of hiding an explosion; and, when an appropriate earthquake is found, detonate a nuclear device that has been prepared and waiting for months at just the right time to minimize the probability of detecting the explosion in the earthquake coda at all seismic stations. The simplest type of HIE evasion is to wait for a large earthquake somewhere in the world, but if a regional seismic network is available, there would be few opportunities for HIE evasion each year. To illustrate the difficulty, consider hiding a 1-kt tamped or a 10-kt muffled explosion from a single regional seismic station in the coda of an earthquake a few thousand kilometers distant. The station would detect a much larger high-frequency signal (5–10 Hz) from a nearby explosion than from a distant earthquake of the same size; therefore, the explosion signal must be much smaller than the earthquake signal so that even the high-frequency explosion signal will be hidden. There would be fewer than one opportunity per year in the Soviet Union to hide an explosion with an m_b of 3.7 from a network of fifteen internal seismic stations.[67] Against a network of twenty-five internal seismic arrays with better high-frequency detection capability, tamped explosions of at most a few tenths of a kiloton could plausibly be hidden in explosions. Using earthquakes close to the test site does not help much; although smaller earthquakes can be used, fewer earthquakes occur in small regions. The only region in the Soviet Union with enough seismicity for this purpose is the Kamchatka-Kurile region. Evernden estimates that only two to three shallow earthquakes per year with an m_b greater than 5.0 would occur within 300 kilometers of a test site on Kamchatka, which may be just sufficient to hide a 1-kt tamped explosion from a single station.[68] The opportunity to hide the same explosion from a network of sophisticated seismic stations would come only once every several years. Hiding both the seismic and the hydroacoustic waves of explosions on Kamchatka may be impossible.[69] The opportunities for evasion in the southern tectonic belt would come much less frequently unless the explosion was decoupled.

The chance of successful evasion could increase dramatically if one could predict the time and location of major earthquakes far enough in advance so that the nuclear explosive could be emplaced near the earthquake epicenter; but this capability is nowhere in sight. Predictive ability is not required to place an explosive near the aftershocks that occur during the weeks and months following a major earthquake, but the maximum size aftershocks are often about one m_b unit below that of the main earthquake, and many earthquakes have maximum aftershocks two m_b units less.[70] Since the aftershock would have to be one to two m_b units greater than the explosion, aftershocks from a shallow earthquake with an m_b of at least 6.5 would be required to hide a 1-kt tamped explosion. These earthquakes occur only about once every five years in the Soviet Union. Furthermore, the explosion would have to take place within 50 kilometers of the earthquake to be plausible as an aftershock, but this may be difficult or impossible in the Kamchatka-Kurile region, since most of the earthquakes occur offshore. Any drilling or mining activity near the site of a major earthquake would be suspicious. The Soviets could claim that an earthquake study was being conducted, but they would still run the risk of an OSI request.

Simulating an Earthquake

Most evasion scenarios have focused on avoiding seismic detection; however, an evader may also consider the riskier strategy of complicating event identification. By this strategy, an evader hopes that a signal detected by the monitoring party will be interpreted as an earthquake. The earliest of these evasion ideas was to set off several nuclear explosions of various yields in sequence to simulate the seismic signature of an earthquake. But the spectra of earthquakes and explosions are very different, especially at high frequencies, and setting off a few explosions together will not change this. A related concept is to explode the nuclear device in a seismic region displaying very high tectonic stress release, so that the explosion signal will be mixed with long-period earthquake-like shear and surface waves. Although stress release can complicate identification of explosions (i.e., it has made some past explosions appear somewhat earthquake-like), this is difficult to predict in advance with high confidence. Furthermore, since the amount of stress released is rarely of the same order as the explosive energy released, such events would still appear in the tail of the earthquake distribution when analyzed by spectral discriminants, making them more likely to be classified as explosions.

Hiding in Chemical Explosions

A more plausible way to avoid identification is by hiding a nuclear explosion in one or more chemical explosions. For example, an evader could detonate a large chemical explosion deep underground at the same time as a nearby decoupled nuclear explosion. The chemical explosion could be associated with an industrial activity, such as stimulating natural gas production. If an OSI was demanded, the evader could demonstrate that a large chemical explosion had taken place. The relationship between m_b and the energy released by an explosion is uncertain by at least a factor of 2 at low magnitudes without special calibration; therefore, even if one could somehow determine the size of the chemical explosion, this would not provide evidence of cheating.

As mentioned above, most large industrial explosions in the United States are ripple-fired. But even if most Soviet explosions are ripple-fired and can be distinguished efficiently from single explosions (neither of which is now known), concerns about evasion would not disappear, since large, single chemical explosions are occasionally fired in both countries. Single blasts of up to 5 kilotons have been fired in the past, and single explosions of up to 100 tons may not be uncommon.[71] Nevertheless, evasion opportunities could be limited by controlling large chemical explosions as part of a CTBT. For example, the treaty could specify that single blasts larger than 20 tons must be announced in advance and would be subject to on-site inspection during the explosion. OSI procedures similar to those specified in the PNET could verify the absence of a simultaneous nuclear explosion. Ripple-firing could be defined in the treaty so that it could be observed by an in-country network. It is not known to what degree mining operations could adapt to such restrictions. The proposed Underground Nuclear Explosions Control Act of 1987 introduced by U.S. Senator Mark Hatfield requires " . . . at least thirty days advance notice of . . . the coordinates, dates, times, and yields of industrial explosions larger than 20 tons of high explosive. . . ."[72]

Underground Evasion in General

It is unlikely that an evader would use only one of the methods outlined above. Several would be combined, and care would be taken to evade detection or identification by nonseismic as well as by seismic means. For example, the clandestine explosion could take place in a large mining zone in a seismic region, near or within a sensitive military installation if possible, and as far as possible from seismic monitoring stations. The Caucasus region would be appropriate because of the large amount of seismic and economic activity in the area. A cavity of 20- to 30-meter radius could be constructed 1 kilometer below the earth's surface, although mineralization in these areas could make it difficult to construct a large cavity that would not vent. Care would have to be taken to dispose of the spoil properly — it would not be sufficient simply to fill up a nearby valley, for that could be noticed by photoreconnaissance. If the excavation takes place over two or three years, the spoil could be hauled away with a few dozen truckloads per day. The entire operation might cost about a hundred million dollars. A cavity in salt might be larger and cheaper, but the detection threshold near salt domes is likely to be much lower than in seismic areas, and the monitoring party would be watching activity in salt domes very carefully.

The decoupling properties of the cavity could be tested with chemical explosives and a sensitive seismic network deployed around the site. The first nuclear test could be 0.1 kiloton, which, by extrapolating from chemical explosion data, might be certain to evade seismic detection. For an extra margin of safety, the test could be conducted during an earthquake, or a large chemical explosion could be fired nearby. The volatile radioactive gases from the nuclear explosion could be pumped into a sealed containment facility, and remote monitoring equipment used to inspect the cavity. Subsequent tests could slowly increase in yield up to about 1 kiloton, when the detection threshold at the seismic monitoring stations would be crossed. A few months before this test, a decoy test site could be set up 5 or 10 kilometers from the actual test site, complete with a large drilling rig and other equipment normally associated with nuclear testing. By hiding in earthquakes or large (100-ton) nearby chemical explosions, it may be possible to test in the cavity up to 5 kilotons before the monitoring party would become suspicious. Even if suspicions were aroused, the monitoring party might request an OSI at the decoy site, or the evader might convince the monitoring party that the events were really due to nearby chemical explosions or earthquakes. The test site would have to be abandoned after this, of course, since additional suspicious events at the same location would be identified as explosions by technical experts. If an OSI is requested for the test site, the evader could claim that the area to be inspected includes a sensitive military installation. This is an extreme scenario, but not impossible. It is doubtful that any party would go to such extremes unless testing at these yields was extremely valuable. There appears to be no technically plausible evasion scenario that would permit successful clandestine underground testing at yields greater than 5 kilotons, and certainly not more than 10 kilotons, under a CTBT.

Testing in Space

Clandestine underground testing is limited to fairly low yields, but clandestine testing in space is possible at any yield — one simply must go far enough away from the Earth. The monitoring party could deploy nuclear burst detectors on satellites to guard against this type of evasion, as the United States did in the early 1960s with the Vela satellites, but there will always be a distance beyond which these detectors cannot see. The capabilities of the Vela satellites and the detectors on the new Navstar satellites are classified, but a simple estimate of the detection threshold can be made. Assuming that the sensitivity of a detector is limited by the cosmic ray background, the X-rays from a 100-kt nuclear explosion could be detected over one billion kilometers away, or roughly the distance between the Earth and Saturn.[73] To escape detection one would have to wait at least three years after the launch to detonate the weapon, which is presumably too long an interval for a weapon development program, even if several weapons are tested at the same time.

The detection of explosions much closer to Earth might be avoided if the tests were conducted behind the Moon, the Sun, or one of the nearby planets. The space probe containing the nuclear weapon could fly behind the planet while two sensor probes fly to either side. The detonation would be observed by the sensor probes, which would then relay the information to Earth. (Communications could be done so that there would be a very low probability that the monitoring party would intercept them, or they could be encoded to look like normal satellite transmissions.) Large Soviet boosters are capable of launching several weapons and sensor probes into other planetary orbits, although care would have to be taken to hide the mission or to disguise the launch as part of a legitimate space exploration program. Such a mission would cost at least a hundred million dollars, and would take two months to two years to execute, depending on the planet chosen and its position relative to the Earth.

Testing behind the Moon is an often mentioned possibility, but the delayed gamma-rays emitted by the radioactive debris as it emerged from behind the Moon could be detected by satellites in Earth orbit.[74] Testing behind planets could be defeated by the careful deployment of additional detection satellites. Tests behind Venus, Mercury, or the Sun could be detected by a constellation of three or four satellites in orbit about the Sun. Testing behind Mars could be detected by a satellite orbiting the Sun just behind Mars or by two satellites orbiting the planet. The cost to maintain such a satellite constellation might be about a hundred million dollars per year, assuming that each satellite costs one to two hundred million dollars and has a lifetime of ten to twenty years.

Asteroids, of which there are about 40,000 with diameters larger than a few kilometers, may be safer to hide behind since it would be extremely expensive to design a satellite system to monitor the entire asteroid belt. It would take about a year for a spacecraft to reach the asteroid belt, which is about 400 million kilometers from the Sun. The delayed gamma-rays emitted by the radioactive debris as it emerged from behind the asteroid could not be detected at such large distances.

Instead of hiding behind a planet or asteroid, one could deploy a shield between the explosion and the detection satellites to absorb the X-rays. No reasonably sized shield could completely stop the gamma-rays and neutrons emitted from the explosion, so this technique would only be useful at distances greater than the detection threshold for these radiations, which is at least 3 million kilometers for a 100-kt explosion.[75] A shield with about the same mass as a warhead should be able to shield the X-rays emitted by a 100-kt explosion at this distance from detection satellites orbiting the Earth. If, on the other hand, detection satellites were deployed in orbits about the Sun, as suggested above, shielding would be impractical at distances of less than 300 million kilometers from the Sun, or about as far away as the asteroids.[76]

A simple and inexpensive measure to prevent all space testing, no matter how cleverly hidden, would be mandatory inspections of all space launches with sensors designed to detect the radiations emitted by fissile material. The United States and the Soviet Union would be reluctant to have military payloads inspected, but the detection devices could be made so sensitive that the inspection could take place from a distance of tens of meters; thus, it would not be necessary to reveal any sensitive information about the shape or size of the payload.[77] If the two countries are unable to agree on mandatory inspection of all launches, perhaps they could agree to inspect only those objects leaving Earth orbit, although a good space tracking system would then be required so that objects that were not inspected could not leave Earth orbit without detection.

LOW-YIELD THRESHOLD TEST BAN VS. CTB

The preceding discussion of evasion techniques clearly indicates that one cannot verify the absence of all nuclear testing. Depending on how much money evaders are willing to spend and how much risk they are willing to take, there will be a low probability of detecting and identifying underground tests with yields less than 0.01 to 1 kiloton, and, with a great deal of luck and defiant confidence, perhaps up to 5 kilotons. It was argued above that even a series of tests with yields below 1 kiloton would be unlikely to alter the military balance. Although tests of several kilotons might be significant, it appears that no one could have high confidence in cheating at this level. A large segment of the defense and arms control community, however, now favors banning only those activities that can be verified with high confidence. Most test ban proponents, for example, now advocate a low-yield threshold test ban treaty (LYTTBT) instead of a CTBT. Since decoupled nuclear explosions with yields less than 1 kiloton cannot be reliably detected (let alone identified), the most common threshold suggested has been 1 kiloton, although thresholds of 3, 5, 10, and 15 kilotons have also been proposed.

The idea of banning only testing that can be verified with high confidence is flawed because the risk of an imperfectly verifiable ban is not weighed against the cost of openly permitting imperfectly verifiable activities. Most people would agree, for example, that the Biological Weapons Convention of 1972 was in the best interests of the United States despite its lack of verification provisions because the benefits of having an agreement outweighed the risks of cheating by other parties. Suppose, for example, that tests below 1 kiloton had *no* military value but that a complete ban on testing was necessary to gain key political advantages; in this case, it is clear that the advantages of a CTB would outweigh the risks of cheating below 1 kiloton. This example is exaggerated, but demonstrates that the single-minded pursuit of effective verification can be self-defeating. Indeed, an LYTTBT may contain the seeds of its own destruction, since it would allow countries to maintain an active nuclear research, testing, and development program. The existence of such a program would make if far easier to cheat on or to abrogate a test ban treaty.

Testing at yields less than 1, 3, 5, 10, or 15 kilotons does provide some military benefits, of course, but one should note that an LYTTBT would permit unlimited testing at yields that could be achieved only at substantial risk and expense under a CTBT. Testing under the threshold would be sanctioned, and weapon research and development would continue. If the unlimited research and development of nuclear weapons that could take place under an LYTTBT would have as great a negative effect (or, more likely, as little an effect) on U.S. security as Soviet cheating under a CTBT, then there would be little reason to prefer an LYTTBT over a CTBT, even if the Soviets are presumed to cheat. The main advantage of an LYTTBT in this case would be to quiet domestic political opposition which, under a CTBT, might claim that the Soviet Union was making significant progress through clandestine testing. Even if cheating is theoretically possible, however, it will not necessarily occur. When deciding on a threshold treaty for verification reasons, one must consider the probability as well as the consequences of successful clandestine testing.

It is often suggested that an LYTTBT would be easier and quicker to negotiate than a CTBT because the requirements for verification are relaxed, but this is not clear. First, one would need to establish a seismic network around the allowed test site to estimate accurately the yields of nuclear explosions to make sure that the threshold had not been violated. A series of specially monitored explosions — probably using on-site personnel and hydrodynamic measuring equipment — would be needed to calibrate the seismic network. The recent stir in the United States over possible Soviet violations of the 150-kt threshold emphasizes the importance of accurate yield estimation even when military significance is not an issue. Yield estimation would be much more critical for a 1-kt threshold, moreover, because 1 kiloton roughly corresponds to the threshold for boosting. Raising the threshold to 5 or 10 kilotons would avoid this problem, but at the expense of greatly increasing the amount of weapon research and development that could take place under the threshold.

Second, a network of seismic stations scattered across the Soviet Union would still be required to monitor the absence of testing outside of the allowed test site. But the network could be somewhat smaller and less sophisticated than that needed to monitor a CTBT because there would be no reason to cheat outside of the allowed test site unless the yield was substantially greater than the threshold. For example, for a 1-kt threshold one would only have to verify the absence of 3- to 10-kt nuclear explosions outside of the test site, which might require ten internal arrays instead of twenty-five. In addition, the false alarm problem would be ameliorated because the network would detect fewer earthquakes and chemical explosions, and because discrimination is generally better for higher magnitude events. At a monitoring threshold of m_b = 3.0, for example, there would be half as many earthquakes and many fewer chemical explosions than there would be at a threshold of m_b = 2.5.

Perhaps the most persuasive reason to prefer an LYTTBT is that it would allow operational experience to be gained in detecting and discriminating explosions from earthquakes in the monitored country. For this reason, an LYTTBT would be especially useful as a first step toward a CTBT, but this would delay gaining the political advantages of a test ban that are only achieved when the ban is truly comprehensive. It is not clear that a CTBT would be easier to achieve in phases, since each phase would be accompanied by vigorous opposition from those who wish, for various reasons, to continue nuclear testing.

SUMMARY

Is a CTBT verifiable? The answer depends on what one means by the word "verifiable." The absence of all testing can never be verified, but a network of twenty-five seismic arrays could detect decoupled nuclear explosions anywhere in the Soviet Union down to yields of 1 kiloton. Even using elaborate evasion schemes, such as hiding decoupled explosions in earthquakes or chemical explosions, yields greater than 5 to 10 kilotons cannot escape detection. Clandestine testing at yields near 1 kiloton would be expensive and risky, and an evader could not have high confidence that cheating at this level would go undetected. Therefore, unless such tests are considered to be extremely valuable, cheating at this level would be effectively deterred. Clandestine tests of a few tenths of a kiloton may escape detection with high confidence and less cost, but the military significance of such testing is questionable. Although many uncertainties remain, it appears that such testing could be identified with a moderately high probability while suffering a reasonably low false alarm rate, but only if chemical and nuclear explosions can be efficiently discriminated.

Most analyses of the verification problem do not take full account of the potential of nonseismic techniques to increase verification effectiveness. Photoreconnaissance satellites may be able to reduce the number of misclassified earthquakes by up to an order of magnitude and to detect signs of testing activity for on-site inspection requests. The possibility of atmospheric detection of radionuclides from a shallow explosion forces a cheater to drill deep and close the hole carefully, which increases the chance of detection by satellites.

Unless a cheater was extremely careless, on-site inspection could not detect testing. If an OSI were requested for the wrong site, or if the cheater was sure that the test was well hidden, an OSI could be allowed and nothing would be found. If an OSI was requested for the site of a test that was not well hidden, the request would be refused and the monitoring party would have to act without positive proof of a violation. On the other hand, OSIs would be important to deter cheating because the refusal of an OSI request would amount to an admission of guilt in the eyes of many. OSI would also be useful to build confidence, since parties abiding by the treaty would have every incentive to prove that ambiguous events were not clandestine nuclear explosions.

High-yield testing in space is technically possible at present, but could be prevented at relatively low cost by an agreement to inspect all deep space launches for fissile material, or could be made very difficult at much higher cost by deploying nuclear burst detection satellites in solar orbits or by deploying a space-based space tracking system and inspecting only interplanetary launches.

Since one cannot have high confidence that testing at a certain level is not being done, many analysts argue that a threshold test ban treaty would be superior to a CTBT. This argument has political appeal in the United States, but an LYTTBT would permit unlimited testing at yields that could be achieved only at great risk and expense under a CTBT. It is my judgment, however, that the cheating that would be possible under a CTBT would be no greater a risk to national security than unlimited testing under the threshold, especially if the threshold is high (e.g., 10 kilotons). The verification system required for an LYTTBT would be somewhat smaller than that required for a CTBT, and the misclassification of earthquakes and chemical explosions would be less of a problem, but one would instead have the problem of accurately estimating the yield of explosions at the approved test site. An LYTTBT would, however, be useful as a first step toward a CTBT since it would allow the seismic network to be calibrated.

NOTES

1. Richard L. Garwin, "The Administration's Case Against a Comprehensive Test Ban is Wrong," *Public Interest Report, Journal of the Federation of American Scientists* 39, no. 10 (December 1986): 13. Yields up to 0.3 kiloton may be contained in a reusable facility.
2. Thomas B. Cochran, William M. Arkin, and Milton M. Hoenig, *Nuclear Weapons Databook*, vol. I: *U.S. Nuclear Forces and Capabilities* (Cambridge, Mass.: Ballinger Publishing Company, 1984), pp. 54, 60.
3. Thomas C. Schelling, *Arms and Influence* (Yale: Yale University Press, 1966), pp. 107–116.
4. Frank von Hippel, Harold A. Feiveson, and Christopher E. Paine, "A Low-Threshold Nuclear Test Ban," *International Security* 12, no. 2 (Fall 1987): 144.
5. Jack F. Evernden, "Study of Seismological Evasion, Part I: General Discussion of Various Evasion Schemes," *Bulletin of the Seismological Society of America*, 66, no. 1 (February 1976), 246–48.
6. A.L. Latter, R.E. LeLevier, E.A. Martinelli, and W.G. McMillan, "A Method of Concealing Underground Nuclear Explosions," *Journal of Geophysical Research* 66, no 3 (March 1961): 943–46.
7. J.F. Evernden, C.B. Archambeau, and E. Cranswick, "An Evaluation of Seismic Decoupling and Underground Nuclear Test Monitoring Using High-Frequency Seismic Data," *Reviews of Geophysics* 24, no. 2 (May 1986): 170; Jack F. Evernden and Charles B. Archambeau, "Some Seismological Aspects of Monitoring a CTBT," in Kosta Tsipis, David W. Hafemeister, and Penny Janeway, eds., *Arms Control Verification: The Technologies that Make it Possible* (Washington, D.C.: Pergamon-Brassey's, 1986), pp. 253–54.
8. Lynn R. Sykes and Jack F. Evernden, "Verification of a Comprehensive Nuclear Test Ban," *Scientific American* 247, no. 4 (October 1982): 52.
9. W.J. Hannon, "Seismic Verification of a Comprehensive Test Ban," *Science* 227 (18 January 1985): 254 gives $m_b = 3.3$ for 90 percent detection probability for ten internal stations, while Thomas C. Bache, "Seismic Verification of a Comprehensive Test Ban Treaty: A Difficult Problem" (paper for the 1987 Annual Joint

Meeting of the American Physical Society and the American Association of Physics Teachers, San Francisco, 28 January 1987), gives m_b = 3.5.

10. Hannon, "Seismic Verification," p. 254, projects a detection capability of 2.8 for twenty-five internal arrays, while Bache, "Seismic Verification," gives m_b = 2.6 for a high-quality network of ten internal arrays. The results in Evernden and Archambeau, "Some Seismological Aspects," p. 259, correspond to an m_b of about 2.8 for twenty-five internal stations.

11. Charles B. Archambeau, "A Time and Threshold Limited Nuclear Test Ban," in Jozef Goldblat and David Cox, eds., *Nuclear Weapon Tests: Cessation or Limitation?* (Oxford: Oxford University Press, 1988).

12. W.J. Hannon, Lawrence Livermore National Laboratory, personal communication, January 1987.

13. The frequency of earthquakes in a given region can be described by the equation $\log N = a - bm_b$, where N is the cumulative number of earthquakes with magnitude greater than or equal to m_b, and a and b are empirically determined constants for the particular region. Values for b typically range between 0.6 and 1.0, with a world-wide average of 0.9. Using data on earthquake frequency at m_b of 3.8 to 5.0 in Sykes and Evernden, "Verification of a Test Ban," pp. 49–53, Archambeau, "A Time and Threshold Limited Test Ban," and Evernden, et al., "An Evaluation of Seismic Decoupling," p. 211, and assuming that 10 percent of all Kamchatka/Kurile earthquakes are within 25 kilometers of land, there will be about 2,000 earthquakes per year with m_b greater than 2.5 located within 25 kilometers of Soviet territory. The uncertainty in this estimate is about a factor of 2. Evernden, et al. and Archambeau assume b = 0.6 to 0.7, which leads to lower values, while Hannon, "Seismic Verification," p. 255 and Bache, "Seismic Verification," assume b = 0.8 to 1.0, which gives somewhat larger results. A study by D. Racine and P. Klouda, "Seismicity of the Salt Areas of Texas, Louisiana, Oklahoma, and Kansas," AL-79-3 (Alexandria, Va.: Teledyne Geotech, 1979), gives a value for b of about 1.0 and appears to indicate that areas thought to be aseismic actually experience large numbers of low-magnitude seismic events. Little is known about Soviet seismicity at low magnitudes, but if one assumes that it is similar to the seismicity of the region studied by Racine and Klouda, then extrapolations indicate that as many as 7,000 natural events per year would be detected in an area the size of the Soviet Union by a network with a 90 percent detection threshold of m_b = 2.5. Even though these data were collected only on Sundays to minimize the detection of man-made events, most of the events were detected during a few hours in the evening. For example, about 55 percent of the events occurred between 20:00 and 0:00 hours, and 78 percent occurred between 15:00 and 0:00 hours. If the excess events during these hours, which are almost certainly due to human activity, are eliminated from the data set, then the resulting estimates of natural Soviet seismicity agree with other sources—about 2,000 per year. The Racine and Klouda study does, however, emphasize the importance of man-made seismic events in seismic monitoring.

14. Estimated from data in Archambeau, "Time and Threshold Limited Test Bans."

15. Robert S. Norris, Thomas B. Cochran, and William M. Arkin, "Known U.S. Nuclear Tests: July 1945 to 16 October 1986," Nuclear Weapons Databook Working Paper NWD 86-2 (Washington, D.C.: Natural Resources Defense Council, October 1986), pp. 5–6; Sykes and Evernden, "Verification of a Test Ban," p. 49.

16. Sykes and Evernden, "Verification of a Test Ban," p. 49. Deeper holes are few, well known, and too substantial to hide.

17. Ibid. The depth distribution of small-magnitude earthquakes in the Soviet Union is unknown.

18. National Academy of Sciences, *Nuclear Arms Control: Background and Issues* (Washington, D.C.: National Academy of Sciences Press, 1985), p. 216, gives about 100 shallow Soviet earthquakes per year with $m_b > 3.8$, which translates to 600 to 2,000 per year with m_b greater than 2.5 (see note 13).

19. The detection threshold usually refers to the magnitude that can be detected with 90 percent probability. The probability of detecting an event with $m_b > m_b'$ is given by integrating the product of $P(m_b)$, the probability of detecting an event with magnitude m_b, and $N(m_b)$, the number of events in the interval dm_b about m_b. $N(m_b)$ is equal to $-a10^{a-bm_b}$, where a and b are constants described above in note 13. The integral was numerically integrated for $a = 4.75$, $b = 0.7$, with $P(m_b)$ represented by an error function with a mean of 2.3 and a standard deviation of about 0.16. The results indicate that the probability of detecting an event with a magnitude above the 90 percent detection threshold is about 98 percent. For 0.2, 0.4, and 0.6 magnitude units below the 90 percent detection threshold, the probability of detection is 90 percent, 70 percent, and 50 percent, respectively.

20. The decision line in Figure 4–3 was drawn to best separate the explosion population from the earthquake population, but this is not a proper statistical procedure since it takes advantage of bias in the sample population (e.g., testing patterns) to enhance discrimination. If the discriminant is simply $(m_b - M_s)$, then the slope of the decision line should always be equal to one. Many seismologists fail to take this into account, and incorrectly use $(m_b - M_s)$ as a two-dimensional discriminant.

21. For example, a Gaussian fit to $(m_b - M_s)$ for each population for the Landers station resulted in a seven-fold increase in $p(q|x)$ for low $p(x|q)$ compared to that for the Elko station. Data supplied by Eileen S. Vergino, Lawrence Livermore National Laboratory, personal communication, December 1986.

22. Anne Suteau-Henson and Thomas C. Bache, "Spectral Characteristics of Regional Phases Recorded at NORESS" (San Diego, Calif.: Science Applications International, September 1987).

23. S.R. Taylor, N.W. Sherman, and M.D. Denny, "Spectral Discrimination between NTS Explosions and Western United States Earthquakes," *Seismological Research Letters* 58 (1987): 17.

24. Sykes and Evernden, "Verification of a Test Ban," p. 50; Evernden and Archambeau, "Some Seismological Aspects," pp. 231–32; and P.W. Pomeroy, W.J. Best, and T.V. McEvilly, "Test Ban Treaty Verification with Regional Data: A Review," *Bulletin of the Seismological Society of America* 72, no. 6B (December 1982): S89–S129.

25. Ronald E. Glaser, Steven R. Taylor, Marvin D. Denny, and Eileen S. Vergino, "Regional Discrimination of NTS Explosions and Western U.S. Earthquakes: Multivariate Discriminants," UCID-20930 (Livermore, Calif.: Lawrence Livermore National Laboratory, November 1986).

26. Ibid., p. 11.

27. Multivariate analysis of only those events which had $(m_b - M_s)$ available showed perfect discrimination. Ronald E. Glaser, Lawrence Livermore National Laboratory, personal communication, June 1987.

28. Eileen S. Vergino and Steven R. Taylor, Lawrence Livermore National Laboratory, personal communication, 9 April 1987.

29. Glaser, et al., "Regional Discrimination," p. 38.

30. A best-fit line for events with $3.5 < m_b < 5.0$ gives $\log(N) = 3.62 - 0.56m_b$. Data from Ibid., p. 22.

31. Evernden and Archambeau, "Some Seismological Aspects," p. 231.

32. Taylor, et al., "Spectral Discrimination."

33. 1.73 megatons of high explosive was used in 1985, of which about 85 percent was ammonium-nitrate. The most common industrial explosive is ANFO (ammonium nitrate and fuel oil), which has about 90 percent of the energy content of TNT. Charles Davis, U.S. Bureau of Mines, personal communication, 24 April 1987.

34. Paul G. Richards, "Consideration of Chemical Explosions," (paper presented to the Office of Technology Assessment, Washington, D.C., 28 April 1987), presents data for the number and size of explosions at fourteen mines in the western United States. There are approximately 25 explosions per year at these mines with yields greater than 500 tons, 175 with yields greater than 200 tons, and 500 with yields greater than 100 tons. It is not clear how comprehensive or accurate these data are.

35. Ibid. Chemical explosions are roughly twice as efficient in generating seismic waves as nuclear explosions.

36. Extrapolations from data in Richards, "Consideration of Chemical Explosions," based on cumulative yield, with the total cumulative yield limited to 1.5 megatons, give about 15,000 explosions per year with yield greater than 10 tons. Extrapolations based on cumulative number give at least 5,000 per year.

37. Bache, "Seismic Verification." Seventy-two chemical explosions with m_b greater than 2.5 were detected in six months in the northwest corner of the Soviet Union. Since the area observed was only 3 percent of the land area of the Soviet Union, these data are consistent with thousands of chemical explosions with magnitudes greater than that of a decoupled 1-kt nuclear explosion.

38. The typical coal mine in the western United States uses 10–20-ton explosions to loosen the coal. Individual explosive charges, of which there may be 50 to 100 in all, weighing 200 to 300 pounds are placed in holes 6 inches in diameter and 50 feet deep. The charges are fired five at a time, with the firings separated by 25 to 50 milliseconds. The explosion takes place over a period of about 1 second. Richard Dick, U.S. Bureau of Mines, personal communication, 24 April 1987. Richards, "Consideration of Chemical Explosions," reports that for large (> 100-ton) explosions, each hole is filled with less than 1 ton of ANFO, that there are about 10 holes per row, with the rows fired every 200 milliseconds. A 200-ton explosion would therefore take about 4 seconds. S.A. Greenlaugh, "Effects of Delay Shooting on the Nature of P-wave Seismograms," *Bulletin of the Seismological Society of America*, 70, no. 6 (December 1980): 2037–50, reports that iron mines typically use 680 kilograms of high explosive per hole with 10 holes per row. Twenty rows are fired in the typical shot, with 17-ms delays between each hole. A 140-ton shot takes about 3.4 seconds.

39. Suteau-Henson and Bache, "Spectral Characteristics."

40. In his account of test ban discussions during the Johnson administration, Seaborg tells of a meeting at which Herbert Scoville, then ACDA assistant director for science and technology, "presented a very optimistic assessment of the ability of photographic intelligence to supplement seismic methods in further reducing the number of unidentified seismic events." Glenn T. Seaborg, *Stemming the Tide: Arms Control in the Johnson Years* (Lexington, Mass.: Lexington Books, 1987), p. 220.

41. Non-pointing satellites can revisit the same spot on the earth every fifteen to eighteen days, which would allow forty to fifty random events to be photographed. Actually, the number of visits would be greater for the Soviet Union, since there would be substantial overlap at northern latitudes. Satellites that can point, such as SPOT, have a revisit time of only one to four days, thus allowing many more events to be photographed. Ronald J. Ondrejka, "Imaging Technologies," in Kosta Tsipis, David W. Hafemeister, and Penny Janeway, eds., *Arms Control Verification: The Technologies that Make it Possible* (Washington, D.C.: Pergamon-Brassey's, 1986), pp. 78–79.

42. The resolution of SPOT is 10 meters, and that of the planned Atlas-C is 3 to 5 meters. The resolution necessary to detect roads is 9 meters. Ibid., pp. 74–79.
43. *The Concise Columbia Encyclopedia* (New York: Avon, 1983), p. 872, and *World Facts in Brief* (Chicago: Rand McNally, 1986), pp. 124–25.
44. Author's estimate using a map of Soviet Union that indicates navigable rivers.
45. Author's estimate using detailed road maps of California.
46. To prevent a subsidence crater from forming at NTS, an explosion must occur at a depth of at least $160Y^{1/3}$ meters, where Y is the yield in kilotons. Venting, on the other hand, depends on how carefully the hole is filled. W.J. Hannon, Lawrence Livermore National Laboratory, personal communication, 20 October 1987.
47. Stephen I. Warshaw and Paul F. Dubois, "Ionospheric Detection of Explosions," *Energy and Technology Review*, May 1983, p. 43.
48. Warren Heckrotte, "On-Site Inspection for Verification of a Comprehensive Test Ban Treaty," UCRL-95313 (Livermore, Calif.: Lawrence Livermore National Laboratory, October 1986), p. 13.
49. Milo D. Nordyke, "The Test Ban Treaties: Verifying Compliance," *Energy and Technology Review*, May 1983, pp. 6–7.
50. Ibid., p. 6.
51. See note 5.
52. Latter, et al., "Concealing Underground Explosions," p. 945.
53. D. Springer, M. Denny, J. Healy, and W. Mickey, "The Sterling Experiment: Decoupling of Seismic Waves by a Shot-Generated Cavity," *Journal of Geophysical Research* 73, no. 18 (1968): 5995.
54. Ibid., p. 6006, calculates a decoupling factor of 120 for a mined cavity of the same radius, while Evernden, et al., "Seismic Decoupling," p. 149, gives a decoupling factor of 200 for these conditions.
55. Evernden, et al., "Seismic Decoupling," p. 149.
56. J.L. Merritt, "Constraints Imposed by Siting Conditions, Construction Methods, and Cost on the Formation and Use (and Possible Reuse) of Large Cavities," *Proceedings of the DOE-sponsored Cavity-decoupling Workshop*, Pajaro Dunes, Calif., 29–31 July 1985, pp. V-33–V-52.
57. Ibid.
58. Evernden, et al., "Seismic Decoupling," p. 146.
59. Ibid., p. 149.
60. Robert Blandford, "Decoupling Experiments," in Donald B. Larson, ed., *Proceedings of the DOE-Sponsored Cavity-decoupling Workshop*, Pajaro Dunes, Calif., 29–31 July 1985, p. V-3.
61. Evernden, et al., "Seismic Decoupling," p. 177, and David W. Cheney, "Monitoring Nuclear Test Bans," CRS Report No. 86-155 SPR (Washington, D.C.: Congressional Research Service, 23 September 1986), p. 37.
62. Evernden, et al., "Seismic Decoupling," p. 149.
63. L.A. Glenn, A.J.C. Ladd, B. Morgan, and K.A. Wilson, "Elastic Radiation from Explosively-Loaded Ellipsoidal Cavities in an Unbounded Medium," *Geophysical Journal of the Royal Astronomical Society* 81, no. 1 (1985): 231–42; and L.A. Glenn, B. Morgan, A.J.C. Ladd, K.A. Wilson, and J.A. Rail, "Elastic Radiation from Explosively-Loaded Axisymmetric Cavities," *Geophysical Journal of the Royal Astronomical Society* 86 (1986): 119–36.
64. The maximum distance from a set of equidistant points, d, is given by $(a/2.6)^{1/2}$, where a is the area divided by the number of points. For twenty-five stations in the Soviet Union, $a = 900,000$ km^2 and $d = 600$ km. If, on the other hand, the distance to a point within 45° of just one axis is maximized, this is given by $(3)^{1/2}d$, or about 1,000 km.

65. Evernden, et al., "Seismic Decoupling," p. 179.
66. Hannon, "Seismic Verification," p. 252.
67. Jack F. Evernden, "Study of Seismological Evasion, Part III: Evaluation of Evasion Possibilities Using Codas of Large Earthquakes," *Bulletin of the Seismological Society of America* 66, no. 2 (1976): 589, gives three opportunities per year in the Soviet Union to hide a 1-kt tamped explosion in unsaturated hard rock (m_b = 3.7). If the estimate of the m_b of the earthquake is uncertain by only 0.1 units of m_b, then only one opportunity per year is available. If the uncertainty is 0.2 units, or if the m_b of the explosion as well as of the earthquake is uncertain, then this is reduced by another factor of 2.
68. Evernden, "Seismological Evasion, Part III," p. 270.
69. Ibid., p. 275.
70. Ibid., p. 271.
71. Richards, "Consideration of Chemical Explosions," p. 3.
72. Senators Mark Hatfield, Edward Kennedy, Dennis DeConcini, Robert Stafford, John Danforth, Claiborne Pell, Arlen Specter, Alan Cranston, Spark Matsunaga, and William Proxmire, "A bill to provide for a simultaneous, mutual, and verifiable moratorium on underground nuclear explosions above a low-yield threshold," 28 April 1987.
73. A nuclear explosion releases 50–70 percent of its energy in a half-microsecond pulse of X-rays with a blackbody temperature of 1–10 keV. Harold V. Argo, "Satellite Verification of Arms Control Agreements," in Kosta Tsipis, David Hafemeister, and Penny Janeway, eds., *Arms Control Verification: The Technologies that Make it Possible* (Washington, D.C.: Pergamon-Brassey's, 1986), pp. 293–95. The X-ray energy flux at a distance R (km) in space from a weapon of yield Y (kt) is given by $10^{17}Y/R^2$ keV/cm^2. The isotropic cosmic ray background is about 8,000 MeV/cm^2/s, which would give about 4 keV/cm^2 during the X-ray pulse. For a signal to noise ratio of 1, the signal can be detected out to $R = 10^8 Y^{1/2}$. One could reduce the noise level considerably by rejecting high-energy events, but one would still be limited by the necessity of detecting at least several photons from the explosion in each detector. Assuming a detector size of 10 cm^2 and a blackbody temperature of a few keV gives about the same detection threshold as that given above. A 100-kt explosion could be detected out to the orbit of Saturn, which is an average of 1.4 billion kilometers from the Earth. Cosmic ray showers with intensities up to 100 times greater than average occasionally occur, which would reduce the detection range by a factor of 10, but since the particles originate from the Sun, it is doubtful that a plausible scenario for hiding in this shower exists. See the *Geneva Conference on the Discontinuance of Nuclear Weapons Tests: History and Analysis of Negotiations*, Report No. 7258 (Washington, D.C.: U.S. Department of State, October 1961), pp. 367–75.
74. The weapon debris carries away about 25 percent of energy released in a nuclear explosion. Assuming that a 100-kt nuclear device weighs on the order of 100 kilograms, the velocity of the debris is about 1,000 km/s. The radius of the Moon is 1,700 kilometers so the debris would emerge from behind the Moon a few seconds after the explosion. The flux near the Earth of the delayed fission gamma rays emitted at this time — on the order of 1 MeV/cm^2/s/kt — is more than sufficient for detection.
75. About 0.3 percent of the energy from a nuclear weapon is emitted in the form of prompt gamma rays in about 10^{-7} sec. Using arguments similar to those used above for X-rays, the incident gamma-ray energy fluence would be equal to the cosmic ray energy out to a range of about $10^7 Y^{1/2}$. On the other hand, the requirement that at least one photon be collected in each detector would lead to

a threshold 3 to 10 times lower than this, if the detector has an area of 10 cm^2 and the gamma-rays have an average energy of 1 MeV. The detection range for neutrons is similar.

76. A 100-kt nuclear explosion ten million kilometers from the Earth could be shielded by a 100-kg shield deployed a few hundred meters from the explosion, even if the explosion has a high blackbody temperature. The separation between the shield and the explosion would ensure that the shield would not reradiate X-rays that could be detected by nuclear-burst-detection satellites in Earth orbit. If, on the other hand, the detection satellites are in a solar orbit with a radius of 150 million kilometers, then the shield must cover a much larger solid angle. In this case, a 100-kg shield located a hundred meters away could only shield an explosion 300 million kilometers from the earth if the blackbody temperature was low. Steve Fetter, "Shielding Nuclear Explosions in Space," June 1987 (unpublished).

77. Steve Fetter, "Inspection of Space Launches for Fissile Material," October 1987 (work in progress).

5 STRATEGY, PROLIFERATION, AND DETENTE

The discussions of modernization, stockpile confidence, and verification in the previous chapters have been essentially technical. Even so, it may have been apparent to the reader that the basic considerations that divide test ban friends from foes are political, not technical, in nature. The lack of consensus in the United States about the desirability of a test ban is not due primarily to disagreements about the technical feasibility of, for example, using an existing warhead on a new missile or seismic monitoring. Rather, the main reason for this disharmony is that there are fundamental differences of opinion about nuclear strategy, the political effects of arms control negotiations, the aims and trustworthiness of the Soviet Union, the efficacy of superpower efforts to thwart nuclear proliferation, and so forth. It is often more acceptable, however, to discuss political subjects such as the test ban in technical terms — to use technical arguments as proxies, so to speak, for issues of strategy and politics. Thus, one often hears statements about the technical feasibility of accomplishing certain tasks under a CTB that are divorced from any discussion of the political assumptions that underlie these judgments. This insidious tendency should be resisted, for it only serves to divert attention from the real issues at stake and to mislead the citizenry to believe that consensus is impossible only because experts disagree about technical matters.

Previous chapters have pointed out when technical judgments depend on political beliefs. As in most cases, technical judgment is relevant only after one has made more fundamental political decisions. This chapter explicitly considers three nontechnical areas — strategy, proliferation, and détente. The primary purpose is to elucidate the relationship between these topics and the test ban debate, not to argue for a particular political viewpoint.

STRATEGY

Arms control and disarmament proposals, as well as requirements for weapon modernization and stockpile confidence, should flow naturally from conceptions about nuclear strategy, or how nuclear weapons should be disposed in order to achieve national security objectives. Traditionally, strategy has referred to rules and principles of warfare designed to achieve success in military operations. But the advent of nuclear weapons has changed the focus of strategic thought from success in winning wars to success in preventing them. Because of the tremendous destructive potential of nuclear weapons, the primary purpose of virtually every nuclear strategist has been to deter war.

It would be a simple matter if the desire to deter war led inexorably to a single framework for the disposition of nuclear forces, but this is not the case. Although everyone carries the banner of deterrence, theories about exactly how nuclear forces are supposed to deter war vary widely, as do the practical consequences of these theories. All too often strategists, activists, military planners, policymakers, arms controllers, and weapon designers justify a certain proposal simply by saying that it would "strengthen deterrence." To be meaningful, however, such statements must be tied to a specific deterrent strategy and supported by technological and geopolitical realities.

Deterrence theories go by many names, including existential, type I and II, extended, countervailing, war-winning, massive retaliation, mutual assured destruction, and flexible response. It is beyond the scope of this book to describe the evolution of nuclear strategy in detail.[1] To evaluate the connection between strategy and the test ban, it is sufficient to focus on the two basic threads of strategic nuclear thought in the United States since the end of the Second World War, as expounded by Bernard Brodie and Herman Kahn: minimum deterrence and war-fighting deterrence. These two views of deterrence differ in almost every respect: what they seek to deter, the weapons that best deter war, the efficacy of using nuclear weapons in war, the damage resulting from war, and so forth. Nearly every thoughtful view on nuclear strategy falls somewhere between these two extremes.

Minimum vs. War-fighting Deterrence

Minimum deterrence is based on the notion that a nuclear war between nuclear powers could not be won in any meaningful sense. This belief flows from the observation that a single nuclear weapon could obliterate a large city, and only a handful would be necessary to functionally destroy a society as large and diverse as the United States. Since large numbers of nuclear weapons exist, and since a perfect defense (or a perfect preemptive strike) is impossible, the destruction of the homeland cannot be prevented. Hence, the traditional definition of war as a rational means to a political end no longer applies, because there can be no political goal that is worth self-destruction (or even an appreciable risk of self-destruction). Bernard Brodie articulated these ideas soon after the destruction of Hiroshima and Nagasaki: "Thus far the chief purpose of our military establishment has been to win wars. From now on its chief purpose must be to avert them. It can have almost no other useful purpose."[2]

In this view, nuclear war is prevented simply by guaranteeing that an attacker would suffer unacceptable damage in return. This involves acquiring a nuclear force that is sufficiently powerful, reliable, and invulnerable so that a rational adversary could not envision attacking with impunity. Advocates of minimum deterrence differ on the types and numbers of nuclear weapons necessary to deter war, but all agree that the number and variety required is far less than that currently deployed by the superpowers. This conviction was well summarized by President Kennedy's national security advisor, McGeorge Bundy: "In the real world of real political leaders — whether here or in the Soviet Union — a decision that brings even one hydrogen bomb on one city of one's own country would be recognized in advance as a catastrophic blunder; ten bombs on ten cities would be a disaster beyond history; and a hundred bombs on a hundred cities are unthinkable."[3]

Many strategists are not satisfied with the concept of minimum deterrence, or what has commonly become known as mutal assured destruction (MAD). One of the earliest and most vocal critics of minimum deterrence was Herman Kahn, who believed that questions of victory and defeat are not irrelevant in the nuclear age. Kahn's central point was that nuclear war *could* happen. If, despite our best attempts at deterrence, nuclear war does occur, Kahn argued that a policy of targeting cities would be tantamount to committing suicide. In this view, it is irresponsible not to plan for attacks on military targets (i.e., counterforce) in an attempt to reestablish deterrence after the outbreak of war, thus possibly sparing the destruction of cities. If general war was to break out, these counterforce attacks would limit damage to the United States by destroying the ability of the Soviets to retaliate, thus saving tens of millions of American lives.

To show the dangers of accepting MAD, Kahn postulated a nuclear war in which one side attacks and destroys most of the other side's strategic nuclear weaponry in a disarming first strike while sparing its cities. (This scenario was recently revived by the Committee on the Present Danger in the "window of vulnerability" argument.) According to this view, the victim would then be left with a simple choice: retaliate or surrender. Since retaliation would be equivalent to suicide, the rational move would be surrender. Thus, argued Kahn, victory and defeat *are* possible, and the United States should make every effort in its defense planning to assure that the United States has the capacity to fight and win a nuclear war, while denying this capability to the Soviet Union. Minimum deterrence works only if both sides have accepted it; if, as some observers have claimed, the Soviet Union believes that a nuclear war could be fought and won, then the United States has no choice but to adopt a similar posture.[4]

Kahn acknowledged that nuclear war would likely be an unprecedented catastrophe even for the winning side. But, unlike advocates of minimum deterrence, he dismissed the notion that nuclear war could therefore only be inadvertent or the result of gross miscalculation. He believed that a counterforce first strike combined with vigorous strategic and civil defenses could limit casualties enough so that nuclear war could serve a rational goal of national policy:

> To mention one often-used example: 15 to 30 million Soviet citizens were killed in World War II; in addition the Soviet Union lost about one-third of its wealth. It is sometimes pointed out that this was not the result of calculation, and that no alternatives were ever really offered to the Soviets. However, given the nature of the Nazis and their program, I believe that even the average Soviet citizen (not to mention the government), if presented with a choice, would have been willing to accept the cost of World War II in order to achieve the position they have since won, as an

alternative to Nazi domination. They might feel themselves presented with a similar choice someday.[5]

Some Western strategists believe that the United States should be willing to risk tens of millions of lives for the achievement of certain political goals. According to Kahn's intellectual descendants, Colin Gray and Keith Payne:

> An intelligent U.S. offensive strategy, wedded to homeland defenses, should reduce U.S. casualties to approximately 20 million, which should render U.S. strategic threats more credible. If the United States developed the targeting plans and procured the weapons necessary to hold the Soviet political, bureaucratic, and military leadership at risk, that should serve as the functional equivalent in Soviet perspective of the assured-destruction effect of the late 1960s.[6]

Most proponents of a war-fighting posture are not as sanguine as Kahn or Gray about the possibility of limiting damage during a nuclear war. They acknowledge that huge retaliatory forces are invulnerable to preemptive attack and that it may well be impossible to prevent their full use. Nevertheless, proponents of a war-fighting posture believe that maintaining the apparent capability to fight a nuclear war is the best way to deter war. They maintain that preventing general nuclear war, while an important goal, is not the only objective of U.S. security policy and that minimum deterrence is ill-suited for supporting these other objectives. The basic argument is that a measure of nuclear superiority increases the willingness of leaders to threaten nuclear use and, more importantly, increases the credibility and effectiveness of such threats. In order to protect vital U.S. interests, supporters of war-fighting strategies argue that the use of nuclear weapons by the United States in a limited conflict must be credible. This credibility is critical when adversaries have a substantial advantage in conventional forces. For example, a minimum-deterrent posture is inconsistent with the U.S. commitment to initiate the use of nuclear weapons against a Soviet attack of Western Europe: if American strategists believe that a nuclear war would almost inevitably be devastating to the United States, and Soviet strategists are aware of this belief, then how can the threat to use nuclear weapons in the defense of Europe be credible? Similar arguments are made with respect to the defense of other areas of U.S. interest, such as Japan and the Middle East. If, in the eyes of Soviet leaders, the United States cannot make a credible threat to use nuclear force, then some U.S. analysts fear that the Soviets will be emboldened to take military action. Since any large-scale conventional military conflict between the superpowers raises the prospect of nuclear use, they believe that lack of a war-fighting strategy would increase the risk of nuclear war.

Defenders of minimum deterrence contend that the overall risks of war are increased by preparing to fight and win a nuclear war. First, they argue that a war-fighting strategy leads to a destabilizing arms race. Serious implementation of a nuclear war-fighting strategy would require weapons and operational plans designed to destroy all types of Soviet nuclear forces, their command and control systems, and their political and military leadership; it would also require a vigorous effort in ballistic missile, air, and civil defenses to limit damage to the United States. Just as they have in the past, the Soviets would undoubtedly respond with similar deployments of their own. Such capabilities would be especially troublesome during crises, since they increase mutual fears of a preemptive first strike. Even if the United States managed to "win" this arms race while avoiding crisis instabilities, it is not clear that the Soviet Union would become more pliant in other areas. The greatest Soviet challenges to U.S. power in the past—in Berlin, in Korea, and in Cuba—occurred during a period of over-whelming U.S. nuclear superiority. A recent review of past instances of nuclear coercion concluded that the effectiveness of nuclear threats was only weakly correlated with the nuclear balance.[7]

Second, advocates of minimum deterrence believe that war-fighting strategies cannot prevent escalation to general war under realistic circumstances. They maintain that command and control systems would be wiped out during the first few hours of nuclear war, making it impossible to direct the careful attacks called for in many war-fighting scenarios. Even if the national command authorities are safe from destruction, they may not have accurate information about the progress of the war, the disposition of remaining forces, or the damages sustained by either side. Most important, who could be sure that the Soviets would play along with a limited war? Might they not, as most of their writings on nuclear strategy indicate, launch an all-out attack as soon as they were sure that the United States intended to cross the nuclear threshold?

Third, critics of war-fighting strategies do not believe that it is possible to limit damage to levels that permit a meaningful victory during a limited counterforce strike, much less during general war.

Since many military, command and control, and political targets are collocated with population centers, and since ground-burst weapons designed to destroy hard targets would contaminate vast areas with fallout, a limited attack would be devastating to either country. A counterforce attack by either the United States or the Soviet Union, using one quarter to one third of the warheads in their strategic arsenals, would result in 20 to 35 million deaths.[8] In addition, indirect and unquantifiable repercussions caused by disruptions of food supply and environmental effects may dwarf the direct consequences of war. After sustaining damage of this magnitude, how could an adversary determine that it had suffered a "limited" rather than an all-out attack? The urge to retaliate would be overwhelming, and the belief that this urge might prevail would deter any rational opponent from launching such an attack in the first place.

Supporters of minimum deterrence also question the technical feasibility of strategic defense and the efficacy of civil defense in limiting casualties. They claim that the near perfect defense required to prevent the destruction of cities is impossible to achieve against the countermeasures that could be employed by a determined adversary. It has been estimated that only a few hundred warheads (a few percent of either superpower's strategic arsenal) could kill over 50 million people and cause an economic crash from which recovery would not be possible for many decades (if ever).[9] No plausible strategic defense could guarantee a leakage rate smaller than this. Against the most vigorous civil defense efforts, a determined adversary, by targeting the relocated population or by exploding weapons at ground level to maximize fallout, could kill as many as 85 million people in a retaliatory strike.[10]

Fourth, proponents of minimum deterrence believe that advocates of a war-fighting posture have lost touch with political reality. They maintain that even if the theoretical possibility of winning a nuclear war exists, there would still be huge moral and psychological inhibitions against unleasing the greatest slaughter in history. Even if these inhibitions could be overcome, a responsible political leader would have to take into account the many uncertainties surrounding theoretical predictions of nuclear victory. Windows of vulnerability may actually exist, but if the attack is not perfect (and one should remember that nuclear war-fighting systems have never been operationally tested), victory may easily turn into suicide. Proponents of minimum deterrence also point out that although Soviet strategists have made statements that nuclear war can be fought and won (just as American strategists have made similar statements), no Soviet political leader (at least since Brezhnev) has ever been known to express this belief. What possible goal, supporters of minimum deterrence ask, could be worth risking at least tens of millions of lives?

The controversy over the meaning of deterrence in the nuclear age boils down to a debate between a very old idea (deterrence by denial) and a relatively new concept (deterrence by punishment). Deterrence by denial, which has been practiced for millennia, deters attack by presenting an opponent with the prospect of defeat. Deterrence by punishment, on the other hand, makes no attempt to secure victory by preventing one's own defeat; opponents are deterred instead by the prospect of destruction. Beliefs about the effectiveness of deterrent policies based on denial or punishment have their roots in different notions of stability. Strategists who favor denial are mostly concerned with *political* stability, or assuring that adversaries do not take unfavorable political actions of all kinds. Strategists who favor punishment, on the other hand, are mostly concerned with *crisis* stability, or minimizing the incentives for launching a nuclear strike during a confrontation. There is a natural tension between these ideas of stability, because actions taken to assure denial are likely to decrease crisis stability.

The Middle Ground: Limited War-fighting Strategies

In practice, there is a continuum of nuclear strategies between those represented by Brodie and Kahn. In fact, many strategists reject the fundamental assumptions of both extremes of deterrence. They believe, for example, that a policy of targeting cities is immoral and lacks credibility because it is suicidal and that it is of little help in deterring actions short of nuclear war. On the other hand, these strategists recognize that the pursuit of an all-out war-fighting capability could increase the risk of nuclear war by creating dangerous arms race and crisis instabilities. In an attempt to achieve both political and crisis stability, they argue that nuclear weapons should be targeted not against the cities or strategic nuclear weapons of an opponent, but against its military forces.[11] For example, some strategists advocate "limited options" that provide for strikes against a few key military installations, while others call for "soft counterforce" attacks against military bases or "countercombatant" attacks against ground troops. Since the quantity and quality of nuclear weapons required for such strategies is insufficient for a preemptive first strike, crisis and arms race instabilities may be avoided while at the same time reinforcing deterrence by making credible the use of nuclear weapons to achieve limited political objectives. But if deterrence fails, these strategies could only work if collateral damage could be limited and if both sides cooperated in keeping it limited. A policy of limited options would be suicidal if the Soviets plan to launch an all-out attack as soon as the West crosses the nuclear threshold. Similarly, soft counterforce or countercombatant strategies would be suicidal if the resulting collateral damage was so great that an adversary felt that it had little to lose by retaliating against cities. Although minimum and war-fighting deterrence are poles apart, it is not easy to find a stable path between them.

Strategy and the Test Ban

The purpose of this brief review of nuclear strategy has been to elucidate the relationship between strategy and a test ban. Stated simply, support for a CTB flows naturally from a minimum-deterrent strategy. Exponents of minimum deterrence believe that nuclear weapons are unusable; therefore, except insofar as it makes weapon systems safer and more survivable and the maintenance of a minimum level of weapon reliability possible, continued nuclear testing is at best wasteful and at worst dangerously destabilizing. Most advocates of minimum deterrence believe that the contribution of nuclear testing to safety, survivability, and reliability is greatly outweighed by its contribution to weapon system innovations, which they maintain are useless or destabilizing. These innovations include increased accuracy or earth-penetrating warheads for the destructions of silos, nuclear directed-energy weapons to destroy satellites or missiles, and nuclear weapons to destroy relocatable targets. In addition, proponents of minimum deterrence tend to be less worried about the effects of possible cheating under a test ban agreement because they believe that deterrence is quite stable. In other words, they argue that the innovations made possible by nuclear testing strengthen the illusion that a nuclear war could be fought and won, without altering the underlying reality that all would lose.

With equal conviction, supporters of nuclear war-fighting strategies reject restrictions on nuclear testing. In their view, minor differences in weapon system performance can result in large differences in war-fighting effectiveness. Other considerations aside, it would be illogical to cease nuclear testing voluntarily, because testing is necessary to fully realize the potential of new weapon systems that are indispensable to war-fighting strategies. (In the late 1950s and early 1960s, some proponents of war-fighting deterrence were willing to accept a test ban because they believed it would have preserved a decisive U.S. advantage, but this is unlikely to form the basis for a future treaty.) If a war-fighting posture is taken seriously, for example, weapons must be designed to destroy hardened command bunkers, relocatable targets, and attacking warheads. Similarly, war-fighters find it imperative to keep stockpile reliability — and especially stockpile *confidence* — as high as possible. Since they believe that nuclear weapons can be valuable instruments of national power and policy, supporters of war-fighting strategies are more concerned about cheating under a test ban.

Strategists who favor limited options or soft counterforce are divided, but generally favor a CTBT. Limited options require a handful of accurate ballistic missile warheads to destroy key targets quickly. No improvements in warhead design are required to achieve this capability now or to respond to any foreseeable nonnuclear Soviet deployments (assuming that large-scale deployments of strategic defenses remain banned). Similarly, soft counterforce strategies require no new warheads. Attacks against airfields and troops that limit collateral damage require accurate, low-yield warheads, but nothing that does not already exist. Command and control, target acquisition, and retargeting ability may have to be improved, but not nuclear design.

In view of this natural division between supporters and detractors of a test ban on issues of nuclear strategy, a CTB could be a useful way for the United States and the Soviet Union to signal to each other and to the rest of the world a shift in position from deterrence by denial to deterrence by punishment. Many proponents of war-fighting deterrence concede that deterrence by punishment would be safer if both superpowers could be sure that it was the policy of the other side. Issues of verification aside, it would be extremely difficult for a nation to claim that it was not interested in war-fighting strategies (at least the more extreme versions), yet to object to a test ban. A CTB would be a natural complement to cooperative efforts to reduce nuclear anxiety, especially if it is coupled with reductions in less stable strategic systems (i.e., those most capable of preemptive attack) and agreements on defensive systems.

A CTB, however, cannot by itself force a change in nuclear strategy. It is entirely possible for a nation both to accept a CTB and to maintain and augment war-fighting capabilities, because many of the weapon system improvements necessary to increase war-fighting capability do not depend much on nuclear design. These weapon system improvements include increased accuracy; hardened, mobile, or proliferated command, control, and communication systems; ballistic missile and air defenses; and civil defense. Thus, a CTB is a necessary but insufficient condition to decrease mutual fears about war-fighting strategies.

PROLIFERATION

To most Americans, it is axiomatic that nuclear proliferation decreases the security of the United States. The acquisition of nuclear weapons by additional nations not only reduces U.S. leverage in dealing with these countries, but it is also thought to increase the probability that nuclear weapons will be used in anger somewhere in the world, thus increasing the risk of a devastating general nuclear war. Since the birth of the Manhattan Project, every U.S. president has, with varying degrees of enthusiasm and success, sought to impede the spread of the knowledge and materials necessary to build nuclear weapons. The Non-Proliferation Treaty (NPT) of 1968 and the Non-Proliferation Act of 1978 were directed specifically at this goal, but nonproliferation was also a major rationale for many other initiatives, such as the Atomic Energy Act, the Atoms for Peace Program, the Limited Test Ban Treaty, and President Carter's proposed Comprehensive Test Ban Treaty.

A small minority of American nuclear strategists and a somewhat larger fraction of military thinkers in nonnuclear states do not agree that nuclear proliferation necessarily increases the risk of war.[12] They observe that the world is currently experiencing an unprecedentedly long time without great-power war, credit for which they attribute to the possession of nuclear weapons by the superpowers. Despite the deep ideological conflicts between the superpowers and the continual recurrence of crises (many of which, in earlier times, may well have precipitated a major war), direct confrontation has been avoided because of fears of escalation to a nuclear war, the costs of which would far outweigh any political benefit. Why, they ask, should the stabilizing effect of nuclear deterrence not be extended to regional rivalries? If, for example, both Egypt and Israel, Pakistan and India, and North and South Korea possessed nuclear weapons, would not they, like the superpowers, realize that it was not in their best interests to initiate conflicts that would, with high probability, prove suicidal?

Opponents of proliferation believe that such thinking is extremely pernicious. First, many nations may not be as responsible as the current nuclear weapon states have been in controlling their desires for conquest or redress. A Khadafi or Khomeini about to lose a war might not be deterred by the possibility of self-destruction. The probability of madmen coming to power in some nonweapon states is far greater than in the current weapon states. Second, if a regional nuclear war breaks out, the risk of superpower involvement and escalation is not trivial, especially if strategic resources or close allies are affected. Moreover, the possibility that new nuclear states with radical world views would deliberately attempt to catalyze wars cannot be ignored. Such motives were, for example, attributed to China with respect to the superpowers during the 1960s. It would be unwise to assume that all proliferators would, upon realizing the full significance of nuclear arsenals, moderate their behavior and rhetoric as China has done subsequently. Finally, the safety and security of a proliferator's nuclear weapons are unlikely to be as great as those of the superpowers. The probability of an accidental detonation or the unauthorized use or theft of weapons will be much greater as additional nations join the nuclear club.

The success of nonproliferation efforts, which is assumed here to be a positive contribution to U.S. security and global stability, has been linked to the progress of nuclear test ban negotiations almost since these negotiations began. There are two types of links between nonproliferation and a test ban: technical and political. Technically, a ban on nuclear testing hinders the development of nuclear weapons. Politically, a test ban agreement can help reduce the incentives for nuclear weapon development or at least reduce the prestige value of nuclear testing. These two types of connections between nonproliferation and a CTB are discussed below.

The Ability to Develop Weapons

In most cases, a government that is convinced of the value of nuclear weapon development would simply refuse to sign a CTB, in which case the technical contribution of a CTB to nonproliferation is nil. A government may agree to sign, however, if severe political or economic pressures would result from a refusal to sign, or if by signing, it is hoping to persuade a rival to sign as well. If a nation accepts and abides by a CTB, its ability to develop and deploy a reliable arsenal of nuclear weapons would be impaired but not eliminated. It is generally agreed that a first-generation (i.e., fission) nuclear device could be designed and built and that high confidence in the reliability of the device could be obtained without a nuclear test explosion. The type of bomb dropped on Hiroshima was not tested before it was used, for example, and, as far as we know, the first tests of the first nuclear weapons developed by each nuclear nation have all been successful. The basic ideas behind first-generation weapons are now widely available; only the absence of weapons-grade uranium or plutonium prevents many nations from assembling nuclear weapons. Any nation that is capable of obtaining weapons-grade materials, either by enrichment or by operating reactors and reprocessing, is probably capable of building a bomb without resort to nuclear testing.

It should be stressed, however, that a particular nation's judgment about the desirability of a nuclear test will depend on its level of scientific and technological expertise and its strategic rationale for desiring nuclear weapons. Relatively unsophisticated nations, such as Pakistan, are more likely to validate theoretical calculations with a nuclear test than countries with greater technological experience, such as Israel. On the other hand, nations that wish to develop advanced nuclear weapons in order to maximize their war-fighting utility are more likely to test than those that are content with a primitive nuclear capability. The faith of military leaders in the competence of their weapon scientists would also be a key issue. Even if, for example, Brazilian scientists could build a primitive nuclear weapon in which they would have confidence without testing, would Brazil's military leaders take this on faith, or would they want a demonstration?

For the Hiroshima- and Nagasaki-type weapons, which weighed 4,000 to 5,000 kilograms and yielded 15 to 21 kilotons, it is reasonable to assume that a country that had mastered a broad array of other modern technologies would be capable of developing and producing such weapons with high confidence in their reliability without a nuclear test explosion. More sophisticated countries, such as Israel and South Africa, could develop advanced weapons without testing. It is reported that Sweden, in a secret project during the 1950s, designed a nuclear bomb that would have weighed only 600 kilograms, in which it could have had high confidence without nuclear testing.[13] For comparison, the deployment of light-weight nuclear weapons by the United States occurred only after dozens of nuclear tests were done over a period of many years.[14]

There is a limit to what can be done without testing. As demonstrated by the problems that the United States has experienced in designing and testing nuclear weapons, hundreds of bright physicists and fast computers cannot substitute completely for experimental experience. According to many reports, however, Israel has developed very advanced weapons without having been known to have conducted a nuclear test. One report, for example, states that Israel has deployed a warhead weighing only 100 kilograms on the Jericho II missile.[15] It is highly unlikely that a warhead this light could be designed with high confidence without nuclear tests unless its expected yield was very low (i.e., no more than a few tenths of a kiloton). Since the Jericho II is reported to have a throwweight of 750 kilograms,[16] which would be adequate for a much heavier nuclear weapon yielding tens of kilotons (e.g., of the type the Swedes developed without testing), this report is probably false.

Based on details provided by Mordechai Vanunu, a former technician at Israel's secret Dimona reactor site, it is also reported that Israel has designed weapons that rely on nuclear fusion as well as nuclear fission.[17] As interpreted by a former U.S. weapon designer, the information provided by Vanunu is consistent with a boosted fission-type weapon, with lithium-deuteride (LiD) used as the fusion material. This is not implausible, since the Soviet Union successfully tested an LiD-boosted fission weapon in only their fourth nuclear test.[18] Although the Soviet device had a relatively high yield compared to most pure-fission devices (200 to 300 kilotons), it probably did not represent a significant improvement in the utilization of fissile material compared to efficient pure-fission weapons.[19] In fact, there is no evidence that the United States ever tested or deployed a weapon of this type. Modern boosted weapons use deuterium and tritium (DT) as the fusion fuel, which makes it possible to design efficient, low-yield weapons.[20] DT-boosted devices are used as the "trigger" for thermonuclear weapons. Virtually all technical experts in the United States agree that the successful development of DT-boosted weapons would require at least several nuclear tests.

There are three hypotheses about the nature of the Israeli nuclear arsenal: (1) they have a stockpile of efficient Nagasaki-type weapons in which they have high confidence without testing; (2) in addition to Nagasaki-type weapons, they have developed high-yield LiD-boosted weapons in which they have lower confidence; and (3) Israel has conducted nuclear tests or has had access to the test data of others, which has allowed them to develop advanced DT-boosted weapons with high confidence. The last of these hypotheses cannot be ruled out for two reasons. First, it is reported that the French shared data from their first nuclear test with Israeli scientists.[21] Although this would undoubtedly have benefited an Israeli nuclear program, the device tested was probably of the simple Nagasaki variety. The French later developed advanced nuclear weapons, but by this time Israeli participation presumably would have ended. Second, U.S. nuclear-burst-detection satellites detected a signal in the South Atlantic on 22 September 1979 that had the appearance of a 2- to 4-kt nuclear explosion. A panel of experts convened by the White House concluded that the signal probably was not a nuclear explosion, but other equally informed experts came to the opposite conclusion. It has been widely speculated that the signal was caused by an Israeli or joint Israeli–South African nuclear test explosion. If it was an Israeli test explosion, and if the test was heavily instrumented (which would have made test preparations more detectable by photoreconnaissance satellites), then it is possible that the Israelis might have high confidence in high yield-to-weight DT-boosted weapons that would be more suitable for battlefield use. Even so, one or two test explosions would be a frail reed upon which to base a program for the development of advanced nuclear weapons.

The political significance of nuclear weapons is defined by their unique ability to destroy entire cities in a single blow. Although advanced weapon designs, such as DT-boosted or thermonuclear weapons, may permit more destruction for a given amount of money or fissile material, even the most primitive weapon designs can accomplish the objective of indiscriminate massacre. For this reason, most of the political impact of nuclear proliferation is associated with the first nuclear weapon developed by a country. Since a test ban cannot prevent the design and production of simple but effective weapons by moderately advanced countries, the technical contribution of a CTB to nonproliferation is minimal. While it is true that a CTB would prevent advanced nations from developing sophisticated weapons in which they would have high confidence, a nation that is for some reason convinced of the value of sophisticated weapons is highly unlikely to sign a CTB.

The Desire to Acquire Weapons

Why do nations want nuclear weapons, and how can a CTB help abate these desires? In general, there are two basic motivations for the possession of nuclear weapons, both of which are always present: security and prestige. Of the current weapon states, the United States, the Soviet Union, and China were driven primarily by security concerns, whereas the United Kingdom and France appear to have been motivated mainly by a desire to maintain great-power status. The defense establishments of nearly all nations fear for the security of their country; those that want to keep their nuclear options open usually point to the nuclear developments of particular adversaries. The United States started the Manhattan Project because it feared that the Germans would develop a nuclear weapon, the Soviet Union developed a bomb in response to American nuclear development, the Chinese developed nuclear weapons to resist blackmail by both the Americans and the Soviets, and the nuclear efforts of India were triggered by the emergence of a Chinese nuclear arsenal. Thus, nuclear weapons appear to spread like a contagious disease according to the ecology of the community of nations.

Rivalries continue to spread this disease. Pakistan has been stimulated to the nuclear threshold by India, and the widespread belief that Israel possesses a nuclear arsenal may prompt one of the surrounding Arab states to acquire nuclear weaponry. A CTB would be a satisfactory palliative for this disease only if the nonnuclear states in question could be persuaded to accept a CTB, and probably only if it is unlikely that they could develop satisfactory nuclear forces without nuclear testing. This last point requires careful elaboration. It is almost impossible to develop nuclear weapons without rival nations becoming aware of these developments, because the necessary facilities are large and easily identifiable. Even if such developments could be kept completely secret, proliferators would make rivals aware of their new arsenal so that it could be used for deterrence or coercion. Although Israel is not known to have conducted a nuclear test, for example, the belief by its rivals that it possesses nuclear weapons—a belief that Israel has done little to dispel—will stimulate their nuclear efforts.

The recognition that proliferation may continue even if nations do not test does not mean that nuclear testing is irrelevant. In fact, nuclear testing has been a great stimulus to proliferation in the past. The first test by the Soviet Union precipitated a U.S. decision to accelerate development of thermonuclear weapons, and the first Chinese explosion stimulated India's nuclear efforts. Few analysts would argue that Pakistan would have as ambitious a nuclear weapons program if India had not conducted a nuclear test or that the situation in the Middle East would not be much worse if Israel was known to have tested. A nuclear test is a highly visible demonstration of nuclear capability, which rivals cannot ignore. While a wise government may choose to forgo or postpone a nuclear capability even if it is convinced that a rival has developed nuclear weapons, it may not be able to withstand the domestic pressure that would develop in favor of proliferation if the rival vividly demonstrates its capability with a nuclear test. Thus, while the absence of nuclear testing cannot prevent proliferation, it can slow the spread of nuclear weapons to some states.

It does not follow, however, that a CTB would help retard proliferation among nations at the nuclear threshold, because those nations will refrain from testing even if they do not sign a CTBT. Israel, for example, must be acutely aware of the consequences that would flow from a demonstration of its nuclear capability. Not only would an Israeli test greatly stimulate the nuclear ambitions of Arab nations, but it would also trigger economic boycotts and the withdrawal of U.S. aid to Israel. Pakistan also faces the certain loss of billions of dollars of U.S. aid if it tests. In most cases, the legal obligations entailed in signing a CTBT would be an insignificant addition to the inhibitions against nuclear testing that already exist.

Thus, in the case of rivalries where one state is close to or has crossed the nuclear threshold, a CTB will do little to constrain proliferation for security reasons unless the rival states cannot confidently develop weapons without nuclear testing, and then only if they can be persuaded to sign a CTBT. The rival states will be aware of the nuclear capabilities of the proliferator even if a test is not conducted. Although a nuclear test would certainly hasten the nuclear efforts of the rivals, a CTBT is a small addition to the already large inhibitions against testing. A CTB would be more helpful in situations where neither rival is close to the nuclear threshold. In the case of Argentina and Brazil, a CTBT signed by both parties would help alleviate security concerns that the other was developing nuclear weapons.

The existence of a CTBT might significantly lower the prestige value of nuclear testing, especially for those potential proliferators who could be persuaded to sign the treaty. The desire for domestic and international prestige was apparently a major consideration in the decision of Indira Gandhi to actually test (rather than just develop) a nuclear device, and it was the test explosion that spurred Pakistan's efforts. Since India had been a vocal opponent of nuclear testing throughout the 1950s and 1960s, it is reasonable to assume that India would have signed a CTBT if one had been concluded between the superpowers during this time. It is highly unlikely that India would have violated such a treaty, and India certainly would not have gained prestige by doing so. Even if India had nevertheless decided to develop a nuclear device, the absence of a test explosion would have significantly dampened the nuclear competition with Pakistan. Moreover, it is sometimes asserted that a CTBT would, by acquiring the force of international law, restrain testing by even those nations who would not be party to the agreement. Of course, countries that are already "outlaws" (e.g., South Africa) would have little to lose.

It is often claimed that a test ban would strengthen the nonproliferation regime in other, less direct, ways. In particular, it is said that a CTB would fulfill the obligations of states (particularly the superpowers) in Article VI of the NPT to "pursue negotiations in good faith on effective measures relating to cessation of the nuclear arms race at an early date and to nuclear disarmament...." Article VI is widely understood to mean a CTBT, and at the 1975, 1980, and 1985 NPT review conferences the superpowers have been consistently and severely criticized for their failure to conclude a CTBT. In fact, a dispute about nuclear testing almost brought about the collapse of the 1985 conference.[22] The NPT is not of unlimited duration; in 1995, a conference will be convened to decide the future of the treaty. Many experts feel that unless a CTBT is achieved in the meantime, the neutral and unaligned nations may demand that the NPT be renegotiated in view of the failure of the weapon states to fulfill their obligations under Article VI. It would be extremely difficult, if not impossible, to renegotiate a treaty as effective as the current one. It is not inconceivable that the NPT regime would fall apart altogether if there was a call for renegotiation. Many analysts believe that although a CTBT would not be of much direct help in preventing proliferation, the *failure* to achieve a CTBT would significantly undermine other nonproliferation efforts. Of course, the superpowers could fulfill their legal obligations under Article VI in many other ways (e.g., by agreeing to a 50 percent reduction in strategic weapons), but it is not clear whether this would substitute for their widely perceived political obligation to sign a CTBT.

Analysts often maintain that a CTB would be more palatable to many nations than the NPT because it is nondiscriminatory. That is, whereas the NPT recognizes the right of some signatories to possess nuclear weapons but asks that other nations forswear this right, a CTB would apply equally to all parties. Some nations, such as India, Argentina, and Brazil, based their refusal to sign the NPT on the discriminatory nature of the treaty. Although this may have been an excuse designed to retain the option of developing nuclear weapons, a CTB would not be subject to the same failing, and it would therefore be more difficult for these states to refuse to sign. A CTBT signed by the weapon states would also make the NPT less discriminatory, since the weapon states would effectively be giving up the right to develop and test (but not their right to deploy) nuclear weapons. A CTBT may therefore precipitate a decision by some states to sign the NPT as well.

Many test ban opponents claim that threats by neutral or unaligned nations to defect from the NPT because of noncompliance with Article VI are merely bluffs designed to force the superpowers into concessions. They point out that most of these countries would have nothing to gain — but much to lose — by contributing to the demise of the NPT. Since the NPT is in their own best interests, there is little practical recourse for those nations that are disappointed with the lack of progress in superpower arms control. There will undoubtedly be much acrimonious debate at the 1995 conference if a CTBT has not yet been negotiated, but these test ban opponents predict that the NPT will be renewed nevertheless.

Some CTB opponents go even further and claim that a CTBT would contribute indirectly to nuclear proliferation. The core of this argument is that a CTB would weaken the nuclear forces of the United States. This, in turn, would weaken the security guarantees of the United States, which may force some of its allies to consider acquiring nuclear arsenals of their own. In general, these assertions are devoid of analysis. As argued in Chapters 2 and 3, a CTB need not lead to a decline in nuclear prowess or in the ability to deter war. Moreover, the United States presumably would not significantly reduce its reliance on nuclear forces without corresponding increases in its conventional forces or decreases in Soviet conventional forces. Thus, unless U.S. leaders were extremely unwise, there is little reason to suppose that U.S. allies would be more likely to develop their own nuclear arsenals as a result of a CTB. Indeed, most U.S. allies support a CTBT.

A CTB would not provide additional significant restraints to proliferation in those countries that are already parties to the NPT. First, the NPT is a much better constraint on weapon development than a CTB. Parties to the NPT not only agree to renounce nuclear weapons, but, more importantly, to accept safeguards on their nuclear facilities to prevent the diversion of nuclear material for weapons purposes. A country that abrogated the NPT might be months or years away from deploying a weapon, while a nuclear capability can be demonstrated in the same instant that a CTBT is violated. Second, it would be no more traumatic for a state to abrogate both treaties than just one. That is, if a party to the NPT decides to develop nuclear weapons, the fact that it may also abrogate a CTBT would not worsen the political consequences of the decision. For example, the commitment of Iran, Iraq, and Libya to the NPT and other international norms is weak at best, and it is hard to see why they would be less likely to violate a CTBT than the NPT. Thus, a CTBT is significant only for countries that are not parties to the NPT. The hope is that a CTBT could substitute somewhat for NPT membership and that a decision to sign a CTBT could catalyze the signature of the NPT as well.

Table 5–1 shows the voting record of the twenty-eight nonweapon states that have not signed the NPT on resolutions in favor of a CTBT in the U.N. General Assembly from 1984 through 1986. Although two thirds of these countries have voted consistently in favor of CTB resolutions, only one of these — Pakistan — has nuclear facilities under construction or in operation. All of the other potential near-term proliferators — Argentina, Brazil, India, Israel, and South Africa — have abstained from voting on at least half of these resolutions. (South Africa has been barred from its seat in the General Assembly since 1974, but it is reasonable to assume that it would have abstained from voting had it been able to vote.) In addition, Cuba and Spain, which have or are building nuclear facilities, have not voted consistently in favor of CTB resolutions. (Spain accepted full-scope safeguards on its nuclear facilities, which many view as an acceptable substitute for

Table 5–1.   The Voting Record of Nonweapon States That Have Not Signed the NPT on Resolutions in Favor of a Comprehensive Test Ban in the U.N. General Assembly, 1984 to 1986.[a]

Nation[c]	Resolution Number[b]									
	38/62	38/63	39/52	39/53	40/80A	40/80B	40/81	41/46A	41/46B	41/47
Albania	—	—	—	—	—	—	—	—	—	—
Algeria	Y	Y	Y	Y	Y	Y	Y	Y	Y	Y
Angola	Y	Y	Y	A	Y	Y	A	Y	Y	Y
Argentina	A	A	Y	A	Y	A	A	Y	Y	A
Bahrain	Y	Y	Y	Y	Y	Y	Y	Y	Y	A
Brazil	A	Y	A	Y	A	Y	A	A	Y	Y
Burma	A	Y	A	Y	Y	Y	Y	Y	Y	A
Chile	A	Y	Y	Y	Y	Y	Y	Y	Y	Y
Comoros	—	—	Y	Y	Y	Y	Y	Y	Y	Y
Cuba	Y	A	Y	A	Y	Y	A	Y	Y	A
Djibouti	Y	Y	Y	Y	Y	Y	Y	Y	Y	Y
Guyana	Y	Y	Y	Y	Y	Y	Y	Y	Y	Y
India	A	A	A	A	Y	Y	A	Y	Y	A
Israel	A	A	A	—	A	A	A	A	A	A
Mauritania	Y	Y	Y	Y	Y	Y	Y	Y	Y	Y
Mozambique	Y	A	Y	A	Y	Y	Y	Y	Y	Y
Niger	Y	Y	Y	Y	Y	Y	Y	Y	Y	Y
Oman	Y	Y	Y	Y	Y	Y	Y	Y	Y	Y
Pakistan	Y	Y	Y	Y	Y	Y	Y	Y	Y	Y
Qatar	Y	Y	Y	Y	Y	Y	Y	Y	Y	Y
Saudi Arabia	Y	Y	Y	Y	Y	Y	Y	Y	Y	Y
South Africa[d]	—	—	—	—	—	—	—	—	—	—
Spain	A	Y	A	Y	A	A	Y	A	A	Y
Tanzania	Y	Y	Y	Y	Y	Y	Y	Y	Y	Y
United Arab Emirates	Y	Y	Y	Y	Y	Y	Y	Y	Y	Y
Vanuatu	—	Y	Y	Y	—	—	—	Y	Y	Y
Zambia	A	A	Y	Y	Y	A	A	Y	Y	Y
Zimbabwe	Y	Y	Y	Y	Y	—	—	Y	Y	Y

a. Y = voted in favor, A = abstained, — = did not vote.

b. Type 1 CTB resolutions (38/62, 39/52, 40/80, and 41/46) are entitled "Cessation of all test explosions of nuclear weapons"; the remainder (type 2 resolutions) are entitled "Urgent need for a comprehensive test-ban treaty." Type 1a resolutions (40/80A and 41/46A) are essentially the same as the previous type 1 resolutions (38/62 and 39/52), while type 1b resolutions (40/80B and 41/46B) are directed specifically at converting the LTBT into a CTBT. The language of each type of resolution has varied little from year to year. Both types of resolutions call for CTB negotiations, but type 1 resolutions are more insistent, calling for an immediate moratorium on testing and downplaying the importance of additional research on verification.

c. Underlined nations have nuclear facilities in operation or under construction (except for Cuba, all of these have signed the LTBT). Does not include Monoco. Kuwait and Trinidad and Tobago have signed, but have not ratified, the NPT.

d. South Africa has been barred from the General Assembly since 1974.

NPT membership, when it became a member of the Common Market.) Thus, it appears that support for a CTB is most lacking from precisely those nations whose support is most vital to nonproliferation efforts.

There is cause for optimism in some cases, however. The rivalry between Argentina and Brazil is not irreconcilable, and neither fears that the other has progressed very far toward obtaining nuclear weapons. Both have voted in favor of CTB resolutions, although they have favored different types of resolutions (see Table 5–1, note b). The two countries have recently been moving toward rapprochement on nuclear matters. It is likely that both would sign a CTBT, and it is plausible that this would catalyze a decision to sign the NPT. This, in turn, would prompt Chile, and perhaps Cuba, to sign both treaties. India and Pakistan would probably sign a CTBT, but it seems less likely that this would stimulate a decision by either country to join the NPT. Pakistan has repeatedly offered to put its nuclear facilities under safeguards if India would do the same, but India has consistently refused. It is difficult to see how a CTBT could eliminate this impasse, especially since China is unlikely to ever sign either accord. It seems very unlikely that Israel or South Africa could be persuaded to join either treaty.

Summary

The technical benefits of a CTB to nonproliferation are unreliable and do not appear to be substantial. Nations that can acquire, through indigenous capabilities, the required fissile materials should also be able to fashion a reliable nuclear explosive without recourse to nuclear testing. To the best of our knowledge, all of the weapon states succeeded in building a workable device on the first try, and Israel is credited with having a large nuclear arsenal without having conducted a nuclear test. The military establishment of a new nuclear nation may, however, still want proof that the weapons will work, and the existence of a CTBT may therefore influence decisions to develop weapons in the first place. Since rivals would inevitably become aware of each other's nuclear developments, proliferation would continue even without testing. Adherence to a CTBT would prevent the greatest spur to proliferation, but huge disincentives to nuclear testing already exist. The existence of a CTBT is unlikely to weigh heavily in the decision of a country to develop or test nuclear weapons.

The political effects of a CTBT, on the other hand, may be larger. The NPT has been very successful in preventing proliferation, but its continued existence may be threatened by what many see as the disregard of the weapon states for their obligation to end the nuclear arms race. In particular, the superpowers have been criticized repeatedly for their failure to negotiate a CTBT. If a CTBT is not negotiated by 1995, many analysts fear that the NPT regime will be severely weakened. Although a CTBT may not be much of a direct impediment to weapon development, the signing of such a treaty by rivals (e.g., Argentina and Brazil) may alleviate residual security concerns and may even catalyze a decision to sign the NPT. Thus, while the effect of a CTBT on nonproliferation efforts is positive, it is impossible to quantify the magnitude of its contribution.

DETENTE

Arms control treaties between the United States and the Soviet Union are symbols of détente, or a lessening of tensions. For many of the world's citizens, such treaties provide much-needed reassurance that the superpowers can manage their competition without endangering more than is necessary the hundreds of millions of lives that they hold hostage to peace. The signing of a CTBT would undoubtedly be a powerful symbol of superpower reconciliation, since the failure to achieve a test ban after some three decades of effort has become the quintessential symbol of Soviet-American distrust. Moreover, to many observers (especially of those outside of the United States) the test ban is the *sine qua non* of genuine nuclear arms control. The psychological value of a CTB could therefore be substantial.

It is precisely for this reason that many strategists oppose arms control in general, and a CTB in particular. They believe that the primary danger to peace is not the arms race, but Soviet ambitions for world hegemony. Long-term Soviet goals will not change because of short-term accommodations with the United States. These CTBT opponents claim that détente will only lull the West into a false sense of security. Support for the high defense budgets that they belive are necessary to deter Soviet aggression will evaporate. They point to the resumption of testing after the moratorium and the buildup of strategic weapons after SALT I as proof that the Soviets are interested in arms control only as a means to increase their military advantage.

It is impossible to prove whether the dangers of an arms race are greater than the dangers of détente, for it depends on assumptions about Soviet aims that are poorly known. There is, however, substantial evidence that the United States is not lulled by arms control treaties. A recent, detailed study of possible lulling effects of superpower arms control agreements concluded that "military spending did not decline precipitously after U.S.-Soviet arms control agreements were negotiated, and public opinion polls do not show that agreements or negotiations increased opposition to defense outlays. . . . [I]t would be a mistake to argue against future arms control agreements on the grounds that they will inevitably lull the United States into reducing military expenditures."[23] Indeed, the argument over lulling is an almost exact parallel to the debate over nuclear strategy. Almost without exception, those analysts who believe that the United States should maintain a war-fighting strategy also believe that the United States should be spending more on defense; it is not surprising, therefore, that they would fear that an arms control agreement would lead to even lower expenditures.

NOTES

1. See Lawrence Freedman, *The Evolution of Nuclear Strategy* (New York: St. Martin's Press, 1981).
2. Bernard Brodie, "Implications for Military Policy," in Bernard Brodie, ed., *The Absolute Weapon* (New York: Harcourt, Brace, 1946), p. 76.
3. McGeorge Bundy, "To Cap the Volcano," *Foreign Affairs* 48, no. 1 (October 1969): 9–10.
4. See, for example, Richard Pipes, "Soviet Global Strategy," *Commentary* 69, no. 4 (April 1980): 31–39.
5. Herman Kahn, *Thinking About the Unthinkable* (New York: Horizon Press, 1962), p. 51.
6. Colin S. Gray and Keith B. Payne, "Victory is Possible," *Foreign Policy* 39 (Summer 1980): 25.
7. Richard K. Betts, *Nuclear Blackmail and Nuclear Balance* (Washington, D.C.: The Brooking Institution, 1987).
8. William Daugherty, Barbara Levi, and Frank von Hippel, "The Consequences of 'Limited' Nuclear Attacks on the United States," *International Security* 10, no. 4 (Spring 1986): 35; and Barbara G. Levi, Frank N. von Hippel, and William H. Daugherty, "Civilian Casualties from 'Limited' Nuclear Attacks on the USSR," *International Security* 12, no. 3 (Winter 1987): 183.
9. Daugherty, et al., "'Limited' Nuclear Attacks on the United States," p. 5; and Levi, et al., "'Limited' Nuclear Attacks on the USSR," p. 187. With regard to economic effects of limited attacks, see M. Anjali Sastry, Joseph J. Romm, and Kosta Tsipis, "Nuclear Crash: The U.S. Economy After Small Nuclear Attacks," Program in Science and Technology for International Security Report No. 17 (Cambridge, Mass.: Massachusetts Institute of Technology, June 1987), p. 93.

10. Spurgeon M. Keeney, Jr., and Wolfgang K.H. Panofsky, "MAD vs. NUTS," *Foreign Affairs* (Winter 1981/1982): 303.

11. For an excellent discussion of alternate strategies, see Joseph S. Nye, Jr., "The Role of Strategic Nuclear Systems in Deterrence," *Washington Quarterly* (in press).

12. See, for example, Kenneth Neal Waltz, "The Spread of Nuclear Weapons: More May Be Better," Adelphi Paper No. 171 (London: International Institute for Strategic Studies, 1981).

13. Christer Larsson, "Build a Bomb!" *Ny Teknik*, 25 April 1985. Cited in *The Military Balance 1985–1986* (London: International Institute for Strategic Studies, 1985). If the bomb had a yield of about 10 kilotons, the yield-to-weight ratio would be about 0.02 kt/kg.

14. The Mk-5 bomb weighed about 1,400 kilograms and was first produced in May 1952. By this time the United States had exploded 27 nuclear devices, 17 of which were probably fission-weapon development tests. Judging from the reported yields of the test explosions, the Mk-5 probably had a yield of 21 to 31 kilotons, giving it a yield-to-weight ratio of about 0.02 kt/kg. The W31 warhead for the Honest John and Mike Hercules missiles, which was first produced in October 1958, weighed about 500 kilograms and had a yield of 20 kilotons (yield-to-weight ratio of 0.04 kt/kg). The W33 warhead for the 8-inch artillery-fired projectile weighs about 100 kilograms and has a yield of 10 kilotons (yield-to-weight ratio of 0.1 kt/kg). It was first produced in 1957, by which time the United States had conducted eighty-six nuclear test explosions, four dozen of which were dedicated to the development of low-yield weapons. The yield-to-weight ratio of warheads with yields in the 10-kt range has not improved much beyond this. It is generally agreed that it would be impossible to design a warhead comparable to the W33 without nuclear testing. Thomas B. Cochran, William M. Arkin, and Milton M. Hoenig, *Nuclear Weapons Databook*, vol. I: *U.S. Nuclear Forces and Capabilities* (Cambridge, Mass.: Ballinger, 1984), pp. 33, 45–47; Thomas B. Cochran, William M. Arkin, Robert S. Norris, and Milton M. Hoenig, *Nuclear Weapons Databook*, vol. II: *U.S. Nuclear Warhead Production* (Cambridge, Mass.: Ballinger, 1987), pp. 10, 151–56.

15. NBC "Nightly News," 30 July 1985. Cited in Leonard S. Spector, *Going Nuclear* (Cambridge, Mass.: Ballinger Publishing Company, 1987), p. 132.

16. "Israel Said to Deploy Jericho Missile," *Aerospace Daily*, 1 May 1985. Cited in Spector, *Going Nuclear*, p. 144.

17. "Revealed: The Secrets of Israel's Nuclear Arsenal," *Sunday Times* (London), 5 October 1986. Cited in Spector, *Going Nuclear*, p. 136.

18. The fourth Soviet test, "Joe 4," on 12 August 1953 was their first thermonuclear test. The yield was 200 to 300 kilotons, and the fusion material was lithium-deuteride. Jeffrey I. Sands, Robert S. Norris, and Thomas B. Cochran, "Known Soviet Nuclear Explosions: 1949–1985," Nuclear Weapons Databook Project Working Paper No. NWD 86-3 (Washington, D.C.: Natural Resources Defense Council, June 1986), p. 13.

19. York states that the Joe 4 device "evidently involved one of the several possible straightforward configurations for igniting relatively small amounts of thermo-nuclear material . . . with a relatively large amount of fissile material." Herbert F. York, *The Advisors: Oppenheimer, Teller, and the Superbomb* (San Francisco: W.H. Freeman and Company, 1976), p. 95.

20. When using LiD as a fusion fuel, an Li-6 nucleus is fissioned by a neutron to produce tritium; the tritium then fuses with deuterium, releasing a neutron in the process. Thus, LiD does not produce a net increase in the neutron flux (apart from the fact that the neutrons released during fusion, being of higher energy than fission neutrons, produce more neutrons when fissioning uranium) and does not

therefore lead to a much more efficient device. If one uses DT as the fusion fuel, on the other hand, the tritium already exists and each fusion reaction produces a neutron. In this case, however, tritium must be produced from lithium in nuclear reactors.

21. Steve Weissman and Herbert Krosney, *The Islamic Bomb* (New York: Times Books, 1981), p. 113. Cited in Spector, *Going Nuclear*, p. 292.
22. David Albright and André Carothers, "Fragile Consensus on Non-Proliferation Treaty," *Bulletin of the Atomic Scientists* 41, no. 11 (December 1985): 8–10.
23. Sean M. Lynn-Jones, "Lulling and Stimulating Effects of Arms Control," in Albert Carnesale and Richard N. Haass, eds., *Superpower Arms Control: Setting the Record Straight* (Cambridge, Mass.: Ballinger Publishing Company, 1987), pp. 263–64.

6 CONCLUSIONS

Unlike arms control treaties that limit the deployment of particular types of weapon systems, restrictions on nuclear testing are an attempt to thwart research and development on new nuclear weapon systems of all kinds. A ban on research and development can have wide-ranging and perhaps unforeseen consequences that reach into almost every area of nuclear thought, from the arcane realm of nuclear strategy to the harsh realities of domestic and international politics, from the reliability of existing weapons to the feasibility of weapons that yet escape our imagination, from seismic theory to the nitty-gritty of on-site inspection. It is the sweeping nature of testing restrictions that creates such passion and longevity in the CTB debate. Those analysts who believe that war is best avoided through a process of negotiation and arms control generally see the test ban as one way to cut off the arms race at its source; those who believe in deterrence based on military strength believe that a test ban could erode the foundation of our security. Both sides agree that a test ban would rock the nuclear boat, but they disagree about whether it is safer to be in the water or to remain aboard. Advocates of a CTB fear that the ship may sink; opponents claim that the water is filled with sharks.

IN FAVOR OF A TEST BAN

The most important arguments in favor of a CTB are as follows:

Strategy. Arms control proposals and weapon modernization programs should flow naturally from conceptions of nuclear strategy. The debate over a test ban is largely a debate over the political and military utility of nuclear weapons.

CTB proponents generally maintain that the actual use of nuclear weapons could serve no political goal and that their only rational function is to deter their use by others. In this view, possession of a small, survivable nuclear force is sufficient for deterrence; more potent forces make adversaries anxious and decrease stability. Issues of verification and stockpile confidence aside, a refusal to sign a CTBT would be inconsistent with a policy of minimum deterrence.

Other observers feel that the threat to destroy cities is an insufficient basis for deterrence. They argue that weapons and strategies must be available that make the use of nuclear weapons, or at least the threat of their use, appear credible. A CTBT is consistent with the milder variations of war-fighting deterrence (limited options, soft counterforce, countercombatant) since these strategies require no improvements in nuclear warheads. Proponents of war-fighting strategies, however, desire sophisticated weapon systems that would benefit from continued nuclear testing (although it should be noted that the pursuit of such strategies is possible even under a CTBT).

Since I believe that primary reliance on deterrence by punishment, rather than deterrence by denial, is the most appropriate nuclear strategy, I count a CTBT as a large positive contribution to U.S. security.

Proliferation. Few analysts doubt that a CTBT would aid nonproliferation efforts, although there are great differences of opinion about the magnitude of this effect.

A CTBT would have very little direct effect on proliferation. Simple bombs can be designed without testing; nations desiring nuclear weapons that believe that testing is necessary probably would not sign a CTBT. There are already tremendous disincentives to testing; the signature of a treaty is unlikely to weigh heavily in the decision of a country considering weapon development or testing.

The political benefits of a CTBT may be substantial, however. If there is a significant risk of the NPT collapsing during the 1995 Review Conference because many nations do not believe that the superpowers have lived up to their obligations under Article VI, then a CTBT is vital. Even staunch supporters of continued testing agree that preservation of the NPT is essential, but they argue that nations unhappy with the progress of superpower arms control would have little to gain by bringing about the collapse of the NPT.

Based on the reaction to continued nuclear testing at the 1985 Review Conference, it is my judgment that a failure to negotiate a test ban by 1995 would present a significant challenge to the integrity of the NPT, but that this challenge could be managed if there was significant progress in other important areas of superpower arms control.

Modernization.   From the viewpoint of minimum deterrence, sophisticated weapons systems designed to fight and win a nuclear war are not only unnecessary, but, more importantly, they are dangerously destabilizing. Continued nuclear testing would allow the development of several types of weapons that, by increasing the ability to preemptively destroy opposing forces and limit damage to the homeland, would ultimately detract from our security. Earth-penetrating warheads, for example, would increase the vulnerability of hardened targets such as missile silos and command and control bunkers. Third-generation weapons such as X-ray lasers or microwave weapons could destroy satellites or relocatable targets. The superpowers have all the warhead types that they need for simple deterrence. Nonnuclear developments, such as improved air defenses or antisubmarine warfare, may require new delivery vehicles, but not new warheads.

Détente.   The failure to achieve a CTBT after three decades of international effort has become the quintessential symbol of Soviet-American mistrust and misunderstanding. The successful negotiation of a CTBT would be a powerful symbol of superpower reconciliation and could mark a new era in superpower arms control. Although some analysts fear that the euphoria resulting from the ratification of a CTBT would lull the United States into a false sense of security, there is no evidence that this has happened in the past when arms control treaties were ratified. In fact, the large and vocal domestic opposion to a test ban in the defense establishment of the United States almost guarantees that the psychological value of a CTBT would be blunted and raises the danger of treaty abrogation.

AGAINST A TEST BAN

The most important factors weighing against a CTBT are as follows:

Verification. A CTB suffers most especially from verification difficulties. Although militarily significant clandestine testing could be detected and identified with a high enough probability to deter cheating and to protect national security should cheating occur, there remains the important problem of the false alarm rate. The ability of a workable system of seismic stations to rule out all but a few of the thousands of earthquakes and chemical explosions that occur each year in the United States and the Soviet Union as possible nuclear explosions has yet to be demonstrated. Nonseismic techniques, such as photoreconnaissance, appear to be essential to this task, but so far they have received very little attention. Unless the false alarm rate could be kept to less than a few per year, the resulting suspicions and accusations would prove counterproductive and would contribute to the danger of abrogation. A failed treaty would be worse than no treaty at all.

Stockpile Confidence. It will be more difficult to maintain the reliability of the stockpile under a CTB for two reasons: (1) testing will not be available to evaluate potential problems or proposed solutions to problems, and (2) the acumen of weapon scientists will deteriorate without an active development and testing program. Most problems can be solved adequately with inspection, remanufacture, and substitution (especially if precautions are taken several years before a CTBT takes effect), but there remains a small risk of a catastrophic decline in confidence. A belief that a critical weapon system was no longer reliable, coupled with the institutional pressures that would almost certainly exist for the resumption of testing, would probably lead to the abrogation of a CTBT.

Safety, Security, Survivability, and Cost. A CTB would prevent "good" improvements as well as "bad" improvements in nuclear warheads; that is, it would prevent stabilizing as well as destabilizing modernization. In the absence of continued testing, for example, weapons types that lack insensitive high explosive and the most advanced security features will remain in the stockpile. Most experts, however, believe that nuclear weapons are already sufficiently safe and secure. In addition, it may continue to be necessary to design new delivery vehicles in response to nonnuclear Soviet developments that decrease the survivability of the U.S. strategic force. Although this would be possible in almost every imaginable case using existing warheads, the cost of the system would be greater and performance decreased somewhat because delivery systems would have to be designed around existing warheads.

THE EFFECTS OF YIELD THRESHOLDS AND QUOTAS

This book has concentrated on a *comprehensive* test ban — that is, a ban on all nuclear test explosions above some nominal yield — because it has been the central idea of the test ban debate. In the United States, however, attention has recently been focused on a treaty that would permit some types of nuclear tests, in order to make a test ban more palatable to the defense community. There are three main reasons for permitting continued testing at low yields and/or low rates. First, verifying the absence of test explosions is more difficult at low yields. Not only are the seismic signals more difficult to detect, but the number of earthquakes and chemical explosions that could be interpreted as nuclear explosions increases exponentially with decreasing yield. By setting a yield threshold below which nuclear tests are permitted, thousands of small-magnitude seismic events can be ignored, thus making the false alarm problem much more tractable. Second, confidence can be maintained in stockpiled weapon systems at a very low rate of testing. Only one or two tests per year with yields less than 10 or 15 kilotons would be required for this purpose. Third, a program of low-yield testing (e.g., a dozen tests per year with yields less than 1 kiloton) could keep the skills of weapon designers sharp and would allow nuclear effects testing to continue.

Schemes for less-than-comprehensive test bans abound. One proposal that was recently offered in the U.S. House of Representatives as a model for a test ban treaty permitted unlimited testing below 1 kiloton. The 1-kt threshold was justified mainly because of limitations in seismic monitoring; as stated in Chapter 4, decoupled explosions with yields below 1 kiloton could not be detected by a practical network of seismic stations spread throughout the Soviet Union. A similar proposal in the U.S. Senate also permitted two stockpile confidence tests per year with yields less than 15 kilotons. (Of course, it would be impossible to verify that these tests were being used for the purpose of assessing stockpile reliability.) Other analysts have suggested that a threshold of 10 to 15 kilotons would be more practical from both a technical and a political standpoint.

Supporters of threshold and quota proposals do not usually recognize, however, the degree to which these compromises undermine the rationale for a test ban. Additional restrictions on nuclear testing are not good for their own sake; they are only useful insofar as they support policies that decrease the probability of war. Table 6–1 briefly lists the advantages and disadvantages of thresholds at different yields. For example, although a CTB would be open for signature by all nations, a low-yield threshold test ban treaty (LYTTBT) would not be. If the threshold is set at 10 or 15 kilotons (or even if one or two tests per year are permitted at this level), the treaty is unlikely to have any effect on proliferation. A test of a Hiroshima- or Nagasaki-type device, for example, could be conducted below this threshold. If an LYTTBT was advertised as an interim step on the way toward a CTBT,

Table 6–1. The Effect of Nuclear Test Restrictions on Modernization, Stockpile Confidence, Verification, and Policy Considerations as a Function of Yield Threshold.

Effect of a test ban on:	Yield Threshold (kilotons)		
	10–15 (LYTTBT)	1 (LYTTBT)	0 (CTBT)
Modernization	Tactical and small strategic, NDEW experiments	Tactical, weapon effects, skills	No warhead development
Stockpile confidence	No problem	Maintain skills?	Small risk of failure and abrogation
Verifiability	OSIs needed to verify threshold	Operationally, almost as difficult as CTBT	Serious false-alarm problems to be resolved
Strategy, proliferation, and détente	Negligible unless interim step	Moderate effect on strategy and détente	Highest effect on proliferation and strategy

however, it might bolster the NPT regime by demonstrating the willingness of the superpowers to live up to their obligations under Article VI, especially if the threshold is very low (e.g., 1 kiloton). In any case, most nonnuclear countries are unlikely to be satisfied with an LYTTBT and criticism of the superpowers for their failure to achieve a ban on all testing would almost certainly continue. It is easy to see how the continuation of nuclear testing at any level would serve as a ready justification for those who claim that the NPT is discriminatory.

Thresholds and quotas would also undermine the effect of a test ban in signaling a change in nuclear strategy. A threshold of 10 to 15 kilotons, for example, would permit the development of new tactical warheads. By accepting a modest degree of technical risk, testing at this level would also permit the design of new strategic warheads with yields of several tens of kilotons. Coupled with very accurate or earth-penetrating reentry vehicles, warheads with yields of a few tens of kilotons could be as effective in destroying hardened military targets as the MX warhead. Directed-energy experiments, and perhaps eventually weapon development, could continue with testing in the 10- to 15-kt range. Even a low quota of such tests could permit significant modernization, since many experiments could be performed during one test. With time, imaginative weaponeers would undoubtedly think of many things that could be accomplished at these yields that are not now considered possible. In other words, a threshold of 10 to 15 kilotons may only channel the arms race into new areas rather than catalyze a change in nuclear strategy. A threshold of 1 kiloton, on the other hand, while allowing the continued development of tactical weapons, would nearly eliminate the development of new strategic weapons for the foreseeable future.

An LYTTBT or quota treaty may create almost as many verification problems as they solve. If one assumes, as was argued in Chapter 4, that tests with yields much below 1 kiloton are not militarily significant, then the seismic network required to monitor a CTB need not be considerably more sensitive, sophisticated, or costly than that required to monitor a 1-kt threshold. The number of false alarms would not be significantly reduced by a 1-kt threshold agreement. Unlike a CTBT, however, an LYTTBT would require verifying compliance with the threshold. It is not easy to accurately measure low-yield explosions with seismic monitors, even if the equipment is near the test site. Since 1 kiloton is near the threshold for boosting, tests with yields two or three times higher than the threshold could be significant violations. Intrusive on-site inspections would likely be required to verify strict compliance with the threshold, which would introduce new verification problems. In addition, an LYTTBT would allow one to maintain the infrastructure necessary to conduct clandestine high-yield tests or to abrogate the treaty at short notice. The main advantage of an LYTTBT would be that continued testing would be available to calibrate the regional seismic network and improve its discrimination capability, thus making it easier to verify a CTBT at a later time.

There is little doubt that threshold or quota agreements have a better chance of acceptance by the U.S. Senate than a CTBT. Many CTB advocates support an LYTTBT because they reason that a CTB is not politically possible and that an LYTTBT is a step toward their goal. The important question is, however, not whether an LYTTBT is better than nothing, but whether it is worth the price. The opposition of the defense community to a 1-kt threshold would be nearly as great as that to a CTB. In the long term, verifying compliance with a 1-kt threshold will not be much easier than verifying compliance with a CTBT. A threshold of 10 or 15 kilotons would be considerably more acceptable to the defense community, but at the price of surrendering nearly all the benefits of a CTB. Worse, an LYTTBT may forever derail efforts to achieve a CTB, just as the LTBT defused pressure for a CTB without changing the nature of the nuclear competition.

In my opinion, the only sensible alternative to a CTBT is an agreement in which the yield threshold or test quota is lowered in phases. One could, for example, set the threshold at 10 or 15 kilotons initially, for which it would be relatively easy to obtain the support of the Senate. The treaty would then commit the superpowers to review the efficiency of the seismic monitoring system every two or three years, with the purpose of lowering the yield threshold to the minimum supported by the data. In this way, it might be possible to achieve a CTBT by 2000, at which time the treaty could be opened for signature by all nations. This type of treaty was proposed recently by Paul Richards and Allan Lindh.[1] A phased treaty would allow the seismic network to be calibrated with great accuracy. Most importantly, it would avoid the Senate ratification process each time the threshold is lowered. For this very reason, however, a phased agreement may not be acceptable to the Senate, since it would relinquish influence over the treaty after its initial ratification.

SUMMARY

Deciding the wisdom of a CTBT requires judgments that are inescapably subjective in nature. The debate about the *desirability* of a CTBT is almost entirely an argument over nuclear strategy. It is my conclusion that a CTB would serve the security interests of the United States by pointing away from dangerous strategies of nuclear warfighting and by reinforcing the nonproliferation regime. The debate over the *practicality* of a CTB is almost entirely an argument about the efficiency of available verification technologies. Support for a CTB should be conditioned on the demonstration of a practical system for seismic verification that can discriminate between earthquakes, chemical explosions, and nuclear explosions without generating a large false alarm rate that could fatally wound the confidence-building process. Viewed from the perspective of a minimum-deterrent strategy, the risks of stockpile unreliability or decreased safety, security, or survivability that would result from a test ban are minimal. Finally, I believe that the only sensible alternative to a CTB is a phased agreement, in which the yield threshold is lowered progressively, without renegotiation and reratification, as technology and monitoring experience improve. Although a 10- or 15-kt LYTTBT may be significantly more acceptable to the defense community than a CTBT, it has very few of the advantages of a CTBT and would derail efforts to achieve a more beneficial agreement. A 1-kt LYTTBT does not capture all of the advantages of a CTBT, yet it would be nearly as difficult to achieve. I believe that we should reach for the full prize and secure our future through a comprehensive test ban.

NOTES

1. Paul G. Richards and Allan Lindh, "Toward a New Test Ban Regime," *Issues in Science and Technology* III, no. 3 (Spring 1987): 101–108.

Index

195

ABOUT THE AUTHOR

Steve Fetter is an assistant professor in the School of Public Affairs at the University of Maryland, College Park. Previously, he was a research fellow at the Center for Science and International Affairs in the Kennedy School of Government, Harvard University, where he completed this book. He received an S.B. in physics from the Massachusetts Institute of Technology and a Ph.D. in energy and resources from the University of California, Berkeley. Dr. Fetter has published articles on fission and fusion reactor safety, radioactive waste disposal, space policy, and arms control verification.